CONTEMPORARY SCHOOLS OF PSYCHOLOGY

By

ROBERT S. WOODWORTH, Ph.D., Sc.D., LL.D.

PROFESSOR EMERITUS OF PSYCHOLOGY,
COLUMBIA UNIVERSITY

REVISED EDITION

THE RONALD PRESS COMPANY · NEW YORK

BF
105
W6
c.1

PREFACE

The major schools of psychology as they existed in 1931, when the first edition of this survey was published, are still contemporary schools. Considerable revision is called for, however, not because any radically new schools have come forward, but because important new developments have occurred in nearly every one of the existing schools. This is notably true of behaviorism, Gestalt psychology, and psychoanalysis. Behaviorism has risen to a more critical scientific level; Gestalt psychology has branched out into new fields; psychoanalysis has changed somewhat in its clinical methods and still more in its theory. The "hormic and holistic" group of schools were nearly all mentioned in the previous edition but are now brought together into a single chapter. The newer associationists, instead of being considered rather incidentally, are now given a chapter to themselves along with their associationist predecessors. It has seemed appropriate to regard as functional psychologists, in a broad sense, most of those who were previously spoken of as being in the "middle of the road"; and for that reason the final chapter under the latter heading has lost most of its content and been reduced to a brief epilogue.

All these revisions and rearrangements have demanded a practically complete rewriting of the book. Certain discussions which were perhaps pertinent in 1931 now appear superfluous and have been omitted, so that the text as a whole has not been much enlarged, though its coverage is certainly more complete. What was said in the first edition to the effect that the book had grown out of a lecture course still remains true, for the author has lectured on these schools every year since then; and he desires once more to express his indebtedness to the many students who have discussed with him these important psychological problems. Special thanks are due to Professor Mary Rose Sheehan for her critical review of the text in the proofs.

The author is grateful also to Dr. H. Horsley Gantt for the photograph of Pavlov appearing in this book; to Mr. Jaques

iii

Cattell for the pictures of Wundt and James; to Mrs. Grace P. Weiss for the picture of her late husband; to Professor Karl Zener for the picture of Stern; to the Psychological Review for the picture of Lewin; and to many living psychologists for pictures of themselves.

ROBERT S. WOODWORTH

Columbia University
  May 14, 1948

ACKNOWLEDGMENTS

For permission to incorporate in the text numerous brief quotations from the works of leading representatives of the schools, the author thankfully records his indebtedness to the following publishers:

To American Book Company, New York, for permission to quote from Goldstein's *The organism,* copyright 1939.

To The American Missionary Association, New York, for permission to quote from M. W. Calkins, *A first book in psychology,* copyright 1914.

To American Psychological Association, Inc., Washington, for permission to quote from *The Psychological Review,* Volumes 30, 39, 44, and 52.

To Appleton-Century-Crofts, Inc., New York, for permission to quote from E. C. Tolman, *Purposive behavior in animals and men,* copyright 1932.

To Clark University Press, Worcester, Mass., for permission to quote from *Psychologies of 1925,* copyright 1926; from *Psychologies of 1930,* copyright 1930; from *A history of psychology in autobiography,* Volume I, copyright 1930; and from *A handbook of general experimental psychology,* copyright 1934.

To Harcourt, Brace and Company, Inc., New York, for permission to quote from K. Koffka, *Principles of Gestalt psychology,* copyright 1935.

To Harper & Brothers, New York and London, for permission to quote from M. Wertheimer, *Productive thinking,* copyright 1945.

To Harvard University Press, Cambridge, Mass., for permission to quote from K. Goldstein, *Human nature in the light of psychopathology,* copyright 1940; and from E. L. Thorndike, *Man and his works,* copyright 1943.

To Henry Holt and Company, Inc., New York, for permission to quote from G. W. Allport, *Personality,* copyright 1937; from J. R. Angell, *Psychology,* copyright 1904; and from W. James, *Principles of psychology,* copyright 1890.

To Iowa Child Welfare Research Station, Iowa City, for permission to quote from *University of Iowa Studies in Child Welfare,* 1940, Volume 16.

To The Johns Hopkins Press, Baltimore, for permission to quote from *Comparative Psychology Monographs,* 1935, Volume 11.

To The Journal Press, Provincetown, Mass., for permission to quote from *Journal of general Psychology,* 1931, Volume 5.

To Alfred A. Knopf, Inc., New York, for permission to quote from J. R. Kantor, *Principles of psychology,* Volume I, copyright 1924.

To J. B. Lippincott Company, Philadelphia, for permission to quote from F. Alexander, *Our age of unreason,* copyright 1942; and from J. B. Watson, *Psychology from the standpoint of a behaviorist,* copyright 1919.

To Liveright Publishing Corporation, New York, for permission to quote from Dr. Wolfgang Köhler, *Gestalt psychology,* copyright 1947. Published by Liveright Publishing Corporation, New York.

To The Macmillan Company, New York, for permission to quote from W. Stern, *General psychology from the personalistic standpoint,* copyright 1938.

To W. W. Norton & Company, Inc., New York, for permission to quote from S. Freud, *New introductory lectures on psychoanalysis,* translated by W. J. H. Sprott, copyright 1933; from K. Horney, *New ways in psychoanalysis,* copyright 1939; from K. Horney, *Our inner conflicts,* copyright 1945; and from J. B. Watson, *Behaviorism,* copyright 1930.

To The Principia Press, Bloomington, Indiana, for permission to quote from J. R. Kantor, *Problems of physiological psychology,* copyright 1947.

To Bureau of Publications, Teachers College, Columbia University, New York, for permission to quote from E. L. Thorndike, *Experimental study of rewards,* copyright 1933.

To Yale University Press, New Haven, Conn., for permission to quote from C. S. Sherrington, *The integrative action of the nervous system,* copyright 1906, 1947.

R. S. W.

CONTENTS

CONTENTS

ILLUSTRATIONS

CONTEMPORARY SCHOOLS OF PSYCHOLOGY

CHAPTER 1

OUR SCHOOLS AND THEIR BACKGROUND

As a science psychology is relatively young, much younger than physics, chemistry, and some branches of biology. As a part of philosophy, to be sure, it goes back to Plato and Aristotle. In the history of modern philosophy it took on an empirical slant and approached more and more toward the status of a natural science. It attained this status in the latter part of the nineteenth century and from that time to this has expanded very rapidly. A worldwide survey at the present time would reveal psychologists working in almost every land along a great variety of lines. Some would be found in laboratories and some in clinics. Some are concerned with learning, perception, thinking, motivation, and other such functions in men and animals. Some are using tests for the study of individual and group differences. Some are investigating child development and some mental derangement. Some are working on social problems and some on problems that lie close to physiology. Some are applying psychology to education, some to industry. Those devoted to a specialty have meetings from time to time and develop distinctive techniques and jargons. Such specialties might very well be called schools, but that is not the way psychologists are accustomed to use the word. For us a "school" is a group of psychologists who put forward a certain system of ideas designed to point the way that all must follow if psychology is ever to be made a genuine, productive science of both theoretical and practical value. We have several such schools pointing in different directions.

Unknown territory obviously calls for exploration in all directions. For the research psychologist the unknown territory is that apparently familiar ground which we call human activity or more precisely the activity of the human individual, with

3

some reference also to man's humbler animal cousins. Some of our explorers are fascinated by one, some by another of the many phases of individual activity; and the schools can to a certain extent be distinguished simply by the activity which they prefer to investigate. More than that, each school believes that hidden in its own field is the true key to a unified understanding of human activity as a whole. For one school the illuminating fact is that man perceives the environment; for another, that he learns by experience; for another, that he feels and desires; and for another, that he acts by use of his muscles and so does something in the world. It may be that desire is the key to action, that perception is the key to desire, that learning is the key to perception. With one kind of human activity chosen as the central fact, a system of methods and concepts can be organized and a comprehensive theory worked out to the satisfaction of at least one school of thought. The majority of psychologists maintain a rather skeptical attitude toward these ambitious undertakings, but still find the schools stimulating and suggestive. Each school explores intensively in its chosen direction and makes concrete discoveries which enlarge the boundaries of the known territory of psychology. Meanwhile each school has to be watched, since its claims are sometimes excessive.

In the following list of schools, some names will be well known while others are unfamiliar to the general public and not very prominent in psychology itself:

Functional psychology: very old, wide in scope and not sharply defined, named in America in 1898

Structural psychology: German in origin, with 1879 as an outstanding date; named and sharpened in America in 1898

Associationism: an old British school, taking stimulus-response form in America in 1898, in Russia in 1903

Psychoanalysis: originating in Austria about 1900

Personalistic and organismic psychologies: originating in both Germany and America about 1900

Purposivism or hormic psychology: originating in Britain in 1908

Behaviorism: originating in America in 1912

Gestalt psychology: originating in Germany in 1912

For most of these schools the major field of interest is clear. Structural psychology centers in sensation, Gestalt psychology in perception, associationism in learning and memory, psychoanalysis in desire, hormic psychology in purposive activity, behaviorism in motor activity. Personalism and organismic psychology focus on the individual as a whole. Functionalism is tacitly accepted by so many psychologists of varied interests that perhaps it should not be counted among the schools, but the reason for including it will be shown in the next chapter.

The dates assigned for the origin or rejuvenation of these schools are worthy of notice. The turn of the century, from 1898 to 1912, saw them emerge and take shape. How can the schools of that bygone age, that dim past scarcely distinguishable in the perspective of the younger generation from the time of Aristotle, possibly be regarded as contemporary schools of the present day? The fact is that most of them are very much alive. They have changed somewhat, a good deal in some cases, but they are still recognizably the same schools. If we could suppress them all for a couple of decades, very likely they would emerge again with the same vitality as before. It must be that they represent points of view that are almost inevitable till some higher synthesis is found capable of combining them all. And they are *the* contemporary schools, for it seems that no radically new ones have arisen since 1912.

Why should the dawn of the present century have been so remarkably prolific in new schools of psychology? To gain perspective [1] we must glance briefly at the state of our science in 1900. Each school began as a revolt against the established order and cannot be fully understood without taking account of its historical background. We should know something of the established order of 1900 against which our schools revolted. That established order was itself young and had been revolutionary not long before. In fact it was an old tradition in psychology to rebel against tradition. Away back at the beginning of the modern scientific movement in the seventeenth century

---

[1] For a fuller perspective reference may be made to the excellent histories by Murphy, 1929; Boring, 1929, 1942; Heidbreder, 1933; and, with special reference to American psychology, to papers by several authors in the *Psychological Review*, 1943, 50: 1-155.

we find such philosophers as Descartes and Hobbes rebelling against the psychology that had come down from the Greeks and Scholastics and so making a start toward modern psychology. Without attempting to divorce psychology from philosophy they endeavored to bring their psychology into line with the new developments in physical science. Early in the seventeenth century Galileo and others revolutionized physics and astronomy by showing that many and perhaps all physical processes could be described in terms of motion and inertia; and Harvey, by discovering the circulation of the blood, made a start toward explaining physiological processes in physical terms. Without delay, Descartes applied the new physics to human and animal behavior. Behavior he based on what we now call reflex action; and a reflex he conceived as the motion of a fluid along the nerves from the sense organs to the brain and out again to the muscles. The soul he located in the brain, and he supposed it to intervene in certain processes between the incoming and outgoing motions in the nerves. In animals, however, as he believed, there was no soul and all behavior consisted purely of physical motion. The human soul, with its faculty of thinking, he held to be nonphysical.

Hobbes went Descartes one better by reducing all mental processes to physical motion. External motion striking the sense organs was communicated to the nerves, brain, and heart, and this internal motion, once started, persisted by inertia in the form of memories and ideas. Hobbes's revolt against the traditional psychology was certainly radical, but it was sketchy in detail; so that the task remained for the English philosophers of the following century to develop this line of thought, as they did in the associationist psychology. They tried to reduce all mental processes to the single process of association, as we shall see in Chapter 3. With many variations in their theory as to the physical nature of associations, with many applications to morals, economics, and the social sciences in general, and in spite of numerous objections raised by their contemporaries, the associationists grew in influence and dominated the field in the early nineteenth century.

The New Psychology of the Nineteenth Century

But just as the physics of Galileo's time exerted an immediate influence on psychology, so, early in the nineteenth century, two newly developed sciences made themselves felt. The wonderful achievements of chemistry led the philosophers of the time to project an analytical psychology which should discover the elements of conscious experience and work out their laws of combination. This was an attractive program and proved to be feasible to a certain extent. More influential, however, was the example of physiology, which began early in the nineteenth century to be an experimental science. Soon it had remarkable achievements to its credit, and some of them bordered closely on the proper domain of psychology. The workings of the sense organs, nerves, and brain were intensively studied by physiologists during the nineteenth century. Their findings gained a place in the current books on psychology, and their methods were taken up by the new group of experimental psychologists. Out of the physiological laboratory grew the psychological laboratory, though it was not till 1879 that the first recognized psychological laboratory was set up by Wundt at Leipzig. Soon there were many laboratories, especially in Germany and the United States, and the "new psychology," as it was in 1900, was experimental psychology.

This new psychology rebelled against the older tradition in respect to methods and scientific standards rather than in respect to theory. Where the earlier psychologist had been satisfied with evidence from his memory and ordinary experiences, the experimentalist insisted on definite recorded data. Experiments on the senses and muscular movements were followed by cleverly designed experiments on learning and memory, and hope was strong that all psychological problems could in time be attacked by the new method.

We have not yet displayed the full scope of the psychology of 1900, and our sketch of the nineteenth century developments would be woefully incomplete if we failed to mention the influence of two other sciences. General biology, and especially the theory of evolution, from 1860 on brought into view a whole mass of problems that were quite foreign to the older psychology and also to physiology, chemistry, and physics. Mental development in the race and in the individual as influenced by heredity and environment, child psychology, animal psychology, differences between individuals and between races, and similar topics began to appear in psychological writings toward the end of the nineteenth century, largely through the influence of Darwin and Galton. Tests for measuring individuals were first invented for use in such studies and were added to the laboratory type of experiments as part of the new psychologist's stock of methods.

The remaining influence that calls for notice came from psychiatry; and the history of psychiatry throughout the nineteenth century would well repay an extended review. Suffice it to say that the treatment of the insane advanced from an utterly unscientific to a highly promising state. All through the century psychiatrists were divided into two main schools, the psychic and the somatic, the one seeking causes in the mental sphere and the other looking for some brain disturbance behind every abnormality of behavior. Brain disturbance was actually found in some kinds of insanity but could not be demonstrated in other kinds. Where it could not be demonstrated the somatists assumed it to exist in some elusive form. On the whole the somatic school dominated psychiatry and had the greater influence upon the psychology of the time.

The new problems and methods tended to break the traditional connection of psychology with philosophy, and one by one the American universities, at least, created separate departments of psychology. The decade of the 1890's was a period of great psychological activity. Laboratories were springing up, journals were started, the American Psychological Association was founded, international congresses were held. Great books were published, fruitful new methods were designed. The psychologists of 1900 were an active and aggressive group, small in size but rapidly recruiting itself from the younger generation, hopeful of its newly acquired technique of tests and experiments, finding new fields to explore year by year, beginning to study the child, the animal, the insane as well as the normal adult, maintaining contact with the workers in several other sciences, and ready to break loose from philosophy and set up an establishment of its own. In theory the psychologists of 1900 subscribed to the orthodox definition of psychology as the science of consciousness; but in practice they were studying man's performances rather than his states of consciousness. In theory they stood for an analytical psychology patterned after chemistry, with elementary sensations, images, and feelings, and with complex thoughts and emotions composed of these elements; but in practice they often disregarded this scheme. In theory they were mostly associationists, but not dogmatically so; the high noon of associationism was already past.

These discrepancies between theory and practice, between orthodox definition and actual research work, were an open challenge to the younger psychologists of the period. Was consciousness the proper subject matter for the psychology of the future, with introspection as the only direct method of investigation? The younger psychologists, during the first decade of the twentieth century, even before the outburst of behaviorism, were more and more inclined to emphasize behavior rather than consciousness and objective rather than introspective methods; and from a totally different angle of approach the psychoanalysts urged that the deeper field for investigation lay not in consciousness but in the unconscious. Was the old slogan, "association of ideas," a true guide to a theory of learning? The connection of stimulus and response might be a much better guide. Was behavior a collection of simple and complex reflexes? Desire and purpose seemed to be left out of this picture, and the unity of the organism as well. Was consciousness itself made up of sensory elements in varied combinations? Here the unity of the person and the consciousness of being oneself were missing, and there was no room even for the unity of a perceived object and the meaning of any experience to the individual.

Apart from these flaws in its general theory, the psychology of 1900 was necessarily open to the criticism of immaturity and meager accomplishment. Such minor defects could gradually be corrected by intensive work on specific problems, and to this sort of work the great body of psychologists has devoted itself during the now-past half century. Hypotheses have been set up and tested. Findings have sometimes been disputed, and opinions have sometimes clashed. But such controversies can be settled by the weight of evidence, while the merits of the different schools cannot be appraised in so direct and scientific a manner. The major tenets of a school can scarcely be proved or even disproved. The test of a school is its long-run fruitfulness or sterility. Each school points the way for psychology to follow; psychology is attempting to advance in all directions; and the questions are which path will yield the great discoveries of the future, and whether synthesis of the different lines of advance will not sometime prove to be possible.

CHAPTER 2

FUNCTIONAL AND STRUCTURAL PSYCHOLOGY

A very genuine psychological interest is apt to awaken in anyone who has the opportunity of watching the development of a young child. How many different things even the little baby can do! He sleeps, awakes, sucks and swallows, breathes, coughs and sneezes at times, cries and vocalizes in various ways, lies placid or throws his arms and legs around. After a while he begins to "take notice," to look and listen, to recognize persons, to reach for things and handle them with increasing skill. Months later he begins to understand words that are spoken to him and a little later still to speak a few words and then more and more words. Dozens of items could be added, as any young parent finds who undertakes to keep a "baby diary."

Such a record, psychologically considered, consists of answers to the question, "What did the child do?" This question "What?" is one of the three type questions that are asked by any inquiring person, as for example by a scientist. The others are "How?" and "Why?" These questions, too, are likely to occur to the observer of a child. How does he creep? Why does he cry? They are harder questions to answer. The "How" question inquires into the process by which a result is reached, and the "Why" question seeks for the cause behind an action. The process may be too complex and rapid to follow with the eyes, besides being partly concealed inside the body and even in the brain. The cause of an action—often we can call it the motive—is very likely to be invisible.

The Beginnings of Functional Psychology

If such a diary should be continued through childhood and youth and on into adult life, the number of things a person does would be so enormous that some kind of classification would be found necessary; and since the interest presumably would be in the *person* rather than in the numerous objects involved in his activities, the variety of objects could be disregarded and the "things done" brought under a relatively few heads according to the results accomplished. All the different words and sentences spoken could be brought under the head of "talking," all the games played under the head of "playing," all the lessons learned under the head of "learning," all the various facts remembered under the head of "remembering." So the final answer to the "What" question would be a more or less systematic list of kinds of results accomplished. Meanwhile the answers to the "How" and "Why" questions would be lagging behind because of their difficulty.

Something like this, as far as we can make out from the record, was the early history of psychology. In the time of the ancient Greek philosophers such classes were recognized as: perceiving objects by the senses, remembering, imagining things never seen, choosing between alternative possible actions, and carrying out one's chosen plan. Knowing and willing seemed to be the most inclusive classes possible above the physiological level of digesting, sensing, and moving. This classification was obviously an answer to the "What" question. Aristotle made an important start toward answering the question how we remember (page 38), and other philosophers gave some very amateurish answers to the question how we perceive objects. The "Why" question received a very general answer from the hedonists, who asserted that all human activity is dominated by a desire for pleasure. On the whole the psychology that came down from the Greeks consisted in a set of broad classes of results accomplished by the human mind.

Aristotle employed verbal nouns equivalent to our *remembering, willing,* etc., as names for his classes. When his works were translated into Latin, a slight change of form was required to fit the Latin idiom. It was necessary to say "faculty of remembering" or something of the kind. The word *faculty* was not intended to add any new meaning, though it does of course imply that a man *can* remember, the evidence being that he does remember. So the list of faculties was nothing more or less than a list of classes of "things done," an answer still to the question "What?" No doubt the great thinkers who spoke of the faculties of the mind were perfectly clear on this matter, but many lesser men, even down into the nineteenth century, were betrayed by the form of expression into supposing that the faculties were processes, an answer to the question "How?" A student who asked the professor how we remember and was told, "By the faculty of memory," was not much wiser. It was as if he had asked how birds fly and obtained the answer, "By their faculty of flight." Birds certainly have the faculty of flying, since they do fly. That is a result which they accomplish, but the question is by what process or operation they accomplish this result.

A list of faculties is a respectable answer to the question "What" but only a list of problems for the psychologist who is beginning to take the "How" question seriously. It is not even safe to assume that to each faculty there corresponds one distinct mental operation. To remember a face so as to recognize it may require an operation different from that of remembering a poem so as to recite it. In terms of operation there may be many memories rather than a single one. Or, on the contrary, there may be fewer fundamental operations than there are faculties. This last view was that of the associationists, who tried to show that all mental operations were essentially the one operation of association (see the following chapter).

A psychology that attempts to give an accurate and systematic answer to the question, "What do men do?" and then go on to the questions, "How do they do it?" and "Why do they do it?" is called a *functional psychology*. Men not only know and will, but also feel, and their emotions as well as their intellectual and executive functions are included in the scope of functional psychology. Just as the physiologist, starting with the digestion of food as a result accomplished, seeks to discover the operations that produce this result, so the functional psychologist starts with the fact that objects are perceived and asks how they are perceived, or starts with the fact that problems are solved and asks how they are solved; or he starts with the fact that men get angry and asks how they get angry. He asks "Why?" as well.

In the United States, where psychology of the armchair variety was a very active academic subject as early as 1830, long before the advent of experimental psychology, a favorite expression was the "workings of the mind" to indicate the subject matter. It was evidently a functional psychology that these "mental philosophers" were attempting to develop. They used whatever results they could glean from the contemporary physiologists and psychiatrists but were after all rather abstract. The ideal which they had before their eyes was well expressed by the chemist Edward L. Youmans in his introduction to an American edition of Alexander Bain (1868, see page 45 in our next chapter):

In the whole circle of human interests there is no need so vital and urgent as for a better understanding of the laws of mind and character. . . . The acquirement of true ideas concerning human nature, the springs of its action, the modes of its working, and the conditions and limits of its improvement, is indispensable for all. . . . The extension of the subject of Mental Philosophy so as to include the physiological elements and conditions . . . is therefore an important step in the direction of our greatest needs. . . . In place of the abstraction *mind,* is substituted the living being, compounded of mind and body, to be contemplated, like any other object of science, as actually presented to our observation and in our experience.

This last sentence was an early expression of the "organismic" point of view taken up in one of our later chapters (page 232). The functional psychologists were not always inclined toward physiology, however, for there was little known of the physiological operations of remembering or thinking but undoubtedly much to be learned by psychological experiments on these processes.

Experimental Functional Psychology

It is all very well to ask the question "How," but the difficulty is to find adequate methods for tracing the hidden process that leads to an observed result. Three general methods were devised during the nineteenth century and still seem to exhaust the possibilities. There are two objective methods which may be designated as (1) the physiological method and (2) the method of varied conditions. And there is (3) the subjective or introspective method. It will be worth our while to examine these methods.

THE PHYSIOLOGICAL METHOD. If the question is how we see, the anatomy and physiology of the eye will give an important part of our answer. The focusing mechanism for getting clear vision, the iris diaphragm for regulating the amount of light admitted, the eye muscles for turning the eyes, the retina with its rods and cones, its photochemical substances, and its connection by the optic nerve to certain parts of the brain—each plays its part in the total complex process of seeing. If the question is how we respond to a stimulus, the answer is partly to be found in the sensory and motor nerves conducting to and from the brain at a rate of about 200 feet a second. If the question is how we get angry, part of the answer is found in the activity of the adrenal glands. If the question concerns general mental activity, part of the answer may be furnished by the new technique of amplified "brain waves." These electrical phenomena, however, give only a vague impression of what is going on in the brain. They tell about as much as you would learn of the operations going on in a factory by listening to the noise coming out through a window. The physiological method does not reveal nearly all we want to know about the processes of perceiving, learning, thinking, choosing, etc., and most of the psychological work has been done with the psychological methods.

THE METHOD OF VARIED CONDITIONS. This is simply the general method of experimental science applied to the performances of an individual. He is given a task to perform, and we wish to discover how he performs it. If he can do it under certain conditions but not under others, or does it better under some conditions than others, we have some indication of his mode of operation. We may have to try out many hypotheses by appropriate control of the conditions before we obtain anything like a complete picture of the process. For example, he perceives the distance of objects in the third dimension. What are his cues or indicators of distance? Several cues are suggested and tested by comparing his success when a cue is present and when it is absent. Does he get any help from using both eyes? Compare his success with one eye open and with both. For a simple test, let him take a pencil in each hand and hold them pointing toward each other about a foot in front of his face. Let him close one eye and bring the pencil points toward each other till they almost touch—and then let him open the closed eye and see if he can improve the setting. Following this lead the physicist Charles Wheatstone in 1838 invented the stereoscope and proved that the somewhat different views obtained by the two eyes were an important cue of distance when the object is within a few feet of the eyes.

Ebbinghaus's pioneer experiment on memory (1885),[1] from which came the well-known "curve of forgetting," is a good example of the method of varied conditions. Is forgetting a gradual process? The condition varied was the elapsed time since the learning of a fixed quantity of standard material (nonsense syllables), and the results showed that when the material had been just barely learned, it was forgotten rapidly in the first few hours after learning, and then more and more slowly. Another variation of conditions was to have the material "overlearned" (more than barely learned) and the result was that it was forgotten more slowly. Another, much more recent experiment was to have the subject go to sleep immediately after learning, and the result showed that forgetting was slower than under the waking condition. The experiment has been varied in many different ways during the past sixty years, for the purpose of getting as complete a picture as possible of the process of forgetting.

One more example is the use of tests for tracing mental growth, the condition varied being age. The results indicate continued growth up through childhood and early adolescence and not much beyond. The age curve differs somewhat with

---

[1] Dates in parentheses can be used to locate the reference in the Bibliography for the entire book, pages 257-268.

the kind of performance tested. The correlation of test results is another outgrowth of this general method.

Other examples could be added indefinitely. In short, the great body of experimental work in psychology, in both the nineteenth and the twentieth centuries, has used some form of this method of varied conditions. In order to keep our historical perspective clear we should take careful note of the fact that this objective method has dominated all through the scientific period of psychology.

THE INTROSPECTIVE METHOD. You are with a friend who is driving to the suburb of a good-sized city. A few miles from the city he comes to a stop at the entrance to a side road and silently deliberates for a while, then takes the side road. You ask him how he reached his decision, and he replies, "I was getting worried about the time and the slow driving through the city. This side road seemed to run in the general direction we want and I figured that, though we might wander around a bit, we should probably lose less time this way than in the city traffic." Your friend has given you an introspective account of his thought process and probably a correct account as far as it goes. At the beginning of the present century when our schools were taking shape, much doubt was expressed regarding the validity of the introspective method and the behaviorists were for discarding it altogether—though they would admit privately that introspective reports like the one just given were wholly acceptable in ordinary life. At the time mentioned, too, a common accusation against the older psychology was that it had been merely introspective; but this was a false accusation in two respects. Many objective experiments had already been carried out, as we have seen; and even the old "mental philosophers" had not depended much on introspection in an exact sense. They had sometimes appealed to the introspection of their audience in support of a statement, as in the famous American controversy over free will. Jonathan Edwards (1754) had offered a strong logical argument against free will: "Nothing ever comes to pass without a cause. . . . The will is always determined by the strongest motive." Several of his successors, as Henry P. Tappan (1841), sought to rescue free will: "We appeal directly to consciousness; and as a result, we find that . . . there is nothing intervening between the will and its act of choice." What we miss here is a report of certain occasions when the subject said, "I was conscious of choosing A rather than B as a perfectly uncaused, unmotivated act." The modern introspectionist would require definite data, not general appeals; and he would feel that such introspections as Tappan called for were too difficult to be reliable.

Strange as it may seem, psychology learned the accurate use of introspection not from philosophy but from physics and physiology. Physics used it in studying light and sound, and physiology in studying the sense organs. Light and sound, we must remember, are not absolutely objective facts, for light is not simply radiation, but visible radiation, and sound is not simply vibration, but audible vibration. There is much vibration that is not audible and much radiation that is not visible. The most convenient way to determine the limits of the visible spectrum is to apply different wave lengths of light to the eyes of an observer and ask him to report when he sees the light and when not. The physicists from Newton's time down were interested in these subjective phenomena of light and sound. With the rapid development of physiology in the early nineteenth century, some of the physiologists began to experiment on the operation of the sense organs. An obvious approach was to apply a suitable stimulus to a sense organ and ask for a report on the sensation produced. This way of securing introspective (or at least subjective) data may be called the method of impression. Apply a stimulus and ask your observer what impression he gets. In the hands of the sense physiologists and later of the experimental psychologists the method of impression has yielded much accepted information.

One general problem in each sense is the search for the elements. The skin sense, for example, gives us any number of impressions: the size, shape, weight and texture of objects, warmth, cold, moisture and dryness, roughness and smoothness, hardness and softness, and still others. But many of these impressions might be complex, while the elementary sensations were much fewer. Experiments finally showed that there were certainly four elementary skin sensations—warmth, cold, pain, and pressure—and that probably all the others were blends of these four. This analysis was accomplished by exploring the skin with different stimuli and finding little spots sensitive to warmth, other spots sensitive to cold, and so on. In somewhat the same way the surface of the tongue was explored and four elementary taste sensations were demonstrated: sweet, sour, bitter, and salty. The numerous "tastes" that we ordinarily speak of are blends of these elements with odor sensations and also with pressure and temperature sensations from the mouth. The taste of cold lemonade is a blend of cold, sour, sweet, and lemon odor. By calling it a blend we mean that in spite of the complex of elements the total impression is unitary.

The sense of smell is more difficult to analyze. The great variety of odors has been reduced to some kind of order, but we are still not sure of the elements. In the senses of sight and hearing the method of impression has yielded many significant results.

The method of impression has been used in many different ways. It got its name in experiments on the feelings, likes and dislikes, and esthetic judgments. You show a person a color and ask whether he likes it, whether it makes a pleasant or unpleasant impression. You show him two colors and ask which makes the pleasanter impression. You show him two pictures and ask which seems to him the more beautiful, or you ask the same question regarding two faces. You cannot call his judgments on such matters either correct or incorrect, though you may be able to trace the effects of prejudice. But you do assume that he reports his actual feelings or impressions. To that extent the method of impression calls for a simple form of introspection.

But is this form of introspection really any different from our ordinary objective observation of external facts? Those psychologists who insist always on objective methods dislike the method of impression as if it were tainted with subjectivism. But it seems perfectly objective to the person who receives the impression and gives the verbal report. You show him a color and he reports, "It is green," rather than that it gives him a green impression or sensation. Even when you ask whether he likes it, he is apt to say, "It is beautiful," rather than that it gives him a pleasant impression or feeling. His attitude is that of the ordinary objective observer.

If the method of impression is unsound, all scientific observation must be unsound, since it makes the same demands on the observer. Let us suppose that a chemist has a great many specimens of water to be examined for traces of iron, and that he adds to each specimen a certain reagent which gives a blue tinge to water containing any iron; and suppose he says to himself, "If I had an assistant with a good pair of eyes whom I could trust to observe accurately, I could save myself much routine work." He advertises, and a young girl applies for the job. He fixes up some test tubes of water containing iron and others with no iron, and tells the girl that the job is to examine each test tube carefully and be sure whether or not it shows any tinge of blue. Suppose he finds her very accurate and puts her on the job. He then places his unknown specimens in her hands and depends on her to report which show the blue tinge and which do not. First he tested the girl; now with the girl's help he tests his specimens. But the girl's task is the same, and her attitude throughout is that of the objective observer. The chemist used her observations first for testing her psychologically, and then for testing the water chemically. At first he used known specimens to find out something regarding an unknown person; later he used the known person to find out something regarding unknown specimens. The data were the same, but they were used first for a psychological purpose and later for a chemical purpose.

The organism is a delicate registering instrument. One of its functions is that of perceiving or registering the environment. In studying this important function the psychologist proceeds as the physicist would in testing such a registering instrument as a new thermometer. The physicist would apply known temperatures and note whether the thermometer registered them accurately. Just so the psychologist applies known stimuli to the organism in order to determine how the organism

WILHELM WUNDT

E. B. TITCHENER

registers them; and if the organism is capable of making a verbal report, the report is used as an indicator of the registering process. Other functions are investigated by the same logic: place the organism in a situation that is controlled by the investigator and secure verbal or other responses, which are your data for indicating how the organism functions in registering the environment, in learning, solving a problem, or meeting an emergency.

FURTHER DEVELOPMENT OF THE INTROSPECTIVE METHOD. The purpose of introspection in functional psychology is to obtain from the person who has done a thing some inside information on how he did it. To be accurate enough for scientific use, an introspective report should be made right after the act is completed and it should not attempt to cover too much ground, since it depends on the person's memory of what has just "passed through his mind." The method of impression is ideal in these respects. Processes that are more complicated and take more time can nevertheless be observed and reported to some extent. There is an old standard experiment in which the subject compares two weights that are almost equal by lifting first one and then the other. Usually all he is asked to report is his impression as to which is heavier. But how can he compare the weight he is now lifting with the one he has already set down? The sensation of lifting the first weight is past and gone. The older theory was that a memory image of the pull of the first weight remained and was compared with the actual pull of the second. But why not have him describe the experience of comparing the weights, as a test of the theory? When the subject did so, the theory was not confirmed. His report was that he did not remember, nor try to remember, the pull of the first weight, but simply felt all ready for the second. When he lifted the second weight, it felt light or heavy and he accordingly called it lighter or heavier than the first—and was usually right. The experimenter by watching the subject's hand could clearly see in some cases that a weight which seemed light to the subject had come up quickly when lifted, while one which seemed heavy had come up slowly. Now if the subject adopted a standard force of lifting, adjusted always to the first weight, the second weight would come up easily if it were lighter than the first, but slowly if heavier. The process of comparison accordingly made use of a muscular adjustment instead of a memory image. This theory, which was confirmed by variations of the experiment, was based on a combination of introspective data from the subject with objective observations by the experimenter. From these experiments came the important concept of a preparatory set or state of readiness, a concept that has a wide range of application.

The type of introspective report first obtained in this experiment stands to the credit mostly of G. E. Müller (1850-1934), one of a small number of German psychologists who, without being pupils of Wundt—being rivals, rather—had started laboratories not long after Wundt. (The experiment cited dates from 1889.) Müller went on to use his new introspective method in his long-continued studies of memory (1911, 1913, 1917). The excellent pioneer work of Ebbinghaus (already mentioned, page 16) had used objective data exclusively. It had seemed to indicate that a list of nonsense syllables was memorized by a mechanical, though very intense, process of linking syllable to syllable, quite in line with the old associationist theory. Müller, entertaining some doubt of this interpretation, required his subjects to report their experiences in memorizing the material. The subjects found a good deal to report. They seemed to be very active while memorizing, by no means receiving the material passively and letting it link itself together by some automatic process. They grouped the items, such as numbers or nonsense syllables, put the series into rhythmical form, noted similarities and contrasts, lugged in meanings where possible, and in general actively organized the material. Müller found the combination of objective and introspective methods an excellent approach to the question of how we learn.

About 1900 another great psychologist, Alfred Binet of Paris (1857-1911), began to use introspection in an experimental study of the process of thinking. In his early days Binet had written a book on the psychology of reasoning, quite in the old style, without bothering to obtain any firsthand data, but trusting to logic and the theory of association to furnish a scheme of the reasoning process. In that book he assumed that reasoning must be a process of calling up and manipulating memory images. In his new work (1903) he based his conclusions on actual thinking processes reported by his two young daughters, girls of high school age. He gave them problems to solve and had them notice and report how they solved them. He would quiz them: "Just how did you think of that object? Did you see it? Or say its name to yourself?" Sometimes his subjects reported images, but in many instances they denied the presence of any images, and Binet was thus forced to abandon the theory that thinking consisted essentially in the manipulation of images. Thinking seemed to go on largely in just "thoughts," "*pensées*"—he could find no better word. These thoughts—"imageless thoughts" they were often called—could be described as "thinking of" a certain object or "thinking that" so and so was the case; but this sort of description was not accepted as expert introspection by all psychologists. Even so, the introspective method had scored two successes: it had disproved an old theory; and it had shown that the general course of a thought process could be reported, even if the details were not adequately described.

Almost immediately a school of *Denkpsychologie* ("thought psychology") arose in Germany under the leadership of Oswald Külpe (1862-1915), a pupil of Wundt who broke away in certain respects from his master's teaching. This school, comprising many distinguished psychologists, flourished in Germany up to the time of the first world war and has been continued independently in Belgium by Albert Michotte (born 1881), professor at Louvain, and his students.[2] This school made systematic use of the combined introspective and objective methods, with more emphasis on the introspective reports which tended to be very elaborate. They fully confirmed Binet's imageless thoughts and added many other facts on the process of thinking; and they found Müller's "preparatory set" important in both simple and complicated thought processes.

---

[2] For a recent example of this work, which is allied also to that of the Gestalt school, see Michotte, 1946.

There can be no reasonable doubt, in spite of the behaviorists, that introspection affords some very good glimpses of the processes of learning, problem solving, and reaching a decision. As was said before, however, the objective method of varied conditions has been the favorite of functional psychologists. Many of them think of introspection as belonging to another school with which they are not in sympathy. But we may well be curious to know what other school there could be in view of the broad scope of functional psychology. What other goal could psychology set before itself except that of discovering what the organism does and how and why?

The Structural Psychology of Conscious Experience

William James (1842-1910), a truly great psychologist, in offering a *Briefer course* in psychology for the college student in 1892, started off with a definition which was regarded as standard at the time: "The definition of psychology may be best given . . . as the description and explanation of states of consciousness as such." A much-used English textbook of the period was *Outlines of psychology,* 1884, by James Sully, who said: "I abide by the old conception that psychology is distinctly marked off from the physical or natural sciences as . . . having to do with the phenomena of the inner world, and employing its own method or instrument, namely, introspection." Wilhelm Wundt (1832-1920), certainly a leader in psychology, said in 1892: "Psychology has to investigate that which we call internal experience—i.e., our own sensation and feeling, our thought and volition—in contradistinction to the objects of external experience, which form the subject matter of natural science." In 1896, however, he replaced the words "internal experience," by the improved formula "immediate experience," so as to include what obviously was a part of psychology's subject matter, our experience of external objects. We are conscious of objects outside us as well as of thoughts and feelings inside us, and a science of conscious experience must cover both. Undoubtedly it is the inner experience that first awakens the interest of students who approach psychology from this angle.

James said in a well-known passage of his larger work, the *Principles of psychology* (1890, I, page 550):

The manner in which trains of imagery and consideration follow each other through our thinking, the restless flight of one idea before the next, the transitions our minds make between things wide as the poles asunder . . . all this magical, imponderable streaming has from time immemorial excited the admiration of all whose attention happened to be caught by its omnipresent mystery. And it has furthermore challenged the race of philosophers to banish something of the mystery by formulating the process in simpler terms.

If conscious experience was set apart as the field for a science of psychology to explore and reduce to order, the project was similar to that of chemistry. Discover the elements of conscious experience and their modes of combination. So it seemed to Wundt anyway, though in James's view, on the contrary, the main requirement was to bring out clearly the fluid, streaming, and personal nature of consciousness. It was Wundt, not James, who mapped out the field of *structural psychology,* which however he called simply "psychology." All our experiences—perceptions of external objects, memories, emotions, purposes—are complex and call for scientific analysis.

The elements of conscious experience, in Wundt's analysis, were of two main classes: the sensations which seem to come to us from outside, and the feelings which seem to belong to ourselves. The elementary sensations were teased out by the sense physiologists—the colors, the tones, the elementary tastes, the elementary skin sensations. For the functional psychologist these sensory elements help to explain how we see, hear, etc., but for the structural psychologist they are significant as being the simplest possible kinds of experience, unless it be the feelings. Of the elementary feelings, the pleasant and unpleasant were universally agreed on, and Wundt proposed two additional pairs: the excited and the quiet; the tense and the relaxed. These elements combine into many blends and patterns. Emotion, for example, is a complex experience composed of feelings and bodily sensations; and the experience of willing is a certain time pattern of emotion, characterized by an abrupt change of feeling at the moment of decision. Throughout Wundt aims to describe not what man does but what his experience is—not his acts but the contents of his consciousness.

Of Wundt's laws of combination the most interesting is his "law of psychic resultants" or "principle of creative synthesis." Combination creates new properties. "Every psychic compound has characteristics which are by no means the mere sum of the characteristics of the elements" (1896, page 375). Something very much like this law is to be found in the teachings of the associationists before Wundt and of the Gestalt psychologists after Wundt.

As the revered head of the Leipzig laboratory, where many of the young leaders were trained at about the turn of the century, Wundt exerted great influence on the psychology of that period. Few of his numerous American pupils seem to have carried away a hearty acceptance of the structural point of view; they remained functionalists at heart. But Wundt had at least one vigorous representative in the United States from 1892 on for over three decades.

Edward Bradford Titchener (1867-1927) an English pupil of Wundt, would have preferred on obtaining his doctor's degree in 1892 to be the pioneer in Britain of the new experimental psychology, but the time was not ripe, the British being skeptical of the new approach to one of their favorite philosophical subjects. Titchener accepted a position at Cornell University and remained there the rest of his life, directing a very active laboratory and training a loyal band of structural psychologists. He promptly took up the cudgels in support of the Wundtian structural psychology as against the functional psychology which he found dominant in the United States. It was Titchener at this time who coined the terms *functional* and *structural psychology* (1898, 1899). We can speak of the structure of a machine and of its function or use. We can speak of the structure of the eye and of the function or operation and use of each part of the structure. In biology we have structural sciences and functional sciences, human anatomy being structural, while physiology is functional. The structure of an organ is what it is; the function is what it does, what it is for. Both kinds of science are important, but the structural would seem to have priority, since the function of an organ could not very well be investigated until the organ itself was known.

Now psychology is the science of consciousness, according to general agreement at that time. This science, like biology, will include a study of structure and a study of function. The structure of consciousness will be what consciousness is, "as such," and the function of consciousness will be what it does, what use it is in the life of the individual and of the social group. Structural study should have priority over functional, for until we know thoroughly what conscious processes are we are not equipped to investigate what they do for the organism. Functional psychology will continue to be speculative till structural psychology has provided a scientific foundation.

Now how shall we describe the structure of consciousness, or better, of any conscious process or experience? Every experience, as Wundt said, is complex and calls for scientific analysis; and when analysis has gone as far as possible and reached the elements of conscious experience, description must advance to synthesis, so as to show how the elements fit together into the concrete conscious experience. You recognize a person in the street as an old acquaintance. Logically this must be a complex experience, some elements being supplied by the sense of sight and other elements by memory. As structural psychologists, however, we are not satisfied with this logical analysis, but insist on observing in the experience what is supplied by memory. Is it an image of some past experience or is it a mere feeling of familiarity? Observational analysis of such everyday experiences may be very difficult and only to be accomplished in the laboratory by well-trained introspectionists. They must be trained to report only what they observe as factually present. They must report only the elements they find in the experience, not the logical meaning or practical value of the elements. They must not be like the person who when asked to describe a certain coin says that it is a shilling, so stating its meaning or value and not what it is in itself. The introspective observer must learn to strip off meanings and values. The meanings and values are indeed present in the experience, but they are not elements; they are elusive compounds which must be analyzed if possible. As would be expected, and as Titchener himself expected, his standards for expert introspection were difficult to enforce in the laboratory. To bring out his point of view he sometimes spoke of his brand of psychology as the "existential."

With conscious experience as the subject matter of psychology, the questions "What?" and "How?" take on a new aspect. "What?" becomes "What are the elements?" and "How?" becomes "How are they combined?" The "Why" question calls for explanation and for fitting conscious experiences into the organism and the world at large (Titchener, 1909-1910, page 41). The question "What for?" has no place in existential psychology, being the appropriate question for a functional psychology, and corresponding to the "What" question of the genuine functional psychology. That is, the genuine functional psychology starts not from consciousness, but from man's doings, and uses introspection to give some indications of how he does what he does. If consciousness is the only proper starting point for any psychology, as was generally assumed in 1900, man's doings can be regarded as what consciousness is for, i.e., as the value, use, or function of consciousness.

The word *function* has two related but rather confusing meanings. It means "use or value"; and it means "operation or process." If you look under the hood of an automobile and discover a certain structure there called a carburetor, you ask, "What is the function of this thing? What is it for? What does it do? What is its use in the running of the automobile?" But if you start with the automobile as a whole, a functional whole, you ask what operations must go on in it, what internal functions (not external uses) it must have; and you see that it has the function of supplying its own energy by burning gasoline. Then you ask how this function is carried out and discover that gasoline and air are mixed in the carburetor. In the same way you could start with a bodily organ such as the stomach and ask what its function is, or you could start with the function of digestion and ask how it operates. At the psychological level you could, as a structuralist, start with memory images and then, turning functionalist, ask what use they have for the organism; or, being a functionalist from the start, you would note that the organism has the function of remembering past events and then, asking how this function is performed, find that memory images played a part. Either approach is legitimate, but the thoroughgoing functional approach seems more promising if what you want in the end is a functional psychology. And the actual work in functional psychology, of which a few samples were cited earlier in this chapter, has approached its problems not from the side of conscious experience but from the side of results accomplished. (There is still a third meaning of *function*, taken over from mathematics, and probably more common than either of the others in present-day psychology. Y is a function of X, i.e., depends on X, varies systematically with X. Appetite is a function of the time since eating; forgetting is a function of the time since learning; intelligence is a function of age. The numerous "curves" which psychological investigators put out to show their results are functions in this sense, or represent functions. They also, to be sure, belong under the head of functional psychology for the most part.)

Though Titchener won quite a number of adherents, especially among his students, his crusade for a structural psychology did not carry the day with American psychologists generally. Instead, great and increasing doubt was voiced as to whether psychology was properly the science of consciousness as such or was not better called the science of behavior (see Chapter 4). Titchener granted that there could be a science of behavior but denied that it was psychology. Instead it would necessarily be a part of biology. According to Titchener (1929) the biological and psychological viewpoints are radically different, since biology views the organism in relation to the environment while psychology views conscious experience in relation to the organism. Conscious experience has direct relations, not with the environment, but only with processes occurring within the organism, especially in the nervous system. But behavior is directly related to the environment and so belongs in the province of biology.

In spite of this attempt to draw a sharp line between genuine psychology and the science of behavior, Titchener still regarded the two sciences as closely related. In his general textbooks (1909-1910, 1915) he introduced functional as well as structural material. He projected a comprehensive advanced treatise on structural psychology; but this project bogged down for some reason, perhaps because of the difficulty of fitting into his scheme the newer developments in introspective psychology. He evidently had considerable sympathy with the *Denkpsychologie* (page 23) but could not accept "imageless thought" as adding anything to the conscious elements of sensation, image, and feeling (1909). He may well have had a similar sympathy for the emerging "phenomenological psychology" (page 34) and even for Gestalt psychology (page 120); but to fit these into his system would have been almost impossible. At any rate, his comprehensive treatise was never completed, and only the introductory groundwork was published (1929). His *magnum opus*, a great contribution to the advancement of our science, was his four-volume *Experimental psychology* (1901, 1905). Here, too, functional as well as structural experiments are included. In fact anyone would find it very difficult to draw the line. The quantitative study of sensation ("psychophysics") can evidently be regarded as belonging to structural psychology, but at the same time it is a study of the *functions* of discrimination and estimation. The same can be said of the valuable work on the "dimensions" of a sensation, such as tonal pitch, loudness, volume, and density (Boring and Stevens, 1936). Titchener's pupils can certainly not be accused of any narrow outlook (Pillsbury, 1911; Washburn, 1916, 1930; Boring, 1929, 1930, 1942; Bentley, 1926, 1930).

The Chicago School of Functional Psychology

Titchener's challenge to the functionalists was promptly accepted by a vigorous group at the University of Chicago under the leadership of John Dewey (born 1859) and James Rowland Angell (born 1869), two of the most distinguished men in our whole list—Dewey the great philosopher, Angell later influen-

WILLIAM JAMES

JAMES R. ANGELL

JOHN DEWEY

HARVEY CARR

tial as an educational administrator. In their stand for a functional psychology they were influenced by William James with his conviction that consciousness was not a mere frill or epiphenomenon but rather a genuine causal factor in life and biological survival. Every sensation or feeling, besides its mere existence, has a function as referring to some kind of an object, knowing it and also choosing or rejecting it. Moreover, "every possible feeling produces a movement," or sometimes an inhibition of movement. Conscious processes are thus tied in with the environment on both sensory and motor sides (1890, I, pages 271, 478; II, page 372).

Like James, the early Chicago functionalists accepted the definition of psychology as the science of consciousness and held that conscious processes should be studied not only as existential facts but also as playing their parts in the life of the individual and his adaptation to the environment. A few citations from Angell's *Psychology, an introductory study of the structure and function of human consciousness* (1904), will bring out the point of view.

Psychologists have hitherto devoted the larger part of their energy to investigating the *structure* of the mind. Of late, however, there has been manifest a disposition to deal more fully with its functional and genetic phases. To determine how consciousness develops and how it operates is felt to be quite as important as the discovery of its constituent elements. . . . The fundamental psychological method is introspection . . . the direct examination of one's own mental processes. . . . We are able to supplement introspection by immediate objective observation of other individuals. . . . Animal psychology is engaged with the study of consciousness, wherever . . . its presence can be detected. . . . We shall adopt the biological point of view . . . we shall regard all the operations of consciousness—all our sensations, all our emotions, and all our acts of will—as so many expressions of organic adaptations to our environment, an environment which we must remember is social as well as physical. . . . If the reflexes and the automatic acts were wholly competent to steer the organism throughout its course, there is no reason to suppose that consciousness would ever put in an appearance.[3]

---

[3] Angell, 1904, pp. iii, 4, 6, 7, 50. See also Angell, 1907, 1936.

Here we see an outspoken functionalism making its debut in psychology, but it was not identical with the latent functionalism of the experimental work mentioned earlier in the chapter. It did not start with results accomplished by the individual and ask how they were accomplished, but it started with conscious processes and asked what their use might be in organic and social life. It sought to discover what needs of the organism were met by sense perception, by memory images, by emotion. Taking the evolutionary point of view, it sought to divine at what stage in the development of the race the need for each mental process must have led to the emergence of that particular ability. The simpler forms of consciousness probably emerged when reflexes were unable to meet the organism's needs, and the higher mental processes emerged when a wider and more flexible control of the environment became necessary. Thus functional psychology aimed to give psychology a place in the general field of biological science. It aimed also to be of practical use, especially in the field of education. Dewey, besides his eminence as the philosopher of pragmatism, was a pioneer in progressive education, which, he said, should be based on an understanding of the child's needs as a childish person.

Believing so strongly in genetic or developmental psychology, the Chicago functionalists soon possessed an active animal laboratory. Consciousness could be assumed, according to Angell's view, whenever an animal adjusted to a novel environment or problem. Without regard to this particular assumption the laboratory became and long remained very productive of experimental work on animal learning. Under the direct leadership of Angell's junior colleague and later successor, Harvey Carr (born 1873), the Chicago group lost most of that great emphasis on introspection and most of those speculative and philosophical interests (Carr, 1930), and it trained and sent out to all parts of the country many productive research psychologists. The Chicago school has been a very important psychological center, though Angell never aspired to establish a "school" in our sense. In the course of time the Chicago brand merged with the "latent" brand, which has remained the dominant

American tendency in psychology, a tendency that is, however, not limited to this country.

European Functionalists

Edouard Claparède (1873-1940) is the best example of a European functionalist, and there are many parallels between his work at Geneva in Switzerland and the practically simultaneous work of the Chicago group. Early in his career he adopted a point of view which he first called biological and later functional. The functional conception, he said, "considers psychical phenomena primarily from the point of view of their function in life. . . . This comes to the same thing as asking one's self : What is their use?" (1930, page 79). Their function is to meet a person's needs and interests. He set up an animal laboratory in his department of the university. Because of his dissatisfaction with the traditional methods of elementary teaching and his belief that "the teacher should learn from the child," he founded at Geneva the now world-famous J. J. Rousseau Institute for the study of the child and for the development of progressive methods of teaching. He found John Dewey's ideas on education very much to his liking. Believing in introspection, he would not by any means restrict it as Titchener did to the observation of meaningless existential content. For the study of thought processes he adopted a method which he called *réflexion parlée* or "thinking aloud" (1943). Claparède had no desire to found a "school" of psychology. A peace-loving man of wide acquaintance among psychologists, for many years the secretary of the International Congresses of Psychology, he regarded the controversies between schools as wasted energy which might better be turned into productive channels. "What is the use of wantonly limiting the scope of psychology, prescribing beforehand the concepts which will be of value to it? I believe one should be eclectic and adopt provisionally all those points of view which would appear to be of practical value, even if they be contradictory" (1930, page 96). There should not be many "psychologies," but a single all-inclusive psychology.

David Katz (born 1884, now at the University of Stockholm), a pupil of G. E. Müller and long his right-hand man in the Göttingen laboratory, later professor in other universities in Germany, the United States, and Sweden, might be classed as a functionalist in the broad sense. He is well known for his animal experiments and for his intimate studies of young children. He has attacked the psychological problems of hunger and appetite. Outstanding are his works on the phenomenology of color sensation (1911, 1930) and of touch sensation (1925). He stands as the promoter of "phenomenological psychology." By *phenomena* we mean "appearances." By *touch phenomena* we mean the impressions an ordinary observer gets from touching and handling objects and various kinds of material. We do not tell our observer about the "elements," warmth, cold, pressure, and pain. We leave him as naïve as possible and simply ask him to report how these things feel. He reports that one thing is smooth and hard, another thing soft and bulky, and uses quite a variety of such descriptive adjectives. The structural psychologist might complain that such data are unscientific, contaminated with meanings acquired in past experience, and not pure sensations. The phenomenological attitude is that these naïve impressions are important for psychology and that we should not restrict our psychology to analysis into elements and synthesis of known elements into compounds. Certainly Katz used the phenomenological approach very effectively and worked out a great deal of good psychology. His work on "color constancy" was particularly important and has been followed up by other investigators in many laboratories.

Edgar Rubin (born 1886, professor at the University of Copenhagen) was a pupil of Müller and Katz at Göttingen and may be counted as an exponent of the phenomenological method. His special contribution was the famous study of figure and ground (1915, 1921). To see a figure as standing out from its background is perhaps as fundamental a characteristic of the process of seeing as to see the elementary colors. The figure is typically compact and at any rate it has some form, while the background appears like unlimited space. The figure is more apt to catch attention, but there is no great difficulty in directing attention to the ground; so that the difference between figure and ground is not merely the difference between the focus and margin of attention. Figure and ground are not peculiar to the sense of sight. A rhythmical drum-beat or the chugging of a motorboat stands out against the general background of vaguer noises; and something moving on the skin stands out from the general mass of cutaneous sensations. The facts are obvious enough, but they were overlooked by psychologists till their significance was demonstrated by Rubin. Figure and ground were quickly taken up by the Gestalt school (page 128) and made a part of their system. Rubin's own attitude toward the schools was much like that of Claparède: "Psychological schools are a nuisance. As a rule the association of the members with each other serves as a help toward the continued belief in some unproved favorite notions which characterize the school. As a rule the founders of a school are not so bad as the pupils" (1930).

Rubin, like Katz, and like G. E. Müller before them, could be broadly included in the functional school except that that school is so very broad as scarcely to be called a school. It is a school, of course, in distinction from the structural school. The phenomenological method of impression, along with the somewhat similar free introspection of Claparède, Binet, and the *Denkpsychologie* group, is a useful tool for the study of psychological functions (cf. MacLeod, 1947). Even the results obtained by the restricted introspection of the structuralists can often be turned to good account in the study of function.

In this chapter we have taken note of two, or really three, approaches to psychology. One is the structural approach, the other two are functional. The structural approach starts from a man's conscious experience and attempts to give a scientific account of it and by analysis and synthesis to work out its composition or structure. The Chicago functionalists also started from a man's conscious experience but were interested not only in its structure but also in its function or use to the man in his dealing with the physical and social environment. The primary fact for this school was conscious experience; the secondary fact was the function of consciousness. This approach can therefore be called secondary functionalism. By contrast, primary functionalism starts with results accomplished and asks by what process they are accomplished. It may appeal to conscious experience for evidence on the process, but its interest in conscious experience is secondary to its interest in functions.

Psychology was formerly defined as the science of the mind. Considered as an entity, "the mind" is a metaphysical concept of no use to an empirical science such as modern psychology. The structuralists, however, could define an individual's mind as the sum total of his conscious experiences. The secondary functionalists could accept this definition, adding that the role in life of consciousness must be considered. The primary functionalists would define mind as the sum total of mental functions, though they would admit the difficulty of drawing a sharp distinction between these and other functions of the organism.

Of the schools next to be considered, associationism and behaviorism certainly belong to the general functional group, while Gestalt psychology originated, at least, as a reform in structural psychology.

CHAPTER 3

ASSOCIATIONISM OLD AND NEW

The topic of learning has a prominent place in present-day psychology, as anyone can see by examining the current textbooks or glancing through the journals that report current research. How we learn—the "we" including animals as well as men—has been for several decades one of the biggest problems for psychological experimenters and theorists. How we learn a poem or a list of nonsense syllables, how we learn to solve a puzzle or to find our way through a maze, how we learn a good or a bad habit, how we learn a face so as to recognize it later, or a scene so as to describe it, or a motor performance so as to execute it with skill and speed—all these and many similar questions have been investigated. Learning is certainly one of the major interests of psychology today.

It is surprising, then, to find no chapter on learning in the older textbooks. Even William James in his great book of 1890, the *Principles of psychology,* had no such chapter, nor did the term *learning* occur in the index of this two-volume work. The older psychologists had a great deal to say about *remembering* what had previously been learned, but they had not begun to experiment on the process of learning. They did, however, have a general theory of the process of learning, and this was the theory of *association.* They started, not with the process of learning, but with the facts of remembering and thinking. They asked where the ideas came from that were used in thinking, and they answered that they came from past experience and largely—some said entirely—from past sensory experience. They asked how it came about that ideas occurred in clusters and often in regular sequences, and they answered that the clusters and sequences had been formed in past experience by the linking together of sensations that occurred together

37

or in immediate succession. This was the teaching of the associationists, a predominantly British school.[1]

The Older Associationism

The germ of associationism can be found even as far back as Aristotle's essay on "Memory." He made the fundamental observation that one thing reminds you of another, and went on to ask this question, in effect: "If A reminds you of B, what is the relation of A and B?" He answered that the relation was sometimes one of *similarity,* sometimes one of *contrast,* sometimes one of *contiguity.* For example, one person reminds you of another because they are so much alike, or because they are markedly different, or because you have seen them together. These three relations were called the "laws of association" by the British associationists, who attempted with some success to reduce them all to the single law of contiguity in experience. If A, a stranger, reminds you of your friend B, the two have obviously never been together in your experience; but if they resemble each other, you must now see something in A which you have previously seen in B, and this something, this common characteristic, furnishes a bridge of contiguity between A and B. Contrast could be plausibly reduced to partial contiguity in somewhat the same way.

While these reductions might be open to question, the concept of association seems too matter-of-fact to arouse controversy or provide the basis for a "school." The British associationists made it the basis of their school by claiming so much for it—by regarding it as the sole mental operation, except for sensation. At once, therefore, they came into conflict with the faculty psychology which assumed a variety of mental operations to account for the various results accomplished. Thomas Hobbes, the first of the British line, had the following to say in his *Leviathan,* 1651:

---

[1] For the full story of the associationist school, see Warren (1921), and for briefer accounts Murphy (1929), Heidbreder (1933), and Boring (1929).

Concerning the thoughts of man, I will consider them first singly, and afterwards in train, or dependence upon one another. . . . The original of them all is that which we call 'sense,' for there is no conception in a man's mind which hath not at first, totally or by parts, been begotten upon the organs of sense. . . . As we have no imagination, whereof we have not formerly had sense, in whole or in parts, so we have no transition from one imagination to another, whereof we never had the like before in our senses. . . . All fancies are motions within us, relics of those made in the sense; and those motions that immediately succeeded one another in the sense continue also together after sense. . . .

But the philosophy schools . . . teach another doctrine. . . . Some say the senses receive the species of things, and deliver them to the common sense; and the common sense delivers them over to the fancy, and the fancy to the memory, and the memory to the judgment, like handing of things from one to another, with many words making nothing understood. . . . Those other faculties . . . are acquired and increased by study and industry. . . . For besides sense, and thoughts, and the train of thoughts, the mind of man has no other motion.

In place of the various faculties, then, Hobbes admitted only three (or two) fundamental operations: sensation, recall, and association which governs recall. Hobbes did not use the word *association* which was introduced by later writers, but when he speaks of "fancies," i.e., thoughts and images, as coming in sequences determined by the original succession of sensations, he is speaking of association by contiguity. Hobbes reduces the two or three fundamental operations mentioned to a single one which he calls "motion." An external object affects the senses through what we now call the "stimulus" of light, sound, pressure, or chemical action—some kind of physical motion—and the motion of the stimulus is communicated into the organism through a sense organ. When the stimulus ceases, the internal motion does not cease but continues by inertia though gradually dying away. The original motion is the sensation, and the residual motion is the retained image. A certain sequence of stimuli leaves behind the same sequence of images and so accounts for a later sequence of thoughts. So Hobbes reduced everything to physical terms: motion, the communication of motion, and inertia. But he was forced to recognize one additional factor in the organism. The organism reacts to the stimulus by muscular movement, and the *direction* of this movement is not communicated from outside but originates within the organism. The reaction is either approaching or avoiding, either toward or away from an external object. Desire is an incipient motion of approach, aversion an incipient motion of avoidance. Some desires, such as the appetite for food, are native, and others are acquired from experience of the properties of objects. Hobbes develops this theme extensively, but most interesting to us is his use of desire as a control factor in association. He made the important distinction between what we now call free and controlled association. Because stimuli occur in different sequences at different times, there are many alternative sequences of thoughts available. From A you may pass to B, C, or D, each of which has followed A at one time or another. So thought is free to wander unless there is some active desire present to exercise a selective and directive influence.

This train of thoughts . . . is of two sorts. The first is 'unguided,' 'without design,' and inconstant; wherein there is no passionate thought to govern and direct those that follow . . . in which case the thoughts are said to wander, . . . as in a dream. . . . The second is more constant, as being 'regulated' by some desire and design. . . . From desire ariseth the thought of some means. . . . And because the end . . . comes often to mind, in case our thoughts begin to wander, they are quickly again reduced into the way. . . . Look often upon what you would have, as the thing that directs all your thoughts in the way to attain it.

Hobbes was concerned with the sequence of thoughts, the *successive association* of later terminology. John Locke, next in the chronological list of the British school, had more to say of what was later called *simultaneous association*. In his famous *Essay concerning human understanding,* 1690, Locke undertook to prove that all our knowledge is derived from experience. He combated the notion that self-evident or axiomatic knowledge is independent of experience and based upon "innate ideas." Instead, he held that all *simple ideas* are derived from experience, mostly from sensory experience of the outside world but partly from experience of our own mental operations. Given these simple ideas as elements, we are able to put them together into *compound ideas* of endless variety.

To test the validity of any idea we have to trace it back to its origin and see whether it is justified by experience. Locke was most interested in this philosophical question of the validity of knowledge, and the philosophical discussion which he started and which continued for a hundred years and more does not concern us here. As to the psychological question of how we combine ideas, he indicates that some are combined because they logically belong together, but others from the mere chance "association of ideas"—this being the first appearance in the literature of that historic expression. He wrote,[2]

> Some of our ideas have a natural correspondence and connexion one with another: it is the office . . . of our reason to . . . hold them together. . . . There is another connexion of ideas wholly owing to chance or custom: ideas that in themselves are not [at all akin] come to be so united in some men's minds that it is very hard to separate them; . . . the one no sooner at any time comes into the understanding, but its associate appears with it. . . .
>
> *Instances.* The ideas of goblins and sprights have really no more to do with darkness than light: yet let but a foolish maid inculcate these often on the mind of a child, . . . possibly he shall never be able to separate them again so long as he lives; but darkness shall for ever afterward bring with it those frightful ideas. . . . Many children imputing the pain they endured at school to their books . . . so join those ideas together that a book becomes their aversion . . . and thus reading becomes a torment to them, which otherwise possibly they might have made the greatest pleasure of their lives.

It is interesting to find what we now call conditioned fears and antipathies appearing so early in the history of associationism. Many other foretastes of modern scientific results could be culled from the authors who followed Locke in the next century and more, if we had the leisure for such historical research. Just a few salient contributions should be mentioned.

George Berkeley in his *Essay toward a new theory of vision,* 1709, made an important contribution, though he did not use the term *association.* Just as the meanings of words are obviously acquired by associating the words with the objects they stand for, so it is with a great variety of signs and indicators.

---

[2] In Book 2, Chapter 33 of the 4th edition of the *Essay,* 1700.

A certain sound means to the listener "a horse trotting along the road"—evidently because of previous observation of horses making that sort of noise. Since the eye furnishes only a two-dimensional picture, and still reveals the third dimension—the distance of objects—the visual appearance must indicate distance by virtue of association with the bodily movements necessary to reach a seen object. All such sign-meaning associations are successive rather than simultaneous, the sign having the role of a stimulus, in modern terminology, and the meaning the role of a response. Because of constant use, however, and because of predominant interest in the meaning, we are scarcely aware of the sign but seem to ourselves actually to see distance, as we even seem to hear the meanings of words spoken in everyday conversation.

David Hume in his two great books, *Treatise on human nature,* 1739, and *Inquiry concerning human understanding,* 1748, carried forward the discussion of the validity of knowledge which had been inaugurated by Locke (and which was later taken up in Germany by Kant and his successors). Hume formulated the problem of the associationist psychology very clearly when he asked whether it was not possible to go behind the "faculties" and discover "the secret springs and principles by which the mind is actuated in its operations." He concluded that such a principle was found in association, a force of attraction between ideas. He recognized the factor of similarity but laid most emphasis on contiguity, especially the immediate succession of one sensation (or "impression") after another. Some sequences of impressions are so frequent and invariable as to become firmly associated, with the result that we cannot see the antecedent occur without expecting the consequent. We then call them cause and effect, and we assume that the effect *must* occur because the cause has occurred. We imagine that we see a "necessary connection" in cases such as the falling of an unsupported body or the putting out of a fire by water thrown upon it—just because we are forced by habitual association to expect the usual consequent after the given antecedent. All our reasoning, except in mathematics, is based on habitual associations. "This is the whole operation of the mind, in all our conclusions concerning matter of fact." [3]

David Hartley, a contemporary of Hume, published in 1749 his *Observations on man, his frame, his duty, and his expectations,* a book that is less philosophical and more psychological than those of his predecessors. He reduced everything to association by contiguity in experience, either simultaneous or successive. Sensations occurring simultaneously tended to coalesce into a complex sensation, like the taste of lemonade, and left behind a corresponding complex idea; and ideas brought together in the mind tended similarly to coalesce. Muscular movements often repeated in the same sequence became associated into automatic habits. Ideas became associated with movements and so furnished the basis for voluntary action. Emotions were combinations of sensations, including especially pleasure and pain, bound into units by simultaneous association. So Hartley developed associationism into an all-round theory, a theory which, though vigorously opposed in certain quarters, was widely accepted and influential for the hundred years following. Though capable of further development, it remained little changed till the early part of the nineteenth century.

Thomas Brown was professor at Edinburgh—the first professor in our list—and his remarkable, though long-winded, *Lectures on the philosophy of the human mind* were published in 1820. By this time the modern science of chemistry had begun to show its power, and to Brown it furnished a guide or analogy in tackling the problem of simultaneous association. Many sensations, emotions, and ideas are complex and call for analysis; and yet they have characteristics which are not found in their elements, as the taste of lemonade is a blend and not simply a sum of sweet, sour, etc.:

As in chemistry it often happens that the qualities of the separate ingredients of a compound body are not recognizable by us in the apparently different qualities of the compound itself—so, in this spontaneous *chemistry of the mind,* the compound sentiment that results from

---

[3] *Inquiry,* Section 5.

the association of former feelings has in many cases . . . little resemblance to these constituents.[4]

This idea of a "mental chemistry" reappeared from time to time in later psychological theories; it was rechristened "creative synthesis" by Wundt and was taken over as a central problem by the Gestalt school.

Brown accepted contiguity in experience as the sole primary law of association but saw that certain secondary laws were needed. Why does A remind me of B at one time, but of C or D at another time, B, C, and D having been contiguous with A at different moments of my previous experience? It depends, said Brown, on such factors as the relative *frequency, recency,* and liveliness (later renamed *vividness*) of those previous contiguities.[5] These secondary laws have remained a permanent possession of psychology.

A third major contribution of Thomas Brown may not belong in a strict associationist psychology, since it recognizes something besides the combination of ideas or impressions. Objects are not merely associated; they are compared, related to each other:

There is an original tendency . . . of the mind, by which, on perceiving together different objects, we are instantly . . . sensible of their relation in certain respects . . . coexistence and succession . . . resemblance . . . difference . . . proportion . . . degree . . . the number of relations, indeed, being almost infinite.[6]

He goes on to show that knowledge consists very largely in perceived relations. Mathematics and indeed all science are concerned wholly with relations.

James Mill's *Analysis of the phenomena of the human mind,* 1829, is regarded as the high point of strict associationism. With his insistence on a rigidly logical and consistent system, Mill discarded mental chemistry and perception of relations, and admitted only simple ideas derived from sensation and mechanically linked by association. When the associations are strong

---

[4] Lecture 10.
[5] Lecture 37.
[6] Lecture 45. Brown probably was indebted to the French psychologist Laromiguière in this matter of perception of relations.

and quick-acting from frequent use, the elements may *seem* to coalesce and the resulting complex idea may seem simple, though it still is composed of all the simple ideas that have entered into it in past experience. The complex idea of a house contains the less complex ideas of walls, windows, doors, floors, roof, and chimney, and these contain the simpler ideas of bricks, boards, and nails, and the still simpler ideas of wood, iron, glass, mortar, etc., combined of course with appropriate ideas of size, shape, position, and strength. Such a complex idea would seem to be unmanageable in any ordinary thinking about a house, without some sort of unifying organization of the total idea. It certainly seemed as if James Mill's logical system amounted to a *reductio ad absurdum* of strict associationism. Accordingly his son, John Stuart Mill, in giving this work a critical revision, reinstated mental chemistry and spoke of the simple ideas as "generating," rather than composing, the complex ones.

Last of the great figures in the British line of associationists is Alexander Bain, whose principal works, *The senses and the intellect,* 1855, and *The emotions and the will,* 1859, have much of the modern atmosphere. But Bain departed in some respects from the strict associationist doctrine. (1) He said that the first step toward building up knowledge from sensory experience was not association but discrimination, the singling out of an item from the mass. Until it has been separated it is not ready to be combined with other items. (2) Associations are established not by contiguity alone but by perception of likeness and difference, cause and effect, utility and other relations. (3) Being interested in motor behavior as well as in sensations and ideas, he could not say that everything is derived from experience; for the infant possesses some definite reflexes as well as a large stock of "random movements" which furnish the raw material for motor behavior. There are no innate ideas, as Locke rightly insisted, but there are surely innate muscular movements. There is such a thing as instinct, defined as "untaught ability" or as "what can be done prior to experience and education." Associationism had tried to trace everything back to experience, but now the factor of heredity had to be added.

The emphasis on heredity was greatly accentuated a little later, when Darwin and evolution began to make an impression on psychology.

British associationism had considerable influence in France but very little in Germany down to the beginning of the nineteenth century. Hume's skeptical theory of knowledge had indeed been a powerful stimulus to German philosophy, but in psychology the faculty theory remained dominant down to the time of Johann Friedrich Herbart and his textbook, *Lehrbuch zur Psychologie,* 1816, and his more extensive treatise, *Psychologie als Wissenschaft* (*Psychology as a science*), 1824-1825. Herbart is said to have administered a knockout blow to the faculty psychology by arguments already used in our preceding chapter (page 13).

Herbart's system, by no means the same as associationism, resembles it in being a theory of the interaction of ideas. The difference is that the associationists assumed a single force of attraction between ideas, while Herbart assumed both attraction and repulsion. Ideas that occur simultaneously in consciousness come together and combine so far as they are congruous with each other, but repel or inhibit each other so far as they are incongruous. These forces are due to the unity and limited span of consciousness, or better of attention. You cannot attend to two ideas at once except so far as they will unite into a single complex idea. When one idea holds the center of the stage, incongruous ideas are forced into the background or off the stage altogether into unconsciousness. They still remain alive, however, and "strive" to get back to the center of the stage, being kept out most of the time by other ideas but being drawn in (recalled) when the dominant idea of the moment is congruous. When two or more ideas have combined, the complex idea behaves as a unit thereafter, being forced out and drawn back as a whole. A combination of many related ideas forms a powerful "apperception mass" which welcomes relevant material but excludes the irrelevant. At this point the theory had an important application to teaching. Before introducing new material, prepare the way for it by building up an apperception mass of familiar and interesting ideas. The Herbartians had much influence on both general and educational psychology for a period of fifty years or more. The concept of inhibition reappears much later, both in the conditioned reflex theory of Pavlov and in Freud's "repression." And inhibition or interference in one form or another comes to light again and again in modern experimental studies of learning and remembering.

The associationists, spread over a period of two centuries, were obviously not a compact school like the Gestaltists or psychoanalysts. There was apparently no personal contact between any of the men mentioned except between John Stuart Mill and his father on one hand and Alexander Bain on the other. More recent psychologists generally accept association as an important fact in psychology without agreeing with the extreme associationists who regarded it as the sole basis for all mental operations.

The Newer Associationism

A new era began in 1885 when Ebbinghaus (1850-1909) published his work on memory (already cited on page 16) which was new not only in being experimental but also in studying the formation of associations, the learning process. The older associationists started with associations as they operate in recall and tried to reason back to the process by which these associations were probably established. The new associationists start with the process of forming associations and then test the strength of the associations by later recall. That is, the older associationists started with effects and tried to infer the causes, while the newer ones start with known causes or conditions and observe the effects. The newer procedure is obviously more complete and trustworthy.

Ebbinghaus wished to follow the formation of associations from scratch and therefore needed items not previously associated. He invented nonsense syllables such as *cag, wom, kel,* which nobody has ever associated together. A single pair of these could be learned in one reading and there would be no observable process to follow objectively. With close attention a series of four or five syllables could be learned in one reading, and after considerable practice a person could perhaps recite six or even seven syllables after a single reading, but that would be his limit, his "memory span." Some kind of inhibition or mutual interference prevented the immediate grasp of a longer series. The interference could be overcome by repeated readings, and the longer the series of syllables the more readings were required. By this and similar methods Ebbinghaus and his successors reduced the law of frequency to quantitative form and worked out the now familiar "learning curves." The law of recency was given quantitative form in the "curve of forgetting." Contiguity itself was found to be a matter of more or less, since associations were formed not only between the adjacent syllables in a series, but also, though less strongly, between syllables lying farther apart in the series. This start toward an exact knowledge of the process of forming associations was quickly followed up by many experimenters.

From Ebbinghaus down the study of learning has used objective methods in the main, and quite a number of ingenious methods have been devised. But introspection also has proved of value in giving inside information on how the learner manages to combine disconnected material such as nonsense syllables. G. E. Müller was especially successful in combining introspection with objective measurement, as we saw in the previous chapter (page 22). Association by contiguity, his results show, is not the whole story. Contiguity is an opportunity rather than a force, and the learner establishes connections largely by perceiving relations.

ASSOCIATION IN ANIMAL BEHAVIOR. The psychological study of animals arose partly from the interest of biologists and physiologists in the sense organs and motor activities of various kinds of animals. There was much experimental work along those lines in the latter half of the nineteenth century. Another very important influence came from Darwin and the theory of evolution. For if all animals are blood relatives in respect to bodily structure, must they not be the same in respect to behavior and mentality? And if the human body has evolved from an ancestral line of animals, must not the human mind have developed from a more primitive animal mind? Such a suggestion was bound to awaken heated opposition not only from the theological side but even from the self-conceit of the common man who regarded himself as radically different from the "brutes," not merely superior to them. The animal was guided by "instinct," not by "reason," which was peculiar to man. To combat this argument the early evolutionists industriously collected instances of animal behavior which seemed to depend on reasoning. There were numerous anecdotes of this sort: A dog, without ever being trained to do it, was observed to open a gate by raising the latch with his muzzle—evidently, so the dog's master felt, because he had figured out the mechanism of the latch or because he had seen it opened by men and reasoned that he could do the same in his own way.

The trouble with such interpretations was that they saw only the alternatives, instinct and reason, instead of the broader choice between instinct and learning. Certainly the dog does not open a gate by instinct, and therefore he must have *learned* to open it. But *how* did he learn the trick? The only way to tell would be to take a dog which has never learned to open a gate, confront him with the problem of opening one, and watch carefully how he attacks the problem. Give him repeated trials and follow his progress till he is complete master of the trick. Such an experimental study of animal learning was projected in the early 1890's by two eminent psychologists of the day, in Germany by Wundt in the second edition of his *Lectures on human and animal psychology,* 1892 (English translation, 1894) and in Britain by Lloyd Morgan in his *Introduction to comparative psychology,* 1894. Both of these men, but especially Lloyd Morgan, had already made some informal homemade experiments and had concluded that dogs learned by forming simple associations (Wundt) or by trial and error (Morgan), and not by reasoning. At least the facts could be explained without the assumption of higher mental processes. And both of these men recommended that animal psychology should observe the *law of parsimony,* "the approved maxim of the exact natural sciences that we should always have recourse to the *simplest* explanation possible" (Wundt)—or in other words that "in no case may we interpret an action as the outcome . . . of a higher psychical faculty, if it can be interpreted as the outcome . . . of one which stands lower in the psychological scale" (Lloyd Morgan's Canon, as it has been called).

These two books no doubt had much influence in turning the attention of the young experimentalists of the time toward the study of animals. Especially in the budding laboratories of the United States animal work soon became established, and of course it tended to change the atmosphere of the department of psychology, which became less philosophical and more biological. Experimental studies of animal learning came out from the Harvard, Columbia, and Clark laboratories before 1900 and from Chicago and several other universities shortly thereafter. This early work can be truly called epoch-making both because of the extensive and fruitful investigations that have followed down to the present day and because of the two theoretical schools that arose from it, Thorndike's connectionism and Watson's behaviorism.

A NEW LAW OF ASSOCIATION REVEALED IN ANIMAL LEARNING. Now we come to a striking instance of that independent but (almost) simultaneous discovery of the same fact or law which has occurred so often in the history of science (evolution, the conservation of energy, photography, the telephone, and many other examples). Thorndike's law of "effect" was discovered about 1898, Pavlov's law of "reinforcement" about 1902. It was many years before the identity of these two laws was fully recognized. The two discoveries were as independent as possible. Thorndike, a young American graduate student of psychology, was following up the evolutionary interest in animal intelligence. Pavlov, an already distinguished Russian physiologist, came upon the "conditioned reflex" in the course of his investigations of digestion and fastened on it as a possible lead toward the understanding of brain physiology. In spite of this great difference in background and aim the two men were alike in scientific spirit, keen alertness, and great energy and persistence.

Edward Lee Thorndike (born 1874, long professor at

Teachers College, Columbia University) was a pupil both of James at Harvard and of Cattell at Columbia, but his selection of animal psychology as a fruitful field for experiment was not due to either of them but probably to study of the books of Wundt and Lloyd Morgan already mentioned. He shares with his contemporaries, Linus W. Kline and Willard S. Small, who worked at Clark University, the honor of introducing the animal into the psychological laboratory. Mazes and problem boxes (or puzzle boxes) were the tasks which they gave the animals to learn. The animal was confronted with the problem by being placed in the maze or puzzle box while hungry, with food present as a reward for the solution of the problem. The animal was left to his own devices, his behavior was watched, and the time required for the first success was noted. He was given trial after trial and the changes in his behavior and the decrease in time of performance were recorded. From these data the animal's progress in mastery of the problem could be plotted in a "learning curve," and some evidence could be obtained as to how the animal learned.

Beginning in 1896 and continuing for several years until his energies were absorbed in educational psychology, Thorndike used these methods with fishes, chicks, cats, dogs, and finally monkeys. His extensive experiments with cats are best known, and his description of the cat's behavior has been so often quoted as to be classic. The cat, usually a young and lively one, was placed while hungry in a slatted cage or box, with food outside as a reward for getting out. The door could be opened in one box by pulling a string, in another by turning a door button, etc.

When put into the box the cat would show evident signs of discomfort and of an impulse to escape from confinement. It tries to squeeze through any opening; it claws and bites at the bars or wire; it thrusts its paws out through any opening and claws at everything it reaches; it continues its efforts when it strikes anything loose and shaky. . . . The cat that is clawing all over the box . . . will probably claw the string or loop or button so as to open the door. And gradually [i.e., in the course of a number of trials] all the other non-successful impulses will be stamped out and the particular impulse leading to the successful act will be stamped in by the resulting pleasure, until, after many trials, the cat will, when put in the box, immediately claw the button or loop in a definite way [1898, page 11].

This "stamping in" or "stamping out" of a response tendency by its favorable or unfavorable results constituted Thorndike's "law of effect," which he formulated as follows a little later (1905, page 203):

Any act which in a given situation produces satisfaction becomes associated with that situation, so that when the situation recurs the act is more likely than before to recur also. Conversely, any act which in a given situation produces discomfort becomes dissociated from that situation, so that when the situation recurs the act is less likely than before to recur.

A companion law was the law of exercise, or of use and disuse, which stated that any response made to a given situation was thereby associated with the situation, that the more it was used as a response to the same situation the more strongly it was associated with it, whereas prolonged disuse weakened the association. This law of exercise was evidently the old law of association applied to connections, not between ideas, but between situation and response. It was the old law of association with its sublaws of frequency and recency.

The study of animal learning showed clearly that the law of exercise did not cover the ground. In a novel situation such as a maze or puzzle box the animal (or man for that matter) is apt to make a number of different responses before hitting on the successful one. Every one of these responses, according to the law of exercise, becomes associated with the situation. Consider the first response made: as soon as it is made it has a recency and frequency advantage over any alternative response which has not been made, and therefore this first response should be immediately repeated and so gain still more advantage. According to the law of recency alone, the animal would never get away from this first unsuccessful response. There must be some factor at work causing him to desist from this first response and try something else. The law of recency must be counteracted by some other factor or the animal would never

EDWARD L. THORNDIKE

IVAN P. PAVLOV

reach success. By the time he does succeed he is likely to have repeated certain unsuccessful responses several times during this first trial, but the successful response is made only once because it terminates the trial. At the start of the second trial, then, the successful response is at a disadvantage in respect to frequency, and according to the law of frequency alone it would remain at a disadvantage trial after trial and no improvement could occur. As a matter of fact, however, the unsuccessful responses gradually lose out in spite of their advantage in recency and frequency, and the successful response is victorious.

The law of effect, announced by Thorndike, encountered much criticism, stimulated a vast amount of experimental investigation, and led to persistent efforts to work out a complete and satisfactory theory of learning. It is not necessary for our purposes to follow this discussion, though we shall catch glimpses of it in connection with some of the other schools. We need consider only the importance of this law in the newer associationism.

The law of effect is a law of association and nothing more. It lays down a certain factor in the strengthening and weakening of associations. When a response is made to a situation, the favorable or unfavorable result of the response is a factor in strengthening or weakening the association of that response to that situation. The early criticisms of the law of effect failed to notice the precise bearing of the law.

It was said, for example, that the law pretended that the outcome of an act worked backward to strengthen or weaken the act just performed. Absurd, of course; but the law asserted, instead, that the outcome of an act strengthened or weakened the continuing association—something calling for neurological explanation, no doubt, but not involving any absurdity.

Again, it was objected that the law assumed blind trial and error in hitting on the successful response. Thorndike seemed to make this assumption, but it has nothing to do with the law of effect, which does not attempt to say how the response is initiated but only that, when initiated and performed, it has results which strengthen or weaken the tendency to make the same response in the future. Perhaps, if an act were done with crystal-clear insight, it would need no further confirmation from successful results; but in the ordinary human cases of partial insight, success certainly has an effect.

It was said, too, that the law had the reprehensible character of being "atomistic"—the cardinal sin to certain schools—but there is nothing atomistic about Thorndike's "situation" and "response," nor about "effect." The total act of a whole organism can have a global effect which strengthens or weakens the tendency to repeat the same total act.

The behaviorists of course took fright at the words *pleasure, discomfort, satisfaction,* and *annoyance* used by Thorndike to indicate the effects of an act and asked what right he had to assume such conscious states in animals or to assume even in man that they could have any effect on the brain so as to strengthen the nerve connections involved in making a certain response to a situation. Thorndike offered possible neural explanations, admitting that they were speculative. Really it is not necessary to work out a neural explanation before accepting a behavioral law such as the law of effect, if only it conforms to the facts of behavior. And it is not necessary to speculate on the animal's conscious states. All we need assume is that success has an effect on the organism, that failure has a different effect, and that these different intraorganic effects can modify the organism's associations or response tendencies. So much as this can safely be assumed in view of many behavioral facts besides the facts of learning.

About thirty years after the original animal experiments which led to the law of effect, Thorndike re-examined the matter by extensive experiments on human learning (1932, 1933). The learner's task in these varied experiments was quite different from that of a puzzle box, except that alternative responses were always possible and that one response was successful or correct and was "rewarded" by the experimenter's saying "Right," while other responses were "punished" by being called "Wrong." The results demonstrated a strong positive effect of reward but no comparable negative effect of punishment. Thorndike accordingly revised his law of effect by assigning much greater weight to reward than to punishment. The effect of punishment, he decided, was not exactly to "dissociate a response from the situation" but rather to cause the learner to try something else until a response was found that was rewarded and so positively associated with the situation. Establishment of the correct response would incidentally and automatically eliminate the incorrect ones.

With the law of effect thus simplified, Thorndike was able to offer a physiologically conceivable explanation. The organism, being "set" for reaching a certain goal, makes tentative exploratory movements aimed at the goal; when one of these movements is actually reaching the goal, the whole organism instantly confirms and intensifies it, so giving it an advantage which remains behind as an association of the successful response with the situation and goal. Or, in Thorndike's words (1933, pages 66-67):

Suppose that in animals possessed of a certain degree of cerebral organization, the acceptability or satisfyingness of a status arouses what we may call the "confirmatory" reaction. . . . Suppose that the nature of this confirmatory reaction is such that it strengthens whatever connections it acts upon. . . . The confirmatory reaction probably is set up and controlled by large fractions of the "higher" levels of the cortex, often by what corresponds to the general "set" and purpose of the animal at the time. . . . The confirmatory reaction will . . . make the animal more likely to repeat the connection when the situation recurs.

Or again (1943, page 33 ff.):

The strengthening by satisfying consequences may have a biological causation. . . . Perhaps all that is required is that the over-all control of a person or animal (what we used to call the "higher" centers) should be able to react to a certain stimulus by a reinforcement of whatever connection has most recently been active, and that the stimulus that sets off this "confirming reaction" should be satisfying to the over-all control. . . . The confirming reaction is not held in reserve for great affairs. . . . You do not have a dozen a week, but more nearly a dozen a minute. To each phrase that I speak you respond by a certain meaning. If this meaning satisfies you by making sense, the connection is confirmed. . . . But if difficulty or confusion arises, the confirming reaction is withheld.

It is not necessary for our purposes to examine Thorndike's numerous and important contributions to such problems as the nature and measurement of intelligence, the influences of heredity and environment, and many others, though in all of these studies he is a thoroughgoing associationist, or "connectionist" as he prefers to call himself. All associations, he believes, have the character of stimulus-response connections. The mere contiguity of two impressions or ideas in a momentary experience does not, he believes, establish an association between them unless some response is evoked. Human genes enable men to establish more connections and larger systems of connections than is possible for animals, and therein lies man's superior mentality. "A good simple definition or description of a man's mind is that it is his connection system, adapting the responses of thought, feeling, and action that he makes to the situations that he meets" (1943, page 22).

THE PAVLOVIAN CONDITIONED RESPONSE. Ivan Petrovitch Pavlov (1849-1936), a clergyman's son (and in this one respect having a background similar to Thorndike's), started to prepare for the priesthood but was deflected by an awakening scientific interest into the study of medicine and particularly of physiology. By 1890 he had definitely "arrived" as a leading physiologist, and from that date until his death he was director of the physiological laboratory at the Institute for Experimental Medicine in St. Petersburg (later Petrograd, Leningrad). For the first twelve years he devoted his laboratory to the study of the digestive glands, their nerves and reflexes. His ingenious and instructive experiments along this line won for him the Nobel Prize in 1904. Meanwhile, in 1902, he made an incidental observation which, after a year of hesitation and soul-searching, changed the whole course of his research. For the study of salivary reflexes in dogs he had devised apparatus enabling him to collect and measure the saliva secreted in response to the stimulus of food in the mouth. In a dog that was being used in these experiments he noticed that the saliva began to flow before the food actually reached the mouth. It flowed at the sight of the food dish, or at the approach of the attendant who customarily brought the food, or even at the sound of the attendant's footsteps in the adjoining room. Now while food in the mouth is a natural stimulus for the reflex flow of saliva, the sight of a dish or the sound of footsteps cannot be a natural stimulus for this reflex. The salivary response to the dish or to the attendant must have been acquired by the dog in the course of the long series of experiments. The sight of the dish or the sound of the footsteps had come to serve as a *signal* that food was coming. Pavlov saw that such signals could play an important role in the adaptation of an animal to any particular environment. This biological lead would not have turned him away from his chosen physiological field of work. But it seemed to him that he had found a promising lead toward research in brain physiology. Physiologists had been trying to study the brain by operations which could not but disturb the normal function, while here he had a method which left the brain intact. The salivary response to a signal he at first called a "psychic secretion," but as he wished to stick to physiology and not get drawn off into assumptions regarding the dog's mental life, he gave up that expression and coined the term *conditioned reflex* (CR). The signal he called the conditioned stimulus (CS).

The conditioned reflex was obviously a learned response, but Pavlov's interest focused on its being a cortical affair, not simply subcortical like a true reflex. It was a compact specimen of the "higher nervous activity," readily available for experiment and measurement. The first step was to discover how a conditioned response could be established. He quickly found the way to build up a conditioned salivary response to any stimulus that would attract the dog's attention without arousing fright or anger. A hungry dog was placed in the familiar apparatus and left quiet for a while. Then a metronome began to tick; the dog pricked up his ears; when the metronome had ticked for thirty seconds, meat powder was introduced into the dog's mouth producing the normal reflex flow of saliva. This exact procedure was repeated at intervals of perhaps fifteen minutes, and after a number of such repetitions saliva began to flow during the thirty-second interval *before* the meat powder was given. This advance flow was the conditioned response; its quantity was small the first time it appeared, but it increased trial by trial to a moderate amount. The metronome in this experiment was the conditioned stimulus; the meat powder was the unconditioned stimulus, also called the *reinforcement* because it produced a much greater flow of saliva than the metronome did even after conditioning.

To establish the conditioned response so thoroughly that it will hold over from day to day may require several days of conditioning, but once well established it is retained over a long period of disuse. It can be temporarily *inhibited* by any distracting stimulus such as disturbs the dog or makes him investigate. Even the experimenter should be kept out of the dog's sight. Pavlov drew plans for a special conditioned reflex laboratory in the country with elaborate provisions for excluding extraneous sights, sounds, odors, gusts of air, etc.; and, in spite of his being no politician but rather an outspoken critic of the government, the Soviet recognized his scientific importance and built him his laboratory.

Besides distraction, another kind of inhibition came to light. One of Pavlov's most important discoveries was the *extinction* of a conditioned response. Even a well-established conditioned response can be extinguished by the same procedure as is used for establishing it, with one important difference: no reinforcements are given. The hungry dog is in the usual apparatus and the metronome begins its usual ticking, the dog giving the usual conditioned salivary response; but when the time for meat powder arrives, no meat powder is given. This procedure is repeated time after time, with never any reinforcement, and the saliva secreted in response to the metronome decreases from trial to trial till it ceases altogether. The conditioned response has been extinguished by repetition without reinforcement. This "extinction," however, is not a complete loss or forgetting, but is only temporary, for after a rest of a few hours the ticking metronome will again produce a flow of saliva. The conditioned response has been temporarily inhibited by nonreinforcement. In terms of "signals," the metronome has now become a signal that no food is coming, instead of a signal that food is coming. After being an exciting stimulus it has now become a depressing one. Instead of waking up the dog's brain to a state of readiness for action, it now (partially) benumbs the brain into a state of readiness for inaction. It makes the dog visibly drowsy instead of visibly alert.

Pavlov concluded that he had found out how to produce two opposite brain states, the state of excitation and the state of inhibition. By use of these two recognized physiological concepts he could formulate hypotheses and put them to the test of experiment. He could predict, for example, that if he kept the metronome ticking and the dog waiting for two minutes instead of half a minute before the food was given, making this the regular procedure for a long series of trials, the conditioned response would become a two-phase affair, inhibition followed by excitation. When the metronome began ticking it would be a signal of "no food coming for quite a while" and so would induce drowsiness without salivation; but after the ticking had continued for a minute or more it would become a signal of "food coming soon" and so would arouse the dog to alertness with salivation. The prediction was verified, and this two-phase response was named the *delayed conditioned reflex*.

Another prediction had to do with *stimulus generalization and differentiation*. When the salivary conditioned response to a slowly ticking metronome has been established, the same response (only not so strong) will be made also to a more rapidly ticking metronome. If the regular conditioned stimulus has been a high-pitched tone, and a low-pitched tone is substituted, the conditioned response will still occur. If the regular conditioned stimulus has been a vibrating pressure on the dog's shoulder, a similar pressure on the dog's flank will give the conditioned response. The effective conditioned stimulus, then, is "generalized," and the question is how to get the dog to distinguish or "differentiate" the regular conditioned stimulus from other more or less similar stimuli. Prediction: response to these other stimuli must be subjected to inhibition, i.e., to extinction by nonreinforcement, while the conditioned response to the regular stimulus is being maintained by regular reinforcement. Again the prediction was verified, though it often took very many trials to eliminate the nonreinforced response completely. Dogs were found to differ, some being more excitable, easy to condition, and hard to extinguish, while others were more inhibitable, hard to condition, and easy to extinguish. Such individual differences were no doubt physiological and seemed to Pavlov to open a lead toward a truly physiological and scientific psychiatry (Pavlov, 1941).

When two stimuli have been well differentiated, with a positive response to a high tone, for example, and a negative response to a low tone, there is a chance to test the dog's power of sensory discrimination. In a long series of trials extending through many days, so as not to break down the differentiation, raise the pitch of the low tone by degrees, so making it more and more similar to the high tone, while always reinforcing the high tone by giving food, but never reinforcing the lower tone. By slow, careful work the dog may be brought to differentiate quite small differences in pitch, or in shape, etc. But there is a limit where the dog breaks down and may become emotionally disturbed, with barking, biting the apparatus, and refusal to work any more in the apparatus. This disturbed condition Pavlov called "experimental neurosis," and he interpreted it as due to the clash of cerebral excitation and inhibition aroused by the ambiguous stimulus.

Many other experiments were done by Pavlov and his students, aimed entirely at an understanding of brain processes. He made no claim to be a psychologist; in fact that is about the last thing he would have claimed. Time and again in his lectures he made a remark of this nature:

In conclusion we must count it an uncontested fact that the physiology of the highest part of the nervous system of higher animals cannot be successfully studied, unless we utterly renounce the untenable pretensions of psychology.

When, at the beginning of all this work in 1902-1903, he asked his psychological colleagues what concepts they would use in explaining his results, they suggested desire, expectation, disappointment, and the like; but he did not find it possible to make effective use of such concepts for devising new experiments or predicting results. When he used his physiological concepts of reinforcement, excitation, and inhibition, he made progress. So he concluded that the key to the understanding of behavior lies wholly in physiology. It is true, however, that on becoming acquainted a few years later with Thorndike's animal experiments he welcomed them as akin to his own and recognized Thorndike's priority (Pavlov, 1927, page 6; 1928, page 39). But Pavlov was never very well pleased with the use made by psychologists of his results (Pavlov, 1932).

In view of his general discontent with psychology, it is curious to find that Pavlov's conditioned reflexes have awakened much livelier interest among the psychologists than among the physiologists. One of his best friends among the physiologists wrote him expressing the hope that he would soon drop this conditioned reflex fad and get back into genuine physiology. The psychologists, many of them, have seen in conditioning a simple and perhaps the fundamental form of learning. When they first got to know of the conditioned response they regarded it mostly as providing a useful technique for examining the senses of animals; and it is still used for that purpose. Then, in the 1920's, it began to serve as the basis of theories of learning, and from this angle it has given rise in the last two decades to a vast amount of experimenting and theorizing—much more than we can attempt to analyze here. But we must endeavor to bring out the bearing of the conditioned response on the newer associationism.

There was a time in the 1920's when many of us psychologists uncritically adopted the "substitute stimulus" view of the conditioned response which had been uncritically suggested by Pavlov. His interest was not in learning but in brain conditions of excitation and inhibition. This substitute stimulus theory may be stated as follows: When two stimuli are given simultaneously, and one of them is the natural stimulus which elicits a reflex response, this reflex will with sufficient repetition become attached to the other stimulus (the CS), which thus becomes a substitute for the natural stimulus and elicits the reflex response. Closely examined, this glib statement is seen to be a very inaccurate description of Pavlov's procedure and results.

It is inaccurate in several respects. (1) It speaks of the two stimuli as simultaneous, while actually the CS begins first and arouses the CR before the natural stimulus arrives. Pavlov found it very important to time the two stimuli in this way. Unless the CS began first, the CR would not occur (cf. Spooner and Kellogg, 1947). (2) It speaks as if the reflex were aroused by the CS (after conditioning), whereas the true reflex does not start till the natural stimulus has arrived. (3) It speaks as if the CR were the same as the natural reflex, whereas actually the two responses are quite unlike in certain respects. As far as salivary secretion is concerned the two differ only in quantity, the reflex being more rapid and abundant. But the natural reflex includes a chewing movement which is absent from the CR. Instead the CR includes some sort of approaching movement. Thus the CR, the response to the advance signal of food, is a preparatory act, a getting ready for receiving the food, while the reflex is a final or consummatory act. The preparation is not deliberate or voluntary but it is preparation none the less.

Many other conditioned responses have been established in other laboratories. Liddell and his co-workers at Cornell (1934) found the sheep a good subject and the reflex withdrawal movement aroused by an electric shock a good basis for the establishment of a CR. The shock is delivered through an electrode bound to one foreleg, and the CS is a ticking metronome which starts a few seconds before the shock. After the animal has become conditioned, he responds to the metronome by raising the leg part way and taking a crouching posture, so getting ready to take the shock. When the shock comes, the reflex response is a full raising of the leg followed by relaxation. Here the shock is the reinforcement, and omission of the shock for a series of trials extinguishes the CR.

Several forms of CR have been obtained with human subjects. Hilgard and Marquis (1940) give a good example. A puff of air blown against the front of the open eye elicits a reflex wink. If a signal is given regularly half a second before the puff, a CR develops consisting of a slow, partial wink—a getting ready to take the puff. Though this CR is executed by the same muscle as the reflex wink, the two are quite different movements, the wink reflex being a remarkably quick movement, and the CR relatively slow to start and slow to stop. The reflex wink is governed by a subcortical (midbrain) center, and there is no evidence or likelihood that this center becomes attached to the signal stimulus. Conditioning is a cortical process and builds up a new response which resembles a voluntary wink rather than the reflex. The reflex wink is not "conditioned" or modified in any way.

Probably no subcortical reflex is ever conditioned in the strict sense, though it may be temporarily sensitized and made more easily aroused. The conditioned response is not a reflex attached to a new stimulus, but is a new response. The once-common theory that learned behavior consists of native reflex acts attached to new stimuli is not justified by the facts of conditioned responses. Reflexes are neat little patterns of movement (or secretion), controlled by well-organized subcortical centers provided in the native structure of the organism. Learned movements depend on cortical organization which is not rigidly laid down in the native structure but is shaped by conditioning and other learning processes.

THE INSTRUMENTAL CONDITIONED RESPONSE. In Pavlov's experiment the dog's conditioned response did nothing in the way of securing the food, for the food was provided at the regular time without regard to the dog's actions. The regular sequence of signal and food, controlled by the experimenter, was the essential feature of the procedure. The conditioned salivary response was preparatory in the sense of preparing the organism for the reception of food in the mouth, but it did nothing toward securing the food. Pavlov noted also the motor part of the conditioned response, the movement of approach toward the awaited food, but in his setup this approach movement was not necessary for obtaining the food. If the dog is placed at a little distance from the food pan and left free to move, then the dog, as shown by other experiments (Zener, 1937), responds to the metronome signal by approaching the food pan (salivating meanwhile), and this approach movement is "in-

strumental" in securing the food. An instrumental CR secures
the reinforcement and is necessary, under the experimental conditions, for the reinforcement to occur. Instrumental behavior
acts on the environment by locomotion or manipulation and so
secures rewards and avoids punishments. It is as common as
prose. The successful act in a puzzle box is an instrumental
response—but can it be called a conditioned response with any
propriety? Thorndike's trial-and-error learning and Pavlov's
conditioning appeared for decades to be radically different and
irreducible. The gap between them was bridged by B. F. Skinner when he devised a simplified form of puzzle box, now
widely known and used under the name of the Skinner box
(Skinner, 1938).

As employed in experiments on that favorite laboratory animal, the white rat, a Skinner box is small and bare, with little
opportunity for the varied reactions elicited by a typical puzzle
box. It has a little tin pan in one corner, and outside is a machine which can deliver pellets of food through a chute into the
pan, each pellet making a "bing" as it falls into the tin pan.
When a new pupil is introduced into this schoolroom and has
nosed around and become adjusted, the teacher lets a pellet of
food drop into the pan. The rat responds to the bing by approaching the food pan, and then responds to the pellet by eating it. Pellets are dropped into the pan at intervals, and the rat
soon learns to approach the pan promptly at the sound.

Now let us compare the sequence of events here with that
in the Pavlov experiment. In Pavlov's case we have:

metronome—salivate—food—eat

And in Skinner's case:

bing—approach—food—eat

The two sequences are exactly alike except that the salivary CR
is not instrumental in securing the food, while the rat's approach to the food pan is instrumental. Let us then agree that
this approach movement is a CR, and that the bing is a CS.

In preparation for the second lesson the schoolroom is
equipped with a horizontal bar extending along one wall and
hooked up to the pellet-delivering machine so that downward
pressure on the bar will release a pellet into the food pan. The

pupil is let in and left to his own devices. Sooner or later he is sure to get his forepaws on the bar and exert enough pressure to release a pellet with the customary bing, to which he responds as before by approaching the food pan. As soon as he goes back and presses the bar again—which some rats do at once and others after some wandering around—a second pellet is delivered. The conditioning is soon complete and the rat, left in the box, continues to press the bar and secure pellets as long as he remains hungry. The bar-pressing response can be extinguished, though not very quickly, by stopping the supply of pellets.

The learned sequence in this last experiment is:

bar—press—bing—approach—pellet—eat

The visual or olfactory stimulus from the bar that guides the rat to it is a CS, the bar-pressing a CR, this S-R unit being preparatory to the previously established bing-approach unit, and this in turn preparatory to the consummatory unit, pellet-eat. Both the bar-pressing and the approach to the pan are instrumental in obtaining the reinforcement of food. A longer series of such S-R units can be built up by suitable conditioning, but the principle is the same as in the simpler instrumental conditioning or in Pavlovian conditioning.

How does the rat's mastery of the Skinner box differ from the cat's mastery of the Thorndike puzzle box? The Skinner box offers a minimum of false leads, while the puzzle box offers a number of promising leads that have to be tried and eliminated. The two differ in respect to elimination, which is of course an important matter in many problems, but as far as concerns the positive learning of the successful response there is probably no essential difference. The positive learned sequence in a puzzle box is, for instance:

door button—claw it—door opens—go out—food—eat

which is exactly parallel to the sequence learned in the Skinner box. An extinction test was not part of Thorndike's procedure, credit for this important invention going wholly to Pavlov. But extinction would certainly occur—as it does in a maze—if the setup were altered so that not the door button any longer, but something else, had to be manipulated in order to obtain the reward.

ASSOCIATIONISM TODAY. It has become clear from all this work that Pavlov's "reinforcement" and Thorndike's "reward" are the same. They stand for the same positive factor in establishing an association. Psychologists today are apt to prefer the term *reinforcement,* which does apply more neatly to such cases as the electric shock in the sheep experiment or the puff of air against the eye in the human experiment cited. Can the shock or the puff be called a reward? Well, they do in a sense reward the preparatory adjustment, the readiness to "take" the obnoxious stimulus. They justify the preparation, they confirm it, to use Thorndike's recent terminology. They enable the preparation to do its job, instead of coming to nought as it does in an extinction series.

The law of reinforcement, effect, or confirmation is the principal contribution of present or recent psychology to associationism. The law has a wide scope, holding good not only in the establishment of conditioned responses but also in many other types of learning, perhaps in all. At least it seems likely that some sort of reinforcement is necessary for the establishment of any strong association (Woodworth and Marquis, 1947, page 536).

Another contribution, not so recent, is the experimental verification by G. E. Müller of the old suggestion of Thomas Brown that the perception of relations is an important factor in the establishment of an association (pages 22, 44). This suggestion has not been much followed up by recent associationists, perhaps because it introduces a cognitive factor that is inconsistent with a strict associationism. The eminent British psychologist, Charles Edward Spearman (1863-1945), did indeed base a whole system of intellectual psychology mostly on the perception or "eduction" of relations and correlates (1923), but he did not regard this system as a form of associationism. Quite the contrary, he complained that the associationists were "astonishingly crude" in their theory, since they ignored what he called "noegenesis," the discovery of new knowledge and solution of new problems, and practically dealt only with memory. The Gestalt psychologists have made a similar criticism, and their main contribution might be regarded as filling this important gap in the associationist theory.

Meanwhile the experimental associationists have found plenty of valuable work to do on problems lying clearly in their proper field. They have been working out conditions favorable or unfavorable to memorizing, learning curves and curves of forgetting, the mutual interference of competing associations, the transfer of learned responses and acquired abilities from one situation or task to another, and other similar problems (Hilgard, 1948; McGeoch, 1942; Robinson, 1932; Woodworth, 1938).

Of the behaviorists, next to be considered, many could be counted among the associationists, but some not; and of the associationists not all by any means could be regarded as behaviorists. Associationism is a theory of learning and remembering, while behaviorism is—well, we shall see.

CHAPTER 4

BEHAVIORISM

As behaviorism is now approaching forty years of age, it has had time to pass through different stages and to take on somewhat different meanings. It grew out of the study of animal behavior, but to define it as the science of behavior would be to miss the force of the "ism." In fact some of the leading workers in animal psychology—Edward Thorndike, Robert Yerkes, Harvey Carr, and others—never joined the ranks of the behaviorists. Behaviorism started off very definitely and consciously as a "school," opposed to the supposedly dominant school of structuralism, and to functionalism as represented by William James and the Chicago group. As these old controversies have died down, behaviorism has naturally become less negativistic and more a part of the general stream of psychology, while still adhering to behavior methods and behavior concepts. Our aim will be to show what behaviorism was when it started, to follow its development to some extent, and finally to see what it has now become.

Watsonian Behaviorism

John Broadus Watson (born 1878, long professor at Johns Hopkins) was the founder of this school. Having become interested in philosophy during his college years, he went for graduate study in that subject to the University of Chicago, where he switched to psychology, took his doctor's degree, joined the teaching staff, and set up one of the earliest of the animal psychology laboratories. In 1908 he became professor at Johns Hopkins University. By 1912 he was well known for his incisive studies in animal learning as well as for his forceful but winning personality. As a teacher of psychology he became more and more disgusted with the abstract and esoteric material he was supposed to convey to his students, till finally, as he later said (1924-1925, page 6), "the behaviorists reached the conclusion that they could no longer be content to work with intangibles and unapproachables. They decided either to give up psychology or else make it a natural science." All that had been accomplished by Wundt and the other experimentalists in their effort to make psychology a science amounted as far as Watson could see to the substitution of the word *consciousness* for the *soul* of medieval philosophy. He wanted to teach a psychology dealing with visible, concrete facts.

Another cause of his irritation was the ambiguous status of animal psychology, his field of research. According to the orthodox definition at the time, psychology was the science of conscious experience. Now since the days of Descartes it had been recognized that you cannot observe or logically prove consciousness in animals. At best, inference from their behavior to consciousness was reasoning by analogy. Titchener and others (notably Margaret Floy Washburn in her excellent book, *The animal mind,* 1908) granted that some such inferences could legitimately be drawn and that animal experiments could thus throw some light on psychology. At best, however, animal psychology was regarded by the structuralists as only a sideshow. Meanwhile the animal psychologists were obtaining excellent results bearing on instinct and learning—certainly psychological problems—and were more or less resentful at the disparaging attitude of the structuralists. Watson decided to take the offensive with the forceful claim that the animal psychologists were doing the truly scientific work and leading the way for all psychologists to follow—the nonintrospective, nonmentalistic way.

Watson's behaviorist manifesto, as we may call it, was set forth first in some public lectures in 1912, and then in a journal article in 1913 and in his book, *Behavior,* in 1914. A few extracts from this notable document will indicate what behaviorism meant to its founder.

Psychology as the behaviorist views it is a purely objective experimental branch of natural science. Its theoretical goal is the prediction and control of behavior. Introspection forms no essential part of its methods, nor is the scientific value of its data dependent upon ... interpretation in terms of consciousness. ... The time seems to have come when psychology must discard all reference to consciousness; when it need no longer delude itself into thinking that it is making mental states the object of observation. ... Our psychological quarrel is not with the ... structural psychologist alone. The last fifteen years have seen the growth of what is called functional psychology. ... The difference between functional psychology and structural psychology, as the functionalists have so far stated the case, is unintelligible. The terms sensation, perception, affection, emotion, volition are used as much by the functionalist as by the structuralist. ... We advance the view that *behaviorism* is the only consistent and logical functionalism.

It is possible to write a psychology, to define it ... as the "science of behavior," and never go back on the definition: never to use the terms consciousness, mental states, mind, content, will, imagery, and the like. ... It can be done in terms of stimulus and response, in terms of habit formation, habit integration, and the like. ... The reason for this is to learn general and particular methods by which behavior may be controlled. ... Those who have occasion to apply psychological principles practically would find no need to complain as they do at the present time. ... If this is done, work ... on the human being will be directly comparable with the work on animals.

This was a stirring appeal and made a strong impression on many of the younger psychologists, as can be seen from the fact that the American Psychological Association by a plurality vote elected Watson to be its president for the year 1915. Many of the younger generation felt that Watson was changing the atmosphere of psychology by clearing away old mysteries, uncertainties, complexities, and difficulties, a heritage from philosophy which the older generation of psychologists had not been able to shake off. In their enthusiasm they exaggerated the extent of the revolution, and it is important, in order to keep the historical record straight, that we analyze this manifesto and see how much of it was new, original, and progressive. The following points are clearly made:

1. *Definition:* Psychology is to be the science, not of consciousness, but of behavior.

2. *Scope:* It is to cover both human and animal behavior, the simpler animal behavior being indeed more fundamental than the more complex behavior of men.

3. *Method:* It is to rely wholly on objective data, introspection being discarded.

4. *Concepts:* It is to avoid "mentalistic" concepts such as sensation, perception, and emotion, and employ only behavior concepts such as stimulus and response, learning and habit. Presumably mentalistic concepts are suggested by human conscious experience and introspection, while behavior concepts are suggested only by objective observation of animals and human beings. Since behaviorism is to be "the only consistent and logical functionalism," the admissible concepts would apparently be concepts of functions, but this point is not made very clear.

5. *Application:* A scientific basis is to be provided for the practical control of behavior, and this means, as shown in some unquoted passages, a scientific basis for dealing with "behavior problems" as they appear in a guidance or psychiatric clinic.

6. *Philosophy:* The old mind-body problem and the rival theories of interaction and parallelism disappear, as shown in unquoted passages, with the disappearance of mind. There is no mystery in the relation of body and behavior. Psychologists have introduced unnecessary mystery by replacing the mind or soul by the inaccessible brain. Behaviorism must not make a fetish of the brain but must keep its eyes fixed on the peripheral organs, the sense organs, muscles, and glands. Only objectively observable facts are admissible.

This list consists largely of "thou shalt nots": drop the mind, say no more about consciousness, cease introspecting, eliminate mentalistic concepts, stop speculating on what goes on in the brain. It was this negative emphasis that was novel. Objective methods had been in use for a long time, as we saw in an earlier chapter (page 15), and functional concepts had predominated from the first. Animal learning had thrown light on human learning. Objective tests had been devised to aid in the prediction and control of behavior. Watson recognized some of this work and complained only that the conclusions were often tainted with superfluous references to "consciousness"—as was true to a certain extent.

With regard to the proper definition of psychology, the ground had been well prepared for Watson. It is true that around 1900 most psychologists, even when working on functions or performances, gave formal assent to the orthodox definition of psychology as the science of consciousness. These active laboratory workers scarcely attempted to define their science in terms of their work. The first to do so was probably James McKeen Cattell (1860-1944), a pupil of Wundt at Leipzig, a co-worker with Galton in London, the founder of the psychological laboratories at Pennsylvania and Columbia, a pioneer in the development of mental tests, and in some ways the most influential American psychologist of his time, though not much given to theoretical writing. In 1904, however, in connection with the World's Fair at St. Louis, he was designated to make an address on the scope and method of psychology, and expressed himself as follows:

The task has been assigned to me of considering the scope, conceptions and methods of psychology, and it is my business to define the field of psychology or to acknowledge my inability to do so. I must choose the latter alternative. I can only say that psychology is what the psychologist is interested in *qua* psychologist. . . . I am not convinced that psychology should be limited to the study of consciousness as such. . . . I admire . . . the ever-increasing acuteness of introspective analysis . . . but the positive scientific results are small in quantity when compared with the objective experimental work accomplished in the past fifty years. There is no conflict between introspective analysis and objective experiment—on the contrary, they should and do continually cooperate. But the rather widespread notion that there is no psychology apart from introspection is refuted by the brute argument of accomplished fact. It seems to me that most of the research work that has been done by me or in my laboratory is nearly as independent of introspection as work in physics or in zoology. . . . I see no reason why the application of systematized knowledge to the control of human nature may not in the course of the present century accomplish results commensurate with the nineteenth century applications of physical science to the material world.

Watson, if he noticed Cattell's pronouncement, regarded it as too tame for his own purposes, which were not simply to promote objective psychology, but to get rid of everything else. For the same reason he was not satisfied with certain other proposals of the same period.

The first man to define psychology as the science of behavior was apparently the young English experimentalist, William McDougall, whom we shall meet again in a later chapter (page 216). In his little book on *Physiological psychology,* published in 1905, he had this to say on the matter of definition:

Psychology may be best and most comprehensively defined as the positive science of the conduct of living creatures. . . . Psychology is more commonly defined as the science of mind, or as the science of mental or psychical processes, or of consciousness, or of individual experience. Such definitions . . . express the aims of a psychologist who relies solely upon introspection, the observation and analysis of his own experience, and who unduly neglects the manifestations of mental life afforded by the conduct of his fellow-creatures.

Here he used the word *conduct,* but in 1908, in his *Introduction to social psychology,* a book which immediately gained a wide audience, he added the word *behavior* to his definition:

Psychologists must cease to be content with the sterile and narrow conception of their science as the science of consciousness, and must boldly assert its claim to be the positive science . . . of conduct or behavior. . . . Happily this more generous conception of psychology is beginning to prevail.

In those years, say from 1904 to 1912, just before the advent or outbreak of behaviorism, there were many psychologists strongly inclined toward this new and broader definition of psychology. An influential representative of this tendency was Walter Bowers Pillsbury (born 1872, professor at Michigan), one of Titchener's early pupils who devoted himself more to functional than structural investigations. Pillsbury published in 1911 his *Essentials of psychology,* a standard college textbook, and his definition was acceptable to a large share of his contemporaries:

> Psychology may be most satisfactorily defined as the science of human behavior. Man may be treated as objectively as any physical phenomenon. . . . Viewed in this way the end of our science is to understand human action. The practical end is . . . to discover means of increasing man's efficiency. . . . Even if we regard the understanding of human behavior as the ultimate end of psychology, consciousness must still play a very important part in our science. By consciousness we mean a man's awareness of his own acts and their antecedents. . . . Behavior is to be studied through the consciousness of the individual and by external observation.

Pillsbury was saying, in effect, that conscious experience was valuable to psychology for the light it threw on behavior, while the structuralists said that behavior was valuable for the light it threw on conscious experience. But Watson complained that Pillsbury was "going back on his definition" by allowing any value to introspection and using terms like *consciousness* and *imagery*. For Watson, behavior and consciousness were mutually exclusive, and to define psychology as the science of behavior was to make a radical departure and rule out all introspection, all reference to conscious experience, and so practically all of the psychological work down to 1912.

Why was Watson so dead set against introspection? Primarily, no doubt, because it was put forward by the structuralists as the essential method of psychology, while it was obviously unavailable to the animal psychologist, who was thus left out in the cold. He had other reasons as well. He was suspicious of the accuracy of introspection. Titchener had admitted or rather insisted that only well-trained introspective observers could be trusted. But Watson pointed an accusing finger at the "imageless thought" controversy and other recent examples of divergent results obtained in different laboratories by presumably well-trained introspectionists. If even your best observers cannot agree on matters of fact, he said, how can you ever make psychology a science instead of a debating society? Here Watson was overplaying his hand, for there were many matters of fact on which introspective observers did agree, the examples of disagreement being such as made extra-heavy demands on keen observation—and in the matter of imagery individuals differ anyway and quite properly report different observations. Watson admitted a little later (1919, page 39) that a person can observe his own behavior to some extent so as to report, for example, "that I am writing, that my face is flushed, etc." And in his autobiography (1936) he includes many personal introspections of this type: "I enjoyed . . .," "I hated to leave," "The thought presented itself," "I honestly think . . .," "I still believe . . ." Watson's argument on the score of reliability did not succeed in disproving a conservative statement such as that introspection can be trusted if too much is not demanded of it.

But Watson had a more serious objection to introspection, an objection that began by being very practical and ended by being altogether metaphysical. He wanted to deal with tangibles, visibles, audibles—things or happenings that he could point out to a fellow-observer as the chemist points at the contents of a test tube. He did not want to have anything going on in his laboratory that was not objectively observable. Introspection pretended to report something going on in an organism that was not objectively observable. Now of course there is much going on inside the organism's skin that is practically unobservable—movements of the viscera, secretions of the various glands, minimal contractions of the various muscles, nerve impulses running to and from the brain. All such internal motions and secretions belong under the head of behavior. They are not overt behavior, to be sure, but they are "implicit behavior." In introducing this famous concept of implicit behavior Watson was relaxing his original requirement that everything in psychology should be actually observable, and retreating to the philosophical demand that everything must be potentially observable. All that goes on in the organism is implicit behavior, and all implicit behavior is theoretically observable by physical means. Introspectionists have claimed to observe processes of an entirely different order, not conceivably observable by any refinement of physical instrumentation; but this claim cannot be allowed by the behaviorist. The parallelists have assumed two processes going on in the organism, a conscious (or sometimes conscious) psychical process and a physical process keeping step with the psychical process; but the philosophical behaviorist eliminates the psychical process and admits only behavior all of which, however hidden and "implicit," is of the same order as the actually observable movements of the organism.—All this may be good strong metaphysics but it does not concern the psychologist, and certainly it has no bearing on the use of introspective data when they are trustworthy empirical facts.

Strictly judged, this philosophical behaviorism was "incompetent, irrelevant, immaterial" in a scientific psychology. But equally so, of course, was the opposed philosophy which regarded introspection as revealing an inner reality distinct from the order of nature. By opposing one of these two irrelevancies to the other the behaviorists helped to clear the psychological atmosphere. The atmosphere became more hard-boiled—to mix our metaphors a bit. But the older, semireligious atmosphere had not been created by the structuralists (whose views were wholly naturalistic; see page 28) but had come down from the older "mental philosophy."

Methodological behaviorism—the insistence on objective methods to the exclusion of introspection—loomed very large at first but proved to be of minor importance. It would have been a mistake to do away with all introspection, and Watson himself came to make some use of it under the name of "verbal report," as we shall see. On the positive side the behaviorists had little to contribute, for the excellent reason that objective methods had been a major concern of psychology since it began to be experimental. The psychophysical methods, the memory methods, the conditioned response methods were already in use before the behaviorists came along. Certainly they made contributions to method, but not revolutionary ones, because no revolution was necessary and because there is no fundamental antagonism between objective and introspective methods.

Conceptual behaviorism was more important in the progress of psychology. It helped along the necessary task of sharpening the functional concepts, particularly the "What" concepts.

What does the organism do? Watson's emphasis on muscular and glandular action laid him open to the charge that his behavior psychology was only a little piece of physiology. Against this charge he had a strong defense (1919, pages 19-20):

It has been claimed by some that behavior psychology is really physiology. That this is not the case appears from even a casual examination. . . . Physiology teaches us concerning the functions of the special organs. . . . Certain combined processes are studied, such as metabolism . . . but nowhere in physiology do we get the organism, as it were, put back together again and tested in relation to its environment as a whole. . . . The physiologist *qua* physiologist knows nothing of the total situations in the daily life of an individual that shape his action and conduct.

Psychology, then, should concern itself with the doings of the whole organism in relation to its environment. Structuralism had excluded the environment from the psychological picture on the ground that consciousness had no direct relations with the environment. Angell's functionalism had brought in the environment but scarcely the whole organism, since only the functions of consciousness were to be considered. The actual experiments of many psychologists had placed the individual in known situations and noted his responses, but a definite formula for this kind of work had perhaps not been given. "Behavior of the organism in relation to the environment" was a good framework for the "What" question.

Watson's proposal that psychology should shift its general headquarters from the human to the animal field seemed mere adolescent bravado at first, but in the course of time it exerted no little influence on the conceptual framework of psychology. The fundamental relations of the organism to the environment must be common to men and animals, and probably there are certain fundamental ways of dealing with the environment common to both. If so, the fundamental operations might be more readily discerned in animal behavior than in man's more complicated behavior. From this point of view it would be desirable to have a set of fundamental concepts free from "anthropomorphism" and strictly applicable to animal behavior. Into this framework of basic concepts could be fitted the secondary concepts required for human mental processes. The fundamental laws of learning, for example, should be worked out in animal experiments or at least should hold good for animals. Man's use of language in learning would require additional laws and concepts. The same would be true in the study of motivation and of problem solving. This general standpoint has been adopted by many psychologists who would not call themselves behaviorists and who would not hesitate to employ introspection in human studies.

Undoubtedly it has been a good thing for psychology to prune its fundamental concepts of anthropomorphism and superfluous references to consciousness. Yet this behavioristic tendency has been disadvantageous in certain respects. The organism's relations with the environment are sensory as well as motor. In order to act effectively upon the environment, it has to be aware of the environment—to explore it, perceive it, know it—but these important operations are better observed introspectively than objectively. Exploring movements can of course be observed in animals. We see them look by turning the head and eyes, we see them listen by pricking up the ears, we see them feel or sniff an object. But what do they get out of these exploring movements? We know perfectly well from our own experience what they get. They get to know the environment by seeing, hearing, feeling, and smelling it. Now we must not assume consciousness in animals—though it would be still more hazardous to assume an absence of consciousness —and if we look to the behaviorists for our fundamental concepts of perceiving and knowing, we find them very cautious and disinclined to tackle this part of the subject, because it comes dangerously near to the study of conscious processes. The lead here must be taken by human psychology, though with that lead the animal psychologist can devise behavioral tests for discovering how much the animal perceives. The behaviorist influence for a decade or two was such as to turn the younger psychologists away from this large and important part of the territory to be explored.

With regard, then, to the behaviorist manifesto of 1912-1914, we have seen that its metaphysics was irrelevant, its methodology unimportant, its definition of psychology as the science of behavior not original but still important as an emphatic expression of the tendency of the time. Its attempt to center psychology in animal behavior and to use concepts applicable to animal no less than human behavior was very influential and largely for good. Its desire to find practical applications was shared by many other psychologists, though not by the structuralists. The work of a "behavior clinic," in spite of its name, is not behavioristic in the least, since the subject's feelings in regard to his behavior difficulties are a part of the problem to be examined. The most important forward stride was conceptual behaviorism, and the working out of an adequate set of behavioral concepts was necessarily a long and difficult task in which we cannot expect Watson to have made more than a beginning. Without being too abstractly conceptual ourselves, let us see what Watson accomplished and attempted.

Watson's Views and Concepts

Watson's career as a productive theorist was unfortunately rather brief. Soon after his initial pronouncement in 1912-1914 came the first world war, during which he joined with many other psychologists in contributing to the war effort—and it is significant that psychologists of different schools could do effective teamwork in the emergency. Soon after the war he left the academic field for a successful career in the practical application of psychology, though for a few years he continued to give emphatic and popularized expression to behaviorism. Watson has to his credit quite an array of important contributions to animal psychology and also to child psychology, for he was a pioneer in experimental studies of the young child. His system of behavioristic psychology can be found in his three principal books: the *Behavior,* of 1914; the *Psychology from the standpoint of a behaviorist,* first published in 1919; and the *Behaviorism,* first published in 1924-1925. The first book is devoted mostly to animal psychology, the other two mostly to the behavior of human children and adults. The major tenets of behaviorism can be found in each of these books but perhaps best in the 1919 *Psychology*.

STIMULUS AND RESPONSE. Just as Wundt had said that conscious experiences are complex and call for analysis into simple sensations and feelings, so Watson said that behavior was complex and capable of analysis into simple stimulus-response units which he called reflexes. "Instinct and habit are undoubtedly composed of the same elementary reflexes. . . . In instinct the pattern and order are inherited, in habit both are acquired during the lifetime of the individual" (1919, pages 272-273). Such statements made it easy for the *Gestalt* and organismic schools to accuse Watson of "atomism." Neither his experimental work nor his theorizing, however, ran much to atomism. From his strong emphasis on motor behavior you might expect him to embark on an analysis of complex movements into the action of separate muscles; but, though he does include in his *Psychology* (1919) some account of the striped and smooth muscles, and of the glands, he makes no effort to analyze complex movements into muscular elements, believing no doubt that such analysis is the job of the physiologist and not of the psychologist. In explaining what he means by *response* he starts with the knee jerk and other reflexes but advances to acts such as taking food, unlocking a door, writing a letter, and even building a house. Evidently he is thinking of a response not as composed of muscular elements but as accomplishing certain results in the environment.

In the same way his examples of a *stimulus* start with rays of light thrown into the eyes, sound entering the ears, etc., and go on to objects in the environment and to total situations. His real interest is not in the analysis of behavior into elementary muscular (and glandular) responses to elementary stimuli, but, quite to the contrary, in what the individual will do in a given situation. For example, the stimulus is a stick of candy dangled in front of a baby and the response (at a certain age) is a reaching out and grasping the candy and putting it into the mouth. Or, the stimulus is a baseball thrown by the pitcher, and the response is a fly to the outfield. In strictness we should speak in such cases not of stimulus and response but of objective situation and objective results produced by the individual's response. It is in that sense that Watson should be understood when he says that the goal of behavior psychology is the "ascertaining of such data and laws that, given the stimulus, psychology can predict what the response will be; or, on the other hand, given the response, it can specify the nature of the effective stimulus" (1919, page 10).

Responses can be classified as learned or unlearned, and also as explicit and implicit. It was important for behavior psychology to distinguish between what was instinctive and what was learned, and to discover the laws of learning or habit formation. Still another way of classifying responses is according to the sense organ receiving the stimulus. So an "auditory response" is any sort of motor response aroused by a stimulus to the ears, whether it be a startle response to a pistol shot or a verbal report that a tone is high or low. An "olfactory response" may be a sniffing movement or a verbal report of smelling something like violets or like tar. But how can a speech movement be called olfactory or auditory? It seems a strange use of terms. To see why the behaviorists felt compelled to speak in this queer way we need to examine their attitude toward sensation.

SENSATION AND PERCEPTION. Since we cannot assume consciousness in animals, we have no right to say that they see, hear, or smell. However, since they demonstrably make motor responses to visual, auditory and olfactory stimuli, there is no objection to saying that they make "visual responses," etc., with the meaning just explained. Our objective data in the case of an animal are the stimulus and the motor response. With a human subject before us we wish to be equally objective. His conscious experience, if he has any, is invisible to us. We wish to find out what his "visual response" will be to light of a certain wave length, and to make things simple for him we use the vulgar expression, "Tell me what you see." He replies that he sees blue. This verbal response is a perfectly objective phenomenon. We need not assume that he has any conscious sensation but only accept the fact that he makes the verbal response. If we make the blue stimulus fainter till he says that he no longer sees blue, we learn as much about his power of color discrimination by simply accepting his verbal response as by assuming any conscious sensations in him which we cannot observe. That chemist who employed the young girl to make color tests (page 20) could have been a behaviorist; in which case he would have said, "I don't care whether she *sees* blue or not, if only she *says* blue at the right times and not otherwise. I don't admit," he might continue, "that there is any such thing as seeing, apart from some motor response, any more than I admit that my thermometer feels the temperature which it registers. All I admit, in either case, is a movement which tallies with the stimulus." Well and good—but sometimes the chemist examines his test tubes himself and reports blue or not-blue, and he probably would admit if cross-examined that he reported what he saw. For him to deny or doubt that the other observer's reports are like his own in this respect, or, in general, for the behaviorists to deny that the human subject, at least, is actually seeing or hearing when he so reports, seems pedantic to say the least. The behaviorist certainly admits that he himself can see and hear, for does he not insist that only what he can see and hear shall be accepted as scientific data?

The method of impression (page 18) was an old stand-by of the introspectionists, but Watson believed he could transform it into an acceptable objective method by rechristening it the method of *verbal report*. As an animal psychologist he did not like this method very well and even proposed to substitute for it, as far as possible, the conditioned reflex method which Pavlov had found useful in testing the animal's powers of sensory discrimination. Watson proposed (1916, 1919) to use the motor conditioned response which V. M. Bekhterev (1857-1927), a Russian contemporary and rival of Pavlov, had introduced with human subjects. Bekhterev had written an *Objective psychology* in 1907 which became known to our psychologists through the German and French translations of 1913.

Watson did not care much for Bekhterev's general treatment of the subject, but he did like the motor conditioned response, because it was so purely behavioral and free from any suspicion of introspection. But Watson could not afford to throw overboard all the results obtained in the study of the senses by the method of impression. For example, he did not want to discard the visual after-image as a mere introspective delusion and relic of the old religious psychology. Thus he says (1919, page 91):

> One of the most interesting sets of phenomena to be met with in the whole of sensory physiology appears in the after-effects of monochromatic light stimulation. After the eye has been stimulated for a time by a monochromatic light which is then removed, one of two things may be reported by the subject: The subject may react as though he were stimulated anew by the original light, the so-called "positive after-image"; or, as though he were stimulated by light the wave length of which is complementary to the original light, the "negative after-image." We can illustrate this by data obtained by the verbal report method. If we stimulate with . . . blue and the subject then looks at a gray screen, he will say, "I see yellow." . . . Stating these phenomena in physiological terms, we may say. . . .

From these phenomena, he continues, something can be learned regarding the physiological processes that occur in the eye.

We must be on our guard here, for Watson may be claiming too much and widening the scope of his behaviorism by appropriating data which do not properly belong in his system. So long as he says "verbal response" he remains a behaviorist, for he himself heard the subject say, "I see yellow," and is fully entitled to record that objective fact. But now Watson shifts to saying "verbal report," and we must ask, "Who makes this report, and what does he report?" And we find that the subject makes the report and that he reports "seeing." If Watson accepts this report, he admits "seeing" into his system, while pretending to have a system which excludes all such subjective foolishness. And he cannot pretend that after all he means nothing more than "verbal response," for the mere speech movements of his subject give no indication of the physiological processes in the eye, except so far as they are a report of seeing.

The "phenomena" which Watson finds so interesting and valuable in the after-image experiment are the after-images themselves, not the subject's speech movements. We must conclude that verbal report is not a behavioristic method and that Watson's use of it is practically a confession of defeat for methodological behaviorism. As to conceptual behaviorism, it certainly is not strong and stimulating at this point. For who would devote himself to the study of "visual responses" if he believed he would have to do only with a certain small selection of speech movements? From the history of American psychology following Watson it seems indeed that behaviorism exerted a deadening rather than a stimulating influence on research into human sensation and perception.

MEMORY IMAGES. Behavior in Watson's view is a peripheral and not a cerebral affair; or, rather, it is an activity of the whole organism in which the brain serves to connect the sensory with the motor nerves and so link the sense organs with the muscles. Nerve impulses coming into the brain by the sensory nerves are instantly transmitted to the motor nerves, he believed, and all behavior is sensorimotor. If any process can go on entirely within the brain, it is too inaccessible to be included under behavior. Now memory images, mostly visual, auditory, or tactile, sometimes olfactory, are reported by almost every person who is asked to call to mind a friend's face, or a bit of music, or the feel of velvet, or the odor of peppermint. These images resemble sensations, though they are not produced by any present stimulus to the eyes or ears or skin or nose. They seem to be "centrally aroused sensations," purely cerebral affairs accessible to introspection but not to the behavioral methods of observation. Watson attempted to show (1914 pages 16-21) that the so-called images were really sensorimotor affairs. The visual image could consist partly in after-images from the eye, partly in kinesthetic impulses from the eye muscles, and partly in implicit speech movements.

FEELING AND EMOTION. Like the image, the feelings of pleasantness and unpleasantness seemed to many psychologists to be purely central affairs, without any sense organ to arouse

JOHN B. WATSON

Dishinger-Woodward Studio

KARL S. LASHLEY

Press Association, Inc.

JAMES McKEEN CATTELL

ALBERT P. WEISS

them and without any distinct motor expression. Efforts had been made to discover definite expressive changes in the heartbeat, blood pressure, and breathing, but these efforts had led to no clear result. Watson suggested (1914, pages 21-26) that pleasantness was a true sensorimotor affair, the sensory impulses coming in from tumescent sex organs (or other erogenous zones), and the motor impulses going out to muscles and arousing incipient movements of approach—with the reverse conditions in unpleasantness.

From our point of view as students of the schools, it is not important to decide whether Watson made a good guess or a wild one in his attempt to explain feeling or memory images. It is important for us to notice two things: (1) he evidently did not regard feelings or images as mere unreal ghosts, for then he would not have attempted to explain them; (2) if they were sensorimotor processes, they were behavior and quite acceptable to him, even though both the stimulus and the response were implicit and hypothetical. Nothing must go on in the organism except sensorimotor processes—that was the behaviorist's demand or postulate.

Emotion was universally admitted to be more complex than pleasant or unpleasant feeling, and psychologists had long noticed the rapid heartbeat and breathing and the tense muscles of strong emotion. The old view was that the stirred-up bodily state was aroused by the conscious emotion, while the famous James-Lange theory, dating from 1884-1885, held that the perception of danger, for example, directly caused the bodily changes, and that the mass of resulting bodily sensations was the emotion as we experience it. To convert this theory into Watson's, say simply that the presence of danger causes bodily changes (period). Watson, of course, would not admit any conscious "perception" of danger, and especially he would not admit any "mass of sensations" from the bodily organs. What he says is that emotion consists in "profound changes of the bodily mechanism as a whole, but particularly of the visceral and glandular systems," each separate emotion being a particular pattern of such changes (1919, page 195). "Notwithstanding the fact that in all emotional responses there are overt factors such as the movement of the eyes and the arms and the legs and the trunk, visceral and glandular factors predominate" (1924-25, page 130). Emotion is a form of "implicit behavior," though the hidden visceral changes manifest themselves to some extent by visible changes in pulse, breathing, blushing, and the like, so that emotional behavior can be more directly observed than is possible with the simple feelings.

How much simpler Watson's theory is than that of James! Where James had five items to be fitted into the picture—situation, perception of it, bodily changes, overt act such as running away from danger, conscious state of emotion—Watson, by leaving out the two conscious or cerebral processes, has only three items to consider. He has the situation and the overt response, and the visceral changes. Different emotions can be distinguished on the basis of situation and overt response. So we have flight as an overt response to danger, fighting as an overt response to interference. Each different emotion should have its different visceral pattern. Valiant efforts have been made to identify such patterns of internal behavior by records of circulatory, respiratory, and other changes; but definite patterns have not been found (Landis, 1924). In physiological experiments on animals, anger and fear have shown essentially the same visceral pattern (Cannon, 1929). And recent physiological and clinical findings tend to emphasize the role of the thalamus and frontal lobes in emotion, and to minimize the role of the viscera, thus throwing both the James-Lange and the Watson theories into the shade.

Watson felt that his simplified theory opened the door for a developmental study of emotions in children. He made some important contributions along this line. In very young infants he found three well-marked patterns of emotional behavior, distinguished however in terms of external situation and overt response rather than in terms of implicit visceral behavior. These three primal emotions he called fear, rage, and love. As he could distinguish no others in infants, he regarded these three as the only native emotions, all others being built up by processes of learning. The natural or original stimuli of fear were loud sounds and loss of support (slipping or falling); for rage, interference with the infant's freedom of movement; for love, patting and stroking. Other stimuli could be made effective by the conditioned response technique. He was able to develop a conditioned fear in a child of eleven months by "punishing" with a loud, harsh noise each of the child's efforts to reach a white rat, an animal that up to that time had always got a positive response from the child. The loud noise made the child start and sometimes whimper and give other signs of fear or discomfort; and by repeating the punishment every time the child reached for the rat, the experimenter soon established a conditioned avoiding response to the animal. Moreover, this conditioned fear persisted. Such fears are in fact difficult to extinguish. These early results of Watson's are certainly important, even though they do not exhaust the subject of native and acquired emotions (1924-1925, page 120).

THEORY OF LEARNING. It will be recalled from the preceding chapter that Thorndike had modified the older association theory by adding to the law of contiguity, which he renamed the law of exercise, a new law, the law of effect. Successful responses to a situation, by giving satisfaction to the learner, were gradually stamped in, while the unsuccessful ones were stamped out by the discomfort of failure. Although satisfaction and discomfort could be regarded as physiological states, and although Watson himself suggested a behavioral theory for them (see above, page 85), yet the law of effect seemed to assume conscious feelings in the animal subject and even to allow them a causal influence on behavior. Therefore the behaviorists attempted to eliminate the law of effect by reducing it in some way to the law of exercise. Watson at first pinned his faith to the long-accepted laws of frequency and recency, those sublaws under the law of exercise. He pointed out that an animal learning to run a maze is bound to take the correct path at least once on every trial before reaching the food box, whereas any particular blind alley may be skipped in some trials. Thus the successful response would gradually acquire a balance of frequency over the unsuccessful. Thorndike, in reply, pointed out that the same blind alley was often entered several times in the same trial, so that the advantage in frequency would favor that alley, trial after trial, and the blind alley never could be eliminated on the basis of frequency. Thorndike had the best of the argument (page 53).

Later, Watson came to rely mostly on the conditioned response. He had at first adopted the Pavlov and Bekhterev techniques only as convenient objective methods in certain problems. In 1919 he utilized the conditioned response concept for explaining acquired fears, and we have seen how he developed a conditioned fear in a child. By 1924 he had come to suspect that the conditioned response might afford the key to all habit formation—a suggestion first made, apparently, by Smith and Guthrie in a book with decided behavioristic leanings (1921). But neither these writers nor Watson himself recognized the basic importance of Pavlov's law of reinforcement, which we have seen (page 66) to be practically identical with the law of effect. Watson's theory of learning, therefore, belongs with the older associationism and has few adherents among present-day behaviorists.

THEORY OF THINKING. Among psychologists at any rate, Watson's reduction of thinking to implicit motor behavior is the most famous and distinctive of his theories. He started with his regular postulate that thinking must be sensorimotor behavior of some sort, and it seemed to him that implicit speech movements were the most likely behavior for thinking. People, especially children, often think aloud. The child often says what he is doing as he does it, naming the objects he is playing with and the results he is producing. He gives up talking aloud for whispering to himself, gives up whispering for inaudible lip movement, and finally reaches the stage when his talking to himself is invisible as well as inaudible. He also learns to talk to himself not only about what he is actually doing but also about what he has done or intends to do; and so he reaches the adult form of thinking. Adults often substitute subvocal talking for actual manipulation in the effort to solve a problem, so saving time and effort. Instead of moving the piano bodily to a new position in the room, we silently say to ourselves, "Suppose I moved it over there," and continue, "But it would jut out over the window. That won't do." It seemed likely to Watson, then, that the implicit behavior that was substituted for actual manipulation consisted mostly of minute speech movements. He readily conceded that implicit gestures as well as speech movements might occur in thinking. In the case of deaf people who talk with their hands he held that they would also think in implicit hand movements. He had no radical objection to including other implicit movements, insisting indeed that we think with our whole body, but he always came back to his original emphasis on subvocal talking (1914, page 19; 1919, pages 322-328; 1924-1925, pages 191-199).

Watson's theory of thinking strikes one as reasonable, since most of us can testify that we talk to ourselves more or less while thinking. We are often aware of our own inner speech. The reasonableness of the hypothesis rests on this common introspective observation much more than upon the history of the child's talking which was mentioned. Margaret Floy Washburn, a strong supporter herself of a motor theory of thinking, though by no means a behaviorist, pointed out the absurdity of basing upon introspection a hypothesis designed to bolster up behaviorism (1922).

Because it agrees with our own inner experience, the hypothesis that thinking is silent speech is by no means novel but has been propounded time and again without any reference to behaviorism. What behaviorism requires is that this inner speech must consist of actual little movements of the speech organs. In this requirement it of course goes beyond any introspective evidence. To some persons, inner speech is felt in the mouth and throat and chest as if actual movements were occurring there; while to others it is heard rather than felt, seeming to be auditory rather than motor. Introspection cannot tell whether inner speech involves actual speech movements. Watson, though probably getting his hypothesis from his own introspection, did not propose to test it by introspection. He proposed to apply delicate recording apparatus to the speech organs in the hope of securing objective evidence of speech movements during thinking. The larynx seemed to him at first the most likely "organ of thought" and the best organ to approach with external registering instruments. When his attention was called to persons whose larynx had been removed by surgical means and who were still able to think, he shifted his emphasis to the mouth and tongue.

For a hypothesis of purely theoretical interest, without any possible bearing on the practical question of how to promote better thinking, Watson's suggestion was surprisingly stimulating to the experimentalists. It was a challenge to their technical abilities. Could they demonstrate the supposed implicit movements of the speech organs during silent thought or show conclusively that such movements did not occur? Mechanical recording instruments used by the earlier experimenters failed to yield any conclusive result. They revealed slight movements of the tongue and larynx part of the time but not all of the time while the subject was thinking, and did not show the definite patterns that might be expected. Electrical registration with amplification of the little "muscle currents" that occur when a muscle is even minimally active gave more trustworthy results. By this test the tongue muscle proves to be active during some silent speech but not during all silent thinking (Jacobson, 1932). More accessible are the forearm muscles employed by a deaf person in talking with his hands, and by the electrical test these muscles are apt to show some activity when the subject is engaged in difficult thinking but not when the thinking is easy and smooth (Max, 1937). The evidence for or against the theory, so far, cannot be called conclusive.

Behaviorism does not stand or fall with the fortunes of this particular hypothesis. Even if speech movements were always found during silent thought, there would remain the questions: What kept them going? Was the brain action that kept them going more essential than the little speech movements? On the other hand, if speech movements should be proved nonexistent in some or even most thinking, there would remain other possible muscular movements and tensions to provide the sensorimotor process demanded by behaviorism.

WATSON'S ENVIRONMENTALISM. In the 1920's Watson became widely known for his strong emphasis on environment as against heredity. What at that time appeared to be most characteristically behavioristic was his rejection of instincts and of all hereditary mental traits. "Has the boomerang an instinct to return to the hand of the thrower? . . . Well, why does it return? Because it is made in such a way that . . . it must return." (An argument, by the way, that could be used equally well in support of instinct.) "Let us, then, forever lay the ghosts of inheritance of aptitudes, of 'mental' characteristics, of special abilities." His strongest claim for environment was that he could "guarantee," given a free hand in controlling the environment, to take any normal infant "and train him to become any type of specialist I might select—doctor, lawyer, artist, merchant-chief and, yes, even beggar-man and thief, regardless of his talents, penchants, tendencies, abilities, vocations, and race of his ancestors." He admitted that he was going beyond the known facts and was trying to enlist support for a program of research to check this assertion (1924-1925, pages 82-85). This extreme environmentalism is not logically bound up with behaviorism. It has nothing to do with an insistence on objective methods and a rejection of introspection and consciousness. In 1914 Watson found a great deal to say in favor of animal instincts. In 1919, while critical of the long lists of human instincts offered by James and by Thorndike, he still recognized a number of human instincts and stressed the importance of unlearned activity as a basis for learning and habit formation. Did Watson only gradually realize the full meaning of his behaviorism? Or have we here simply a development of his thinking on a special topic? More likely the latter. The behaviorist cannot be bound for life to the job of continually expounding his main theory and its logical implications. Some behaviorists, it is safe to say, reject Watson's environmentalism, while some who are not behaviorists accept this view. It is not a question between one psychological school and another. It is a question of fact and evidence, and the evidence is still coming in from investigators who work not as behaviorists or as nonbehaviorists, but simply as scientific investigators.

In one way, indeed, extreme environmentalism was a logical stand for Watson. He admits that his conclusion goes beyond the evidence, but he justifies himself on the ground that the hereditarians have been in the saddle "for many thousands of years" without any real evidence in their favor. This urge to shake people out of their complacent acceptance of traditional views is perhaps more characteristic of Watson's behaviorism than any of his special theories of learning, thinking, emotion, and instinct.

WATSON'S POPULAR APPEAL. Watson's later books and lectures were intended to win a public following and were very successful in doing so. A literary reviewer could say in 1930 that behaviorism and psychoanalysis "come near dividing the modern Occidental world between them" and that "of the two behaviorism is probably the better adapted to the American temperament because it is fundamentally hopeful and democratic." There is some literary exaggeration here but interest in behaviorism was genuine and widespread. Why was this? We cannot imagine people getting excited over the psychologist's technical concepts and methods. Why should the public be disturbed to learn that introspection was practiced in certain psychological laboratories, and that certain psychologists pretended to be conscious and to have sensations, feelings, and memory images, and why should the public acclaim the bold knight who set forth to fight these superstitions? Why should great enthusiasm be awakened by the announcement that thinking went on in the neck and not in the head? That part of the public which became involved in college courses in psychology would to be sure welcome the simplifications which behaviorism seemed to introduce. Some of the simplifications were only verbal, and some of the "mysteries" eliminated with a wave of the hand remained in the form of unsolved problems; but other simplifications were genuine, for behaviorism certainly helped on their path to oblivion some unpsychological problems inherited from the old mental philosophy.

But the influence of behaviorism extended beyond departmental boundaries. A sociology textbook of that time was advertised as "frankly behavioristic" because the authors "keep their eyes on concrete problems in American life and discuss them on the basis of verifiable material." And the *Nation* of London had this to say of Watson's *Behaviorism*:

His new book claims to put forward not only a new methodology, not even merely a body of psychological theory, but a system which will, in his opinion, revolutionize ethics, religion, psychoanalysis—in fact all the mental and moral sciences.

What Watson had said (1924-1925) was that behaviorism is a truly natural science which takes as its prospective field all human behavior, to be studied by experimental methods, with the object of controlling man's behavior scientifically. This natural-science approach, he said, is causing philosophy to disappear and become a history of science, is preparing the way for an experimental ethics to replace the old authoritative and speculative ethics based on religion, and will gradually do away with psychoanalysis and develop in its place a scientific control of child development which will prevent the neuroses instead of leaving them to be treated in adult life. He outlined his system in very few words and left it as a program or rather as a hope for future scientific work.

But it was significant that a man who had won the public ear as a representative of science should express this hope so confidently. *The New York Times* said of this same book, "It marks an epoch in the intellectual history of man."

That is doing pretty well for the *Times*. Now let us hear the *Tribune:* "Perhaps this is the most important book ever written. One stands for an instant blinded with a great hope." The reference must be to Watson's strong faith in the environment and to that "guarantee" to make something great of any child whose environment from birth up he was allowed to control. It was only a hope on Watson's part, for if anyone had secured him the full control of a child's environment he would not have known how to proceed, except by way of research. Neither he nor anyone yet possesses the requisite scientific knowledge. But at any rate that may have been the hope that blinded the reviewer.

It was not so much Watson's actual scientific achievements, nor even his system of concepts and methods, that made him a standard-bearer in the forward march of psychology. It was, rather, his boldness, tough-mindedness, scorn of tradition and mystery, along with an optimistic faith in the capacity of science to take charge of human affairs. Behaviorism meant to many young men and women of the time a new orientation and a new hope when the old guides had become hopelessly discredited in their eyes. It was a religion to take the place of religion.

Some Other Early Behaviorists

Though Watson was undoubtedly the **prime** mover in the behavioristic movement and its most prominent representative for two decades, there were a few other eminent psychologists who soon adopted much the same point of view.

Max Meyer (born 1873, long professor at Missouri), writing in 1911 on *The fundamental laws of human behavior,* came rather close to behaviorism, and has since been classed as a behaviorist. Meyer was a pupil of the important German psychologist, Carl Stumpf (1848-1936) of the University of Berlin who, like G. E. Müller, previously mentioned, was one of the younger contemporaries of Wundt who independently started psychological laboratories in the early days. Stumpf specialized in the psychology of hearing and of music, and Meyer has been a prolific contributor to this line of study, which cannot by any means be called behavioristic. But Meyer became intensely interested in the mechanism of the ear and brain and came to believe that the only true science of psychology must deal with such matters. What he did in his book of 1911 was to develop laws and schemes of nerve action to explain the facts of conscious experience and of behavior.

During the past few decades the conviction became general that a science of the subjective, an introspective science, because of its limited possibility of generalizations, hardly deserved the name of a science. In order to remedy the defect which had been discovered, objective methods, like those in the physical sciences, were introduced into the mental sciences, to supplement the subjective method of introspection. . . .

Not the study of the individual's consciousness, of the "structure of the mind," but the study of the nervous laws of behavior will enable us to understand the significance of human action for human life in the individual and in society. The scientific value of introspective psychology consists merely in the fact that it aids us in discovering the laws of nervous function.

Meyer's view, much like Pillsbury's of the same date (page 74), was that introspection should be used for throwing light on function, rather than for attempting to build up a science of conscious experience.

Another of Meyer's books, published in 1921 as a college textbook, is called *The psychology of the other one*. The title at first seems odd for a general work on psychology; you would think it indicated some special topic. But it embodies the author's view that the proper object of psychological study is "the other one." He is the individual to be observed. The author thus urges the student away from the traditional view of psychology as primarily the study of oneself. It should be primarily a study of other people. You are personally concerned about your own doings and likely to be biased in your observation. A clinical psychologist, an experimental psychologist, a social psychologist needs to study other people.

One of Meyer's pupils was Albert P. Weiss (1879-1931) who was certainly a behaviorist, as well as an active experimentalist and student of child development. In his book, *A theoretical basis of human behavior* (1925, 1929), he was concerned to find a place for psychology among the natural sciences. He urged psychologists to give up certain pretensions which he believed were alienating them from other scientists. Psychologists should not pretend to have access through introspection to any realities which are immaterial and so inaccessible to the natural scientist. Psychology should freely admit that there are no ultimate entities besides those recognized in physics. Physics at the time recognized the electron and proton as the fundamental entities. Psychology should adopt these and not claim any other fundamental entities. (In a psychological laboratory or clinic, to be sure, we have nothing directly to do with electrons and protons, but we are no worse off in this respect than the biologist or even the chemist who is mostly satisfied with atoms as his fundamentals. Let us all join hands in paying homage to the electron and the proton, and freely admit that all chemical and biological processes, including what we familiarly call mental processes, consist ultimately in the motion of electrons and protons, until physics has something better to offer.) In short psychology should not claim a separate world as its field but should adopt the view that all phenomena, its own included, are natural phenomena subject to the same ultimate laws. Most important, it should not assume any mental forces or factors separate from the biological forces and factors which are themselves reducible to physical terms (1930).

In ordinary common-sense language we imply that the feelings are causes of behavior—we do something because it is pleasant and avoid something else because it gives us pain. Psychologists should not speak in this way unless they are prepared to regard the feelings as physical processes in the nervous system (1928).

Weiss, however, does not wish to confine psychology to physiological concepts. The human organism exists in a social environment. One individual's behavior acts as a stimulus arousing behavior in other individuals, and each individual's development is very largely controlled by the social situation. But while recognizing the social character of human behavior we must not forget that it is biological at the same time. In becoming socialized, man does not become any less biological. All his activities—talking for example—remain just as truly physiological processes as they would be if he were a solitary animal. In order to do justice to both sides, Weiss coined the term *biosocial* to characterize human behavior. The field of psychology is that of biosocial processes, and the appropriate standpoint for psychology is biosocial. Its main task is to trace the development of the human infant into the social adult. In this task such mentalistic concepts as sensation, image, perception, feeling, thinking, striving are not going to be of any help. Rather, they will hamper research. The development of conscious experience cannot be followed from infancy, because we have no direct access to the infant's feelings, for example. We can only use behavioral indicators. Only in behavioral terms, then, can a complete developmental history be worked out. (This line of argument loses its force if we regard perception, feeling, thinking, etc., not primarily as kinds of conscious experience, but as functions defined by results accomplished and calling for investigation as to how they operate.) Weiss inaugurated a comprehensive program at the Ohio State University for following the development of behavior in the young child, but died before the program could be carried to completion.

Walter S. Hunter (born 1889, professor at Brown University), a pupil of Angell and Carr, is another prominent behaviorist. As an experimentalist working with both human and animal subjects he is to be credited with several very significant contributions to the psychology of learning and problem solving, the most noteworthy being perhaps the "delayed reaction" and the "temporal maze." His view on the schools is that in the time of Wundt and Titchener there was reason to expect a structural introspective psychology to be fruitful, but that it has proved to be relatively sterile.

In America we seem to be emerging at last from an era of controversy concerning what psychology is or ought to be. For good or ill the onward march of experiment, which no mere speculation and controversy can halt, has carried psychology along the way of the objective study of human behavior. . . . Psychology seeks to describe and explain, to predict and control, the extrinsic behavior of the organism to an external environment which is predominantly social [1932, pp. 2, 24].

An analysis of conscious experience does not yield much in the way of real discoveries because the main facts are known to everyone. "The discovery of seeing, feeling and thinking . . . was made by common-sense observation at some unrecorded time in the past" (1932, page 5). The great variety of detailed "conscious content" does not appear to the ordinary man as mental at all but appears to belong to the environment.

The . . . Wundtians abstract qualities, intensities, durations . . . from the environment and call the material selected experience. The users of meaning take concrete objects from the environment and call these experience [1926, p. 88].

Or, in other words:

> If we ask any contemporary psychologist [not behaviorist] what he means by the term consciousness, or experience, he will reply by enumerating such things as sweet, red, and kinesthetic strain . . . or he will reply by enumerating such things as roses, books, configurations, and melodies. . . . I wish to point out that consciousness or experience for the psychologist is merely a name which he applies to what other people call the environment [1930, pp. 282-283].

A good stiff argument could be directed against Hunter on this last point, for the environment is not the same thing as the individual's perception of the environment. To perceive the size, shape, color and distance of an object is really a remarkable achievement, and it is a task for functional psychology (in the broad sense, page 13) to discover how this result is accomplished. Hunter, however, is engaged here in combating the structural, not the functional, psychologist.

Karl S. Lashley (born 1890, professor at Harvard), a pupil of Watson, can best be called a neuropsychologist, as will appear shortly, but has always been classed as a behaviorist. He so announced himself in an early theoretical paper (1923). He opposed subjectivism and any pretension of introspection to reveal a unique mode of existence not conceivable in objective terms. "The subjectivist claims a universe of nonmaterial things as the subject of his study. The behaviorist denies sensations, images, and all other phenomena which the subjectivist claims to find by introspection." This was the regular behavioristic stand. But Lashley went on to show that all genuine findings of the introspectionists could be expressed in objective terms and so find a place in a behavioristic psychology. This conclusion is interesting in two ways. It would show that subjectivism was entirely unnecessary in psychology; but it would also show that the behaviorists, after all, should make no fundamental objection to introspection. They might well be cautious in using so slippery a method of observation, but their objection could not be fundamental if they could utilize some of its results in their own system.

Lashley has devoted many years to an untiring investigation

of the brain in relation to learning and other psychological functions. Localization of functions in the cerebral cortex had been a major enterprise of the physiologists in the latter part of the nineteenth century, and they had shown that each of the senses is connected to a definite cortical area. Besides these sensory areas, a motor area was identified. But all these areas, sensory and motor combined, made up but a small proportion of the cortex in man. Plenty of cortex remained for the higher functions. If these were to be localized, it was time for psychologists to unite their forces with the physiologists. Credit for initiating this neuropsychological line of investigation belongs to Shepard Ivory Franz (1874-1933), a pupil of Cattell and fellow-student with Thorndike. After mastering Thorndike's methods of studying animal learning and the physiologist's methods of studying localization, Franz devised a combination of the two. To discover, for example, whether the cat's frontal lobes were concerned in learning to escape from a puzzle box by turning the door button, he had the animal learn the trick, removed the frontal lobes and allowed time for recovery from the operation, and tested the animal for retention of the trick. If there was no retention, the animal was given the opportunity to learn the trick over again. Franz's results showed that with loss of the frontal lobes there was a loss of the previously learned trick, but no great loss of the ability to learn the same trick again. This is but a sample of Franz's important results (1902, 1907, and many later papers).

Lashley started on this line of investigation as a collaborator of Franz. In 1917 they applied the combined method to that favorite laboratory animal, the white rat, a very convenient animal for such experiments, though its brain is so much smaller and less complicated than that of man. Lashley has continued this line of work on the rat and other animals, with striking though somewhat baffling results. Certainly his results, like those of Franz, perplex anyone who expects—as Lashley did at first—to find a small localized center for each learned performance. While the loss of any considerable amount of the cortex slows the rat's maze learning, it seems to make little difference to the rat what particular part of the cortex is removed and what part is left for him to learn with. He apparently learns the maze as well with one part as with another. The greater the amount of cortex removed, the more is he hampered in his learning. Easy tricks are learned rather quickly with only half of the cortex left, but not difficult tricks, which require a larger mass of cortex. Lashley summarizes his findings under two principles (1929):

1. The principle of equipotentiality: one part of the cortex is potentially the same as another in its capacity to learn a maze or other performance. There are some exceptions: visual perception of a shape or pattern can be accomplished only by the occipital (rear) area, though within that area the parts are largely equipotential.

2. The principle of mass action: the more cortex left, the better the learning.

Lashley himself was surprised by these results and checked them over very carefully. He started this work with the expectation of finding definite sensorimotor connections, definite paths through the cortex, laid down by heredity for instinctive reactions, established by conditioning for learned reactions. But the whole tendency of his results is against accepting the simple reflex arc as the basic unit in brain function. Superimposing the conditioned reflex on the native reflex cannot give us the key to learned behavior. The brain must function in some other way not yet clearly discerned.

Regarding the change in his own views Lashley has this to say (1931, page 14):

I began life as an ardent advocate of muscle-twitch psychology. I became glib in formulating all problems of psychology in terms of stimulus-response and in explaining all things as conditioned reflexes. . . . I embarked enthusiastically upon a program of experiments to prove the adequacy of the motor-chain theory of integration. And the result is as though I had maliciously planned an attack upon the whole system. . . . The conditioned reflex turned out not to be a reflex, not the simple basic key to the learning problem. . . . In order that the concept of stimulus-response should have any scientific value it must convey a notion of how a particular stimulus elicits a particular response and no other. . . . When viewed in relation to the problems of neurology, the nature of the stimulus and of the response is intrinsically such as to preclude the theory of simple point-to-point connection in reflexes.

The last sentence refers to such facts as these: (1) in looking repeatedly at the same object, you change your fixation point and so bring into play different rods and cones and different nerve fibers leading to the brain, and yet the object appears the same and gets the same response; (2) the motor response, too, varies in the exact muscles used and still produces the same result. The cat that has learned to turn the door button of a puzzle box gets somewhat different stimuli and makes somewhat different responses, neurologically, from one trial to the next, and still her behavior remains essentially the same. The brain, therefore, must do something more than merely switch incoming nerve currents over into outgoing nerves. Watson in his desire not to make a fetish of the brain had allowed it only this switching function, and the early conception of the conditioned response had envisaged specific sensorimotor connections established in the brain. Lashley's own experiments and his critical survey of other results led him to view the brain as having a more active role. "This evidence seems to favor the older doctrine of imagery and to throw us back upon the concept of activity maintained within the central nervous system for an understanding of serial habits and the mechanisms of thinking" (1934, pages 482-483). Nor can Watson's extremely negative view of instinct and heredity be maintained (1947).

No doubt Lashley's views and findings came as a shock to many behaviorists, who liked the reflex and the conditioned reflex as furnishing a simple scheme of behavior and banishing "mystery." Yet it must be said that behaviorism is not bound to any single hypothesis or explanation so as to be seriously shaken when that hypothesis is displaced by one that is more adequate. Concepts must be allowed to change provided they remain true to the spirit and attitude of behaviorism. Lashley's concepts are dictated in part by the requirements of neurophysiology.

In one of his papers Lashley gives a graphic description of the behavior of rats after removal of some of their cerebral cortex, in comparison with the behavior of normal rats in the same situation, the "latch box," a form of puzzle box; and in this connection he indicates the kind of concepts which have real value in his neuropsychology (1935, pages 31-35).

The behavior of animals with cerebral lesions in the latch box situations suggests two more general defects which may have contributed to their poor records . . . a general reduction in sensitivity . . . and . . . exploratory activity . . . a lack of aggressiveness. . . . In addition to these differences between normal and cerebral operated cases a third may be significant. The normal rat rather quickly modifies his reactions to the latch so that, whereas his original movement in springing it may have been a random stumbling, his subsequent movements are directly adapted to operating it with a minimum of effort. . . . Such behavior suggests that the normal rat . . . comes to identify the movable latch as a distinct object connected with the opening of the door. . . . Whatever the explanation of behavior of this character, animals with extensive cerebral lesions show a limitation in acquiring it. Their behavior is more stereotyped in that they tend to repeat the movements which were first successful. . . . The observations may be summarized by the statement that the rats with extensive cerebral lesions are less observing, have less initiative, and show less insight into the relations of latch and door than do normal animals.

In previous discussions of the effects of cerebral lesions I have striven to avoid such psychological interpretations of behavior. They do not give us any understanding of the cerebral mechanisms involved and tend to obscure the issues by presenting a pseudoscientific explanation in terms of empathy. . . . I therefore present the above psychological interpretations, not because they have any explanatory value, but in order to make the dynamic concepts of cerebral function sound less strange by identifying them with terms which, though scientifically meaningless, are familiar.

In observing animal behavior we tend by "empathy" to put ourselves in the animal's place, even while avoiding anthropomorphism as far as possible, and we say that the animal seems to perceive objects and relations. But we cannot apply such concepts directly to brain processes. The concept of "connections" can readily be applied to the brain, which shows in its microscopic structure innumerable nerve fibers connecting one part of the cortex with another. But Lashley's work indicates that connections do not tell the whole story. "The unit of functional organization seems to be not the reflex arc . . . but the mechanism, whatever be its nature, by which response to a ratio of intensities is brought about" (1934, page 493).

One interesting aspect of Lashley's findings is that they bring behaviorism and Gestalt psychology—which we shall consider in our next chapter—closer together than once appeared possible. We might even find more in common between Lashley and the Gestalt psychologist Köhler than between Lashley and the behaviorist Hull. Indeed, our present behaviorists differ considerably among themselves. Their work has not been neuropsychological. There are some very productive neuropsychologists at work, but they are not identified closely with behaviorism.

The Later Behaviorists

The division into early and later behaviorists is rather arbitrary, since two of those just considered, Hunter and Lashley, are definitely present-day behaviorists. The distinction, such as it is, rests on the fact that behaviorism seemed to have a new birth about 1930, with new names becoming prominent and new forms of behaviorism emerging. As far as age goes, Hunter and Lashley are a little younger than Tolman and Hull, the next two on our list.

Edward Chace Tolman (born 1886, professor at California) was really one of the early converts to behaviorism. As early as 1920 and 1922 he was calling himself a behaviorist or sometimes a "purposive behaviorist." There was some doubt in the minds of most psychologists whether his *purposive behaviorism* could properly be called behaviorism. As the experimental work in Tolman's active animal laboratory proceeded, the methods were seen to be behavioral methods, beyond doubt, and the behavioral basis of his system of concepts was rather convincingly set forth in his 1932 book on *Purposive behavior in animals and men.* From that time to the present, purposive behaviorism has been generally recognized as truly a form of behaviorism, though differing from the original Watsonian variety.

Tolman's espousal of behaviorism was from the beginning coupled with rather severe criticisms of Watson's views. Watson had waved "purpose" aside as an introspective superstition of no interest to a behaviorist. Tolman, less impatient and more subtle, believed he could discern an objective purposiveness in behavior itself.

Watson had been far from clear and consistent in his definition of behavior. He had insisted that behavior was something that could be seen, objectively observed; yet he had postulated implicit behavior which could not actually be observed. He had emphasized the role of muscles, glands, and the viscera; and yet, to distinguish behavior study from physiology, he had said (1919, page 195) : "It is perfectly possible for a student of behavior entirely ignorant . . . of the glands and smooth muscles . . . to write a thoroughly comprehensive and accurate study of the emotions." He had distinguished fear, rage, and love as the emotions observable in infants without making any attempt to get at the visceral processes in the infants so as to discover whether there actually were three distinct patterns of visceral behavior. Instead, he had observed three types of overt behavior aroused by three types of external situation. He had observed, for instance, that the infant screamed and made slashing or striking movements of the arms and legs when his movements were hampered by the experimenter. The angry behavior was a fighting against interference. The stimulus varied and the response also varied and still the behavior was clearly angry. A critical review of this work led Tolman (1923) to draw a significant conclusion: "It is not a response, *as such,* nor a stimulus situation, *as such,* that constitutes the behavior definition of an emotion, but rather the response as affecting . . . the stimulus situation." Behavioristically, an emotion is a "tendency toward a particular type of behavior-result." What Watson actually described was the infant's behavior in the true sense; what he said he ought to describe amounted to visceral and other physiological processes (Tolman, 1922).

As Tolman put the matter later (1932, pages 6-7) :

In short, our conclusion must be that Watson has in reality dallied with two different notions of behavior, though he himself has not clearly

seen how different they are. On the one hand, he has defined behavior
in terms of its strict underlying physical and physiological details. . . .
We shall designate this as the *molecular* definition of behavior. And,
on the other hand, he has come to recognize . . . that behavior, as such,
is more than and different from the sum of its physiological parts. Behavior, as such, is an "emergent" phenomenon that has descriptive and
defining properties of its own. And we shall designate this latter as the
molar definition of behavior.

Physiological analysis of a behavior act, perfectly legitimate
and desirable in its place, does not bring out the behavioral
character of the act. Clutching at your hat when the wind
threatens to blow it off is a behavior act, a relatively small one
and yet big enough to involve a host of physiological details.
As a bit of behavior it has a start and a finish: it starts from a
certain situation and terminates in a certain change effected in
the situation. Watson's three emotional patterns in the infant
started from different stimulating situations and tended toward
different results. Often a behavior act proceeds through several
stages on its way to the end-result or goal. Several steps may
be taken, several minor acts performed, all advancing toward
the goal.

An animal's trial-and-error behavior in the maze or puzzle
box is visibly goal-directed or purposive. If the goal is not
reached by one route, some other route is taken, and still others
till the goal is reached. In a series of trials the blind alleys are
eliminated, and shorter paths adopted instead of longer ones
leading to the same goal. The animal learns something. And
what does he learn? The route to a goal—the means to an end.
This learning is the real evidence of purpose. For if the animal
after rummaging around in the maze comes upon food and
stops to eat, there is nothing so far to indicate that he has been
seeking that result. But when in a number of trials in the same
maze he comes to take the most direct route to the food box, his
behavior is clearly steered toward that goal. It shows purpose,
and it also shows knowledge, acquaintance with that situation
built up by the trial-and-error process of exploration. When he
dashes by a certain route to the food box, he is behaviorally as-

serting that he is taking a good route toward the goal (1932, pages 10-21).

As can be readily imagined, Tolman had to entrench himself against serious attacks from behaviorists and introspectionists alike, both contending that knowing and purposing could not be attributed to animals except on the assumption that the animals were conscious. Tolman insisted that he neither knew nor cared what knowing and purposing felt like to the animals. If a rat has any conscious foresight of the goal or any conscious preference for the shortest route, it is his private affair and we have nothing to do with his private feelings. Even in the case of human beings, Tolman went on to say, the "raw feel" of their sensations and emotions is their private possession and incommunicable. If I try to describe to you my sensation of the color red, I find it cannot be done. I can point to a red object, I can say that red is somewhat like orange or purple, and very different from green and blue, quite a gay, stimulating color, very nice for a tie but a little too gay for a professor's overcoat —I can put red in many such relations but I cannot describe the sensation itself. I should have the same difficulty in trying to describe my feelings of pleasantness. Now what is essentially private cannot be made the subject matter of science, for science is social. The data of science must be public or capable of publication. The "mentalists" have tried to create a science of private experience, while the behaviorists of all varieties reject any such possibility. Only to the extent that private experience can be *reported,* made public, can it have any place in science.

This apparently clear distinction between behaviorism and mentalism, however, does not stand up very well under analysis. The structuralists, who seem to be the typical mentalists, do insist on verbal report of all introspective observations. Their data are made public and on this basis should be acceptable to the behaviorists. If so, the behaviorists have no real quarrel with the structuralists, except so far as the structuralists attempt (or once did attempt) to rule behavioral data out of psychology. Similarly, the structuralists have no real quarrel with the behaviorists except so far as the latter attempt to rule the former out of scientific psychology. From the broad functionalist point of view (page 24) both kinds of data can throw some light on the difficult "How" question, and accordingly both structuralists and behaviorists are accepted for their positive contributions, while both are rejected for their negativistic tendencies. Tolman, it must be said, is less negativistic than most other behaviorists. He is open-minded toward all the schools and finds concepts that he can utilize even in the theories of such antibehavioristic schools as Gestalt psychology and psychoanalysis (1932, 1942, 1948).

Indeed Tolman seems to claim for "behaviorism" any psychological work using objective methods or objective concepts, concepts that can be expressed in behavioral or even in hypothetical physiological terms (1935). If behaviorism becomes so imperialistic as that, it ceases to be behaviorism and merges into the general body of functional psychology, as has been pointed out in a critical review by Tilquin (1935).

Tolman apparently has the credit of first clearly formulating the concept of *intervening variables* (1935, 1938). The primary task of any psychological experimenter is to observe what a given individual does in response to a given situation. What the experimenter knows in advance is the situation and such facts about the individual as his heredity, age, and past experience (this ideal being more attainable in animal than in human experiments). In a series of experiments the situation is varied or individuals of varying heredity, age, or experience are compared. Whichever factor is varied is the "experimental variable," also called the independent variable, while the resulting behavior shows the dependent or behavior variable. The experimenter's task is to observe the behavior under the different experimental conditions—to discover the relation of the behavior variable to the experimental variable—to work out the "function" (in the mathematical sense, page 29), represented schematically by the equation,

$$B = f(S,A)$$

where B stands for behavior variables, S for situation variables, and A for antecedent variables such as heredity, age, and previous experience.

So far, what the experimenter has is an elaborate answer to our question "What?" But he would like also to attack the question "How?" He tries to imagine the internal process leading from the given situation to the observed response. In terms of another familiar formula, S—O—R, he tries to imagine what goes on in O between S and R. The intervening process must vary with the experimental variables, and so give rise to the behavior variables. The intervening variables, which he imagines, have no scientific value unless they can be tied in with the experimental variables on the one hand and with the behavior variables on the other. The best example is hunger, conceived as a demand for food or an active tendency to seek food. The animal's demand for food is not directly controlled or observed, but it can be tied to a certain experimental variable, the time since last feeding. And it can be tied to a certain response variable, speed of eating when food is found. Tolman finds at least two kinds of intervening variables useful in explaining animal behavior: demand variables and cognitive variables. In the class of demands are sex hunger, demand for a safe spot in face of danger, and demand for a good bed after prolonged activity. The cognitive or "know-how" variables include perception of objects, recognition of previously explored places, motor skill, etc. The cognitive variables might be called abilities and answers to the question "How?" while the demands would be motives and answers to the question "Why?" If the hypothetical intervening variables can be successfully tied in with the experimental and behavior variables, they make up an acceptable theory of behavior.

We said that Tolman had no real quarrel with many psychologists not properly regarded as belonging to the school of behaviorism. His main quarrel (1938) is with the associationists, both old and new, especially perhaps with Thorndike, Pavlov, and the behaviorist next on our list.

Clark L. Hull (born 1884, professor at Yale) was well known as a productive psychologist for a decade before he came out as a champion of behaviorism. Unlike the other prominent behaviorists he was not a graduate of the animal laboratory. Tolman might have claimed him as a behaviorist on the strength of his important experiment on the establishment of concepts (1920), since that was a purely objective study. Without disparaging the introspective work of his predecessors in the study of concepts, which had yielded only qualitative results, Hull pointed out that the "functional and quantitative" development of the subject still awaited the invention of suitable objective methods, and he showed how the Ebbinghaus memory methods could be adapted for the purpose. This work was notable for the excellence of its experimental design, though it was later criticized from the Gestalt standpoint because it defined each class of objects by a "common element" present in each member of the class rather than by a "common form" of the members. That Hull did not at the time consider his work behavioristic is shown by his incidental use of mentalistic terms like *mental activity, focus of consciousness, memory images,* and *unpleasantness.* But the emphasis was strongly on objective methods and functional laws.

Hull's early work was directed also to the projection of an elaborate system of aptitude tests (1928) and to the development of practical statistical methods, including the invention of a machine for computing correlations (1925). Also notable was his experimental work on hypnosis and suggestibility (1933). Brother psychologists were surprised to see him desert these early interests and devote his energies to the working out of a theory of behavior based on Pavlov's laws of conditioning.

Always the inventor, Hull was evidently fascinated by the problem of designing a well-geared conceptual machine, a theoretical system from which definite laws of behavior could be logically deduced for submission to the test of experiment. The conflicting schools meant to him that psychology had not yet advanced to a truly scientific stage of development. Various broad theories were being offered, but only in very sketchy outline, none of the theorists having the patience to work out the implications of a theory far enough to make sure whether it could predict phenomena not yet observed. Good work was being done by the experimentalists in the testing of particular hypotheses, but what was lacking was a comprehensive system of concepts, a "hypothetico-deductive" system. Such a system, much like geometry, starts with certain postulates and definitions which can be combined and yield logical deductions. The deduced propositions must be as logical as those of geometry, once the premises are granted. Of course in an empirical science like psychology the deduced propositions must be put to test in the realm of observable facts. When the predicted results are not verified the postulates and definitions must be re-examined in the hope that some minor revisions will save the system as a whole. The enterprise may run on for many years, paying its way as it goes by the mass of scientific knowledge gathered by the experimenters who test the hypotheses derived from the system (1935).

The postulates of the system, or some of them, may be known in advance to be true statements of fact—so much the better—but some of them will probably be "intervening variables," only to be validated indirectly as essential parts of the whole system. Hull gives credit to Tolman for the fruitful idea of intervening variables as well as for the concept of molar behavior (1943, page 31). One of Hull's important intervening variables is *drive,* akin to Tolman's demand. On the whole, however, Hull's system is very different from Tolman's. Where Tolman regards cognition as a fundamental factor in behavior, Hull believes this function can be derived from his fundamental postulate of stimulus-response association (1930). Hull is definitely one of the "new associationists," while Tolman's negative attitude toward association is much like the attitude of the Gestalt school.

Hull gave a brief "miniature" view of his system in 1937, a rigidly "mathematico-deductive" presentation in 1940, and a more complete and generally intelligible treatment in 1943. He makes full use of Pavlov's principles of reinforcement and extinction. He means also to make full use of Pavlov's law for the establishment of a conditioned response, but it must be said that he does not follow Pavlov very closely. He accepts the substitute-stimulus theory of the conditioned response, which we have discussed on page 61. One of his main postulates (1937, page 16; 1943, page 178) is that any stimulus occurring "in close temporal contiguity" with a reinforced response becomes connected with that response so as to evoke it later (after enough repetitions of this event). This statement implies that the conditioned response is the same as the unconditioned response, only attached by conditioning to a new stimulus; whereas the conditioned response usually, perhaps always, differs to some extent from the unconditioned and has, indeed, the characteristics of a preparatory response. Hull's statement does not specify, as Pavlov's did, that the conditioned stimulus must begin *before* the unconditioned. And while Hull says that *any* stimulus occurring close in time to a reinforced response becomes connected with it, Pavlov says that the conditioned stimulus must be such as to get the animal's attention. Of course Hull is at liberty to deviate from Pavlov in choosing his own postulates, but then he has the job of explaining Pavlov's results, which would seem to be quite contradictory to Hull's postulates.

Hull does not often speak of himself as a behaviorist, believing perhaps that the name of behaviorism properly belongs to Watson's system, which differs greatly from Hull's both in form and in content. Hull often calls his concepts "objective" or "naturalistic," and he endeavors to free them from any trace of introspection, mere intuition, and anthropomorphism. For Thorndike's "satisfaction," which seemed to imply a conscious state, Hull substitutes "cessation or reduction of a need." All admissible concepts, even though referring directly to "molar" behavior, must refer ultimately to bodily processes. And nothing should be assumed to go on in the organism that could not go on in an elaborate physicochemical robot (1943, page 27). What we ordinarily call mental processes must be regarded as complications of physicochemical processes. Now that we are becoming familiar with calculating machines capable of doing certain kinds of "mental work," it is easier to believe that learning machines and thinking machines could be invented. Hull himself devised a machine that could work out syllogisms, and with his students he indicated how some of the simpler learning processes could be mechanically or electrically imitated (1937, page 29). No attempt was made to discover the actual brain processes in learning, but the fact that a physical mechanism could "learn" was regarded as significant. Hull believes that his system of behavior concepts can cover the facts of expectation, purpose, and guiding ideas. "What, then, shall we say about consciousness? Is its existence denied? By no means. But to recognize the existence of a phenomenon is not the same thing as insisting upon its basic, i.e., logical priority. Instead of furnishing a means for the solution of problems, consciousness appears to be itself a problem needing solution." He goes on to challenge anyone to start with well-defined conscious processes and work out a logical system that will predict actual behavior in animals or men (1937, page 30).

Whatever may be the merits of his system, Hull soon gathered around him at Yale a very active and productive group of young investigators, a new school of behaviorism. And his system has awakened lively interest in his fellow-psychologists in many places, though it must be added that his chief fellow-behaviorists, as Tolman and Lashley, have been sharply critical, and so has Skinner, the last behaviorist on our list.

Burrhus Frederic Skinner (born 1904, professor at Indiana and at Harvard), while younger than the other behaviorists mentioned, was an active contributor in the early 1930's to the new birth of behaviorism which occurred at that time. In 1931 he laid down a program for the study of behavior from the experimenter's point of view. What the experimenter can do is to apply known stimuli and note the organism's response. He can describe behavior in terms of correlated stimulus and response. Skinner proposed to regard any S-R unit as a "reflex" in a broad meaning of that term. Traditionally a reflex is limited to unlearned and involuntary responses, but Skinner proposed to prune away these restrictions and to call any S-R unit a reflex. In this sense all behavior is composed of reflexes, or at least the experimenter's task consists in the study of such units.

The psychological experimenter is concerned with overt behavior and not with the internal mechanism of the behavior. He is not concerned with the physiologist's reflex arc nor with the synapses in the nerve centers. Skinner thus adopted the "molar" point of view.

Besides the stimulus, other conditions are under the control of the experimenter, and his job is to discover how the response depends on these other experimental variables as well as on the stimulus. His entire job is to work out the relations schematically represented by a formula which we have already considered (page 107):

$$R = f(S,A),$$

where A stands for a condition controlled by the experimenter and made the experimental variable in an investigation. The laws of behavior will be statements of the variation of response produced by known variations of the stimulus and other experimental conditions. These laws will be "functions" in the mathematical sense and will be made as quantitative and mathematical as the data permit.

For an easy example, take the familiar reaction time experiment with human subjects. The subject is to react as quickly as possible to a sound. If the sound is very weak, the reaction is slow; increase the sound intensity and the reaction becomes quicker. Vary the sound intensity systematically and you can work out a function or curve showing the relation of the reaction time to the intensity of the stimulus, an S-variable. For an A-variable you might take the age in children and work out an age curve. In reaction time work the R-variable is the reaction time itself, also called the latency of the response. Another R-variable often used is the strength of the response; for example, the amount of saliva secreted in Pavlov's conditioning experiment (page 57). In an "extinction series" the stimulus in question is the conditioned stimulus, say the sound of a bell, but this is held constant, the variable condition being the number of trials since the last reinforcement, an A-variable. The strength of the response diminishes as the extinction series advances.

So far there is no special novelty in Skinner's behaviorism, except perhaps for the use of the word *reflex* to cover all varieties of stimulus-response units. Novelty appears in his introduction (1932) of the simplified form of puzzle box which is known today as the Skinner box. This experiment, as we have already seen (page 64) bridged the apparent gap between Pavlov's conditioning and Thorndike's trial and error. Learning of this simplified problem was very rapid, but extinction was slow, and the many studies since made with this apparatus are largely concerned with the rate of extinction under different conditions. This type of experiment gave Skinner occasion to divide his "reflexes" into two classes, the *respondents* and the *operants*. In a respondent a known stimulus elicits a response; in an operant there is no known stimulus, but an apparently spontaneous response is "emitted" by the organism. No doubt there may be some internal stimulus, such as a hunger pang, but from the experimenter's point of view there is no stimulus because he does not apply or observe any. The eliciting stimulus is beyond his control and so is not one of his experimental variables. His concern is wholly with the A-variables, and the functions he works out come under the simplified formula $R = f(A)$.

The experimenter does of course provide stimuli. When the rat presses the bar that secures food, stimuli from the bar show him where to press; these are guiding or discriminative stimuli, but not eliciting stimuli. It would be equally reasonable, of course, to say that stimuli from the bar elicit the response of pressing when the rat is in the state of hunger. But Skinner wishes to avoid any reference to inner states of the organism and to deal wholly with controllables and observables. Accordingly he says that the bar-pressing response is simply emitted by the organism, though guided by stimuli from the bar and other objects.

The operant has another property not included in the definition but implied in the name. It operates on the environment; it is instrumental (page 63); in the Skinner box it procures food. The typical respondent, such as the conditioned flow of saliva in Pavlov's experiment, may prepare the organism for what is to come, but does not produce environmental effects (unless the interior of the mouth is regarded as part of the environment). Behavior consists mostly of operants, and the study of conditioned operants and their extinction is presumably the best lead toward a science of behavior. Such a science will be engaged in studying operant behavior—its acquisition, guidance, and extinction—in relation to experimental conditions.

Obviously Skinner's behavioristic program differs from Hull's or Tolman's. He does not, like Hull, set up a system of hypothetical concepts from which deductions are made to be tested by experiment. Skinner goes so far as to say that he does not make any use of hypotheses (1938, page 44), but a careful reading of his book will detect some hypotheses very usefully employed. Without guiding hypotheses, it would seem, the experimenter would be reduced to trying out any and all A-variables, perhaps in alphabetical order, and assembling his results in a long series of graphs. Skinner certainly would not subscribe to any such mechanical program of research, but he does not make very clear what principles should be the guides in selecting significant experimental variables. Presumably he would be guided as other scientific workers are by the current state of the science and the problems which are leading to significant results. What he does make clear is his judgment that Hull's hypothetico-deductive program is less promising than a program of working out the relations of behavior to known environmental conditions (1944). Skinner's hope undoubtedly is that the simpler laws or "functions," when well established, will prove to be related in such a way that they can be combined into higher and more inclusive laws. For example the laws of conditioning and of extinction may be combinable into higher laws covering both conditioning and extinction. It seems to be impossible in any science to predict the future course of investigation far in advance—to lay down once and for all a systematic plan of what is to be undertaken—so much depends on the impact of new and unexpected discoveries. Skinner's system, aside from the limited set of behavioral laws which he regards as already established, amounts to a methodology, a set of principles governing the collection and treatment of data and the choice and definition of behavioral concepts.

Tolman's system is regarded by Skinner (1938, page 437) as in many respects similar to his own, but as suffering from the use of the maze experiment, which requires behavior of much greater complexity than the Skinner box does, with the consequence that elementary laws of behavior never come out clearly. Besides, the heavy use of "intervening variables" in Tolman's system does not appeal to Skinner, who makes only sparing use of them and then only for convenience. Hunger, for example, is a convenient term to use because the hungry state affects behavior in several ways, but to define hunger we must report the time since last feeding, the rate of feeding (i.e., of bar-pressing in the Skinner box), or some other observed fact. So the hunger variable is reduced to the status of an actually observed variable; and the same can be said of such an intervening variable as anxiety (1938, page 24; 1940; Estes and Skinner, 1941). In speaking of an animal's state of hunger or anxiety we are prone to mean something akin to our own subjective feelings and desires, but such "empathy" must be avoided if we wish to limit our psychology to laws of behavior.

Skinner does not by any means intend to limit his psychology to the rat in the box, though he finds this setup excellent for fundamental investigations. Human verbal behavior, he believes, can be brought under the same laws of conditioning and reinforcement. Quite a number of the younger psychologists declare themselves adherents of his type of behaviorism.

"OPERATIONISM" IN PSYCHOLOGY. If Skinner's school is to have a name, "radical operationism" could be suggested, but his right to any exclusive claim on such a name would immediately be challenged by adherents of many other schools. In a symposium on operationism as viewed from several angles, Skinner had this to say (1945, page 270):

Operationism may be defined as the practice of talking about (1) one's observations, (2) the manipulative and calculational procedures involved in making them, (3) the logical and mathematical steps which intervene between earlier and later statements, and (4) *nothing else.*

It is this underlining of the negative aspect of the operational principle that is characteristic of Skinner. The principle is accepted also by Tolman and Hull, but they make freer use of hypotheses and intervening concepts than he would allow.

The operational principle was clearly formulated by the physicist P. W. Bridgman in 1927. It has to do with the meaning of scientific concepts, and provides a logical method of stripping from a concept irrelevant shades of meaning that may have become attached to it and of ruling out of court any concept that is not truly based on scientific observation. The principle is that the meaning of a concept is limited by the operations required to observe and measure the phenomenon in question. "In general, we mean by any concept nothing more than a set of operations; the concept is synonymous with the corresponding set of operations." What do we mean by *length*, for example —the distance between two points? Yes, but by what operation do we measure the distance? As physics has extended the measurement of length from ordinary terrestrial distances to astronomical distances at one extreme and to subatomic distances at the other, very different methods of measurement have come into use, and the question arises whether *length* means the same thing when measured in these different ways. Some operation is required for checking the results of one method against those of another. This problem and the parallel one of time measurement became acute in physics in connection with the theory of relativity.

In psychology the importance of operational definitions was promptly appreciated. In fact psychologists had already been insisting on such definitions in relation to certain important measurements. In memory experiments, for example, the attempt is made to measure "retention" so as to work out the curve of forgetting. Now retention may be measured by the recall method or by the relearning or saving method, but the saving method gives higher retention scores than the recall method. In presenting your results, then, you must specify the method used. According to the operational principle, *retention* means nothing but the recall score or else the saving score, until by some further operation the two scores are correlated.

The more notorious psychological example is that of intelligence. What is intelligence? Psychologists found it difficult to frame an acceptable definition. But in regard to intelligence testing it was clear enough that "measured intelligence is what the tests measure." And it was necessary to specify the particular test by which intelligence was being measured, since the intelligence quotients obtained by different tests did not agree exactly, because of differences in their materials and construction. The IQ values obtained in a given study are defined by the "operation" comprising the specific test used, the mode of administration, and the standard arithmetical computation.

However, the idea that intelligence is "what the tests measure" and nothing else, is unsatisfactory and really absurd. Consider the situation of a psychologist who undertakes to construct a new intelligence test. "What is intelligence?" "It is defined by the operation I am going to use in measuring it; it is what my test will measure, and nothing more can be said." His whole concern, then, would be to construct a test that will measure what it measures, i.e., in the psychologist's terms, a test with good "reliability." He has no concern with "validity"; as a strict operationist he does not care whether his new test will predict the intelligence measured by other tests, or school success, or success in any vocation. Actually the testing psychologist does care a great deal about validity; he works out the correlations of his test results with certain "criteria" according to the scientific or practical use to be made of the test. In general a scientific concept is a *tool,* and the scientist wants to know not only how the tool is constructed but also what it will do. In psychology anyway a concept must be tied to a measuring operation on one side and to its use, scientific or practical, on the other. Perhaps the same can even be said of physical length and time.

The requirement of operational definitions has been hailed by the behaviorists as speaking in their favor. For, they argue, the meaning of a concept depends wholly on the experimenter's operations in securing the relevant data. The experimenter arranges a certain objective situation, applies certain stimuli, and records the subject's responses. All these operations are strictly objective. Even if the experimenter gives a human subject certain verbal instructions, as in the method of impression (pages 18-21), and if the subject reports seeing or not seeing the given stimulus, still the experimental operations are overt, objective and public. A visiting scientist looking on could verify all the experimenter's operations and records. Here we encounter the same difficulty as once before (page 83) : the crucial part of the whole operation is the observation by the subject, and this cannot be verified by the visiting scientist nor by the experimenter either, since it is a private event in the subject's organism which, however, he is able to report. The concept of a visual after-image, for example, cannot be validated unless the subject's report is accepted as evidence of a visual event. Therefore the complete operation cannot be stated in objective terms. But the same thing seems to be true of any scientific operation. Always there is an observer reporting what he sees or hears. Always this private event is an essential part of the whole operation. The operational principle, so understood, can be accepted by any school of psychology and has indeed been accepted by those whose work on sensation and perception lies quite outside the genuine province of behaviorism (Boring, 1945; Stevens, 1935, 1939).

CHAPTER 5

GESTALT PSYCHOLOGY

If we were required to name the most significant date in the history of our contemporary schools of psychology, we could not do better than to select the year 1912. Simply as the date of Watson's first promulgation of behaviorism that year would be of outstanding historical importance. But several other important developments took place at just about that time. The debate between structuralists and functionalists had perhaps begun to die down a little. The modern associationism of Thorndike and of Pavlov had made its appearance a decade earlier and was very much on the upswing. Thorndike made the full statement of his views (the earlier ones) in 1911 and 1913, and the psychological significance of Pavlov's conditioned reflex was just beginning to be appreciated. Psychoanalysis, too, was already a decade and more old, but the year 1912 was a turning point in its history, for it was just about then that the cleavage between Freud and two of his early adherents, Adler and Jung, took definite shape, and it was just about then that Freud began to revise his earlier views and shift over to his quite different later theory. McDougall's purposivism, first emerging to view in 1908, received its full formulation in 1912; Adolf Meyer's organismic psychology had already been announced, and the name *psychobiology* was proposed a few years later; and Mary Calkins was just putting the finishing touches on her self psychology. Finally, the year 1912 saw the first announcement of the important school of Gestalt psychology.[1]

---

[1] For much fuller accounts of the Gestalt psychology than the one given here see Ellis, 1938; Elmgren, 1938; Hartmann, 1935; Petermann, 1932.

Founding of the Gestalt School

In 1912 it happened that three young German psychologists, who had previously been together for some years as research students at the University of Berlin, were located in and near the city of Frankfurt. These three men were Max Wertheimer (1880-1943), Kurt Koffka (1886-1941), and Wolfgang Köhler (born 1887, now professor at Swarthmore). Each of them had already produced psychological work of some distinction. Wertheimer had shown how the free association test could be used for the detection of an individual's hidden knowledge, as in examining persons suspected of a crime. Koffka had done important work on imagery and thought. Köhler had specialized effectively on problems of hearing. These three friends had become profoundly discontented with the dominant psychology represented by Wundt, the "brick-and-mortar psychology" as they called it, the bricks being the sensory elements and the mortar mere association by contiguity. A collection of elements deprived of meaning and plastered together by meaningless associations seemed to them a travesty of the meaningful experience of human beings. Conscious experiences are not only complex—as Wundt had said—but they are also meaningful, and the type of introspective analysis which pushes the meaning aside in order to get at the bare sensory elements may do good service for the special student of the senses but at the cost of losing the larger values of psychology. These men did not share Watson's disgust with all introspection; quite the contrary, they believed that excellent psychological data could be gained from "direct experience" and that the dynamics of behavior was more clearly revealed in direct experience than in external observation. And they admitted that analysis was necessary, only the analysis must not destroy the meaning and value of experience or behavior. Science in spite of its magnificent achievements seemed to many young intellectuals of the day to be depriving human life of all significance by reducing its values to mere illusions; but our three friends believed the trouble to lie in the scientist's infatuation with "elements" and in his effort always to work "from below upward" and never "from above downward," from the meaningful whole down to parts which are still meaningful because of their role in making up the whole. If a cause and its effect are taken as separate events, Hume was right in asserting that no necessary connection between them can be seen (page 42), but if the entire happening, cause and effect included, is viewed as a whole, it makes sense and cause and effect are meaningful parts of the whole. The Humean and associationist skepticism should not blind the psychologist to the reality of meaningful experience. Wertheimer and his two younger associates were convinced that they had the germ of a new and revolutionary method of attacking all the problems of psychology.

In the Frankfurt laboratory in 1911 and 1912, Wertheimer was conducting experiments on the seeing of motion, and Koffka and Köhler were serving as subjects. The problem was to account for the motion we see in looking at a motion picture. The motion picture camera takes a rapid series of snapshots which are "stills"; nothing moves perceptibly in any one still or the result is a blur and not an appearance of motion. In projection each snapshot stands still on the screen, and the light is cut off while the shift is made from each frame to the next, for if the picture were allowed actually to move on the screen you would see a blur rather than a moving object. Therefore if you saw what is physically presented on the screen, you would see a rapid series of snapshots separated by intervals of darkness. You do not and cannot see what is physically taking place on the screen. You cannot see the dark intervals because the visual sensation outlasts the physical stimulus and holds over till the next exposure, provided the interval is short. (If it is too long, you see some flicker.) Thus retinal lag bridges the time gaps between the successive still views. But what bridges the space gaps and enables you to see an object in the picture moving smoothly along instead of jerking from one place to another as it actually does in the series of views? That is the problem.

Wertheimer was attracted to this problem because the whole experience of seeing an object move in the picture evidently had an important and meaningful property (the motion) which was not to be found in the separate still views. The problem could be attacked by study of the conditions that must be met for motion to appear. He simplified the "picture" to the limit, making it consist simply of a vertical line which could be given an apparent motion to the right or left. The experimenter exposes to view first one line and then a similar line a little to the right or left. A short blank time interval separates the two exposures. Wertheimer found the length of the blank time interval important. If it were as long as one second, the observer simply saw one still line and then the other still line, in full agreement with the physical facts. If the interval were cut down to one fifth of a second the observer continued to see the two still lines in succession. But when the interval was further diminished the observer began to get a glimpse of something moving across from one position to the other; at one fifteenth of a second the motion was very clear, a single line appearing to move across from one end position to the other. With shorter time intervals the motion became less clear, and at one thirtieth of a second no apparent motion remained but the two presented lines seemed to stand side by side. All these effects are even clearer if the two lines, A and B are exposed repeatedly, A-B-A-B-A-B . . ., one at a time in alternation; at the one-fifteenth second interval the side-to-side swing is very striking and at one thirtieth of a second the two lines stand steadily side by side.

Wertheimer varied the experiment in several ways. He exposed a vertical followed by a horizontal line; and the observer saw a line swinging around through ninety degrees. By suitable arrangements he could make one line appear to move to the right and another line simultaneously move to the left—just as in a movie two figures are often seen to move in different directions at the same time. This result was important as ruling out the eye-movement explanation of the apparent motion. It had been suggested that the eyes by moving from one position to the other created the impression of motion; but the eyes could not move in two directions at the same time! Another old explanation was that all you really *see* is the series of still views and that you then *infer* the motion; for if a thing is here one moment and there the next moment, it must have moved from here to there in the interval. Against this theory Wertheimer appealed to direct experience: Are you aware of the separate positions first and then of the motion, or do you get a direct sensation of motion? He could also appeal to the peculiar effects of different time intervals. If the interval is too long, you see two separate lines in succession and do not infer any motion; if the interval is too short, you see two separate lines side by side and no motion; but if the interval is just right you get the clear impression of one line in motion. Wertheimer concluded that when the interval was right, the brain response to the first position merged by a continuous process into the response to the second position, so that there was actual motion in the brain.

Wertheimer's experiment on visual movement was certainly interesting and important, but we may query why it was regarded as important enough to inaugurate a new school of psychology. Well, it was a clear case of a whole which was not a mere sum of parts. An object seen in motion is not merely seen in a series of positions; in fact the separate positions are not seen distinctly because they merge into the motion which is clearly seen. A snapshot of a person running or walking often catches him in what looks like a very odd position. You can scarcely believe that he took that position in the course of his movement; and yet the camera did not lie. You saw him in that position, or rather you saw him passing through that position. You saw his movement as a dynamic whole. Seen movement was important to the Gestalt psychologists as a clear example of the dynamic whole, the whole which dominates its parts. Another clear case was the shape of an object. "Shape" in German is *Gestalt,* and to see why this school called themselves the Gestalt psychologists we need to go back two decades from 1912 and take notice of an important forerunner of the Gestalt school.

Gestalt Qualities, Form Qualities

The fact that we see shapes as well as colors and shades is obvious enough, but the older psychologists made little of this fact. We remember that Thomas Brown early in the nine-teenth century had emphasized the seeing of relations (page 44). Relations are akin to shapes; when we see the front of a church as taller than the rear, we are seeing a relation and we are seeing a shape. It was Christian von Ehrenfels (1859-1932), an Austrian philosopher-psychologist, who in 1890 brought the problem of shape out into the open. What he called a Gestalt quality, or form quality, is present in a whole but not present in any of the parts making up the whole. We are reminded of "mental chemistry" (page 43). Take the same collection of parts and arrange them in different ways and you get different wholes possessing different qualities. For example take the notes of the musical scale: arrange them in one order and rhythm and you have one tune; give them another order and you have a different tune. The tune is not present in the notes taken separately, but only in the whole arrangement. A skeptic might say, "What have you got there besides the notes? —Nothing!" The answer is that the arrangement must be just as real as the notes, since different arrangements give different tunes which have different effects on the listener. If the skeptic is not convinced you can bring forward another fact: the same tune can be made of entirely different notes. That is, the tune can be transposed from one key to another and still be the same tune. If it is transposed into a higher key it may sound more brilliant; if into a lower key, more mellow. But it remains the same tune and is recognized as such. When you recognize a tune, it is not the notes that you recognize but the tune itself. To hear a tune, then, is a real experience, not decomposable into the experiences of hearing the separate notes. The tune has a quality of its own, a form quality.

There are many other examples. Using a dozen red blocks you can build patterns and other structures of many shapes, the patterns and structures being as real as the blocks; and you can "transpose" any one pattern or structure from red to blue, if you happen to have a dozen blue blocks available. A dress-maker can make "the same dress" out of a variety of materials, as well as different dresses out of the same material. The point for psychology is that the same pattern can be seen and recognized in spite of differences of material, and that different patterns can be distinguished in spite of sameness of material. More in general, patterns and shapes can be seen, heard, recognized, and appreciated. They are psychologically as real as the elementary tones and colors.

From 1890 on the psychological theorists were forced to admit the reality not only of sensory elements such as tones and colors but also of shapes and patterns. You hear tunes as truly as you hear tones, and you see squares and circles as truly as you see colors and shades. But by what psychological process do you get the patterns? Do you sense them as you sense tones and colors, or do you construct them by some higher mental process? There soon arose an Austrian Gestalt school which adopted the second alternative (see von Ehrenfels, 1937; Boring, 1929, pages 431-440). In this view tones and colors and other elementary sensations are raw materials provided by the senses, while the patterns are constructed by the observer. The composer constructs a tune by putting notes together in a certain arrangement, and the listener also has to exercise some constructive ability in order to hear a tune rather than a mere jumble of notes.

This theory of the Austrian Gestalt school was rejected by the Berlin Gestalt school, the school which was founded at Frankfurt in 1912 by psychologists who both before and after that date were closely associated with the University of Berlin (and who later came over to the United States). This is the group which is known today as the Gestalt school, without qualification. Their argument was that a higher mental process of combining and constructing was not required in simple cases of seeing or hearing patterns, because the sensory process itself is a process of organization. Sensations are not raw materials. The stimuli reaching the sense organs are raw materials, unorganized, uncombined. But the nerve impulses from the sense organs on reaching the brain immediately interact, attracting and repelling each other and so organizing themselves into patterns. "Organization," a favorite word in Gestalt psychology, is likely to create a false impression. It sounds as if there were an organizer in the form of some higher mental process which

imposed organization on unorganized sensations—the view of
the Austrian school which the Berlin school rejected. Sensations are self-organizing—or the sensory field as a whole is
self-organizing—that is what our Gestalt psychologists mean.

Factors in Organization

In a perfectly uniform visual field, such as you can secure
approximately by closing the eyes in a light room, there is no
observable organization. But as soon as the field is uneven,
spots begin to appear, figures against a background, lines, con-
tours, and other signs of organization (Koffka, 1935, pages
110, 124). They are as directly experienced as colors and tones
or as the motion in Wertheimer's experiment. Organization at
a sensory level occurs whenever shapes and patterns are heard
or seen, while organization at a higher level, more dependent on
the use of past experience, takes place when figures are named
and objects recognized.

As we open our eyes we find nothing in sight, let us suppose,
except a green blotch on a gray background. We unhesitatingly
see the blotch as a coherent whole, a vague shape standing out
from the background. We could scarcely force ourselves to see
part of the green area combined with part of the adjacent gray
as a unit, and we should find it even more difficult to see a part
of the green area united with a more distant part of the gray.
Why is this? Why do we spontaneously see compact, uniform areas as units? The associationists—some of them—
had answered that this manner of seeing was the result of
past experience, that we *learn* to take compact spots for units
because we so often find such spots to be objects that we can
manipulate or that are of some practical importance. If we
have had to learn this lesson, we have certainly learned it well,
for it is almost impossible for us now to see in any other way.
So there is good evidence in direct experience for the Gestalt
theory which says that we do not have to learn to see a compact
blotch as a unit, since the primary brain process in seeing is a
dynamic system and not an assembly of little separate activities.
The visual area of the brain, in the Gestalt theory, is not like a

telephone switchboard, the elements of which remain separate till connected by the operator's cord (corresponding to an association). Instead, the brain switchboard is a dynamic system such that the elements active at a given time interact, those that are close together tending to combine, and those that are similar also tending to combine, while those that are unlike and far apart remain separate.

This primitive organization does not consist simply in combination; separation is equally important. The laws of aggregation are at the same time laws of segregation. William James in a famous passage (1890, I, 488) had vividly insisted on combination but he had not regarded separation as equally primitive. He said,

> The law is that all things fuse that *can* fuse, and nothing separates except what must. . . . The baby, assailed by eyes, ears, nose, skin, and entrails all at once, feels it all as one great blooming, buzzing confusion.

This passage has often been misquoted by omitting the little word "one" in the last line, so giving the impression that James, of all men, was arguing for atomism, which is the very view he combated over and over again. But the Gestalt psychologists are probably right in insisting that things separate as naturally as they combine, according to such factors as distance and dissimilarity. When the baby first opens his eyes upon the world, he certainly does not see a world of objects as he will later, but if there is some compact bright splash in his visual field, due to a face bending over his crib, this probably stands out against the blooming background. If he sees the face as a separate blotch, he is making a start toward seeing it as a face. If he did not naturally take a blotch as a unit separate from the background, his task of coming to know objects by sight would be very difficult (Koffka, 1925, page 145).

Wertheimer (1923) made effective use of dots and lines scattered over the background in demonstrating important factors in aggregation and segregation, also called "field forces" or "principles of organization." Dots are likely to be seen as if falling into groups, and the question is under what conditions a group is easily segregated from the mass. One favorable condi-

tion is nearness or proximity of the dots to each other. Another favorable condition is similarity (including equality) of
the dots. If the field contains dots of two shapes, or better still
of two colors, those which are alike can easily be seen as form-

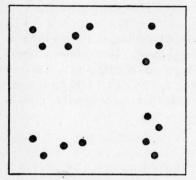

Fig. 1. The Proximity Factor   Fig. 2. The Similarity Factor

Fig. 3. The Closure Factor

ing a group. Another favorable condition is that the dots form
a closed figure or a continuous curve. This principle of "closure" is very important in the Gestalt theory. If a figure is
drawn with small gaps in it, the gaps are apt to be overlooked or
disregarded by an observer. Sometimes, indeed, the gaps stand
out as the striking thing about a figure, but on the whole the

tendency is to close up small gaps. This tendency to close a gap is regarded as revealing a fundamental principle of brain dynamics, a tendency of the brain activity to bridge a gap, like the tendency of an electric current to jump a small gap in the circuit. Tension is built up on both sides of the gap. With the gap present there is a state of unbalanced tensions, but closure brings equilibrium. The sensory brain activity tends toward equilibrium or minimum tension, just as other continuous physical systems do—drops of water, soap bubbles, or electric networks.] The physics of this theory has been handled very competently by Köhler (1938, 1940).

The tendency to close a gap is akin to the tendency to overlook irregularities, and in general to see as "good" or "pregnant" a figure as possible under the given conditions. A figure is "good" if it is symmetrical, simple, or in some such respect appealing to the observer. A figure is "pregnant" if the nature of the whole figure is carried out as fully as possible by the parts. If the star figure shown here is seen as a gappy figure, the observer will tend to emphasize and exaggerate the gaps and make it as gappy as possible. What is sometimes called "Wertheimer's law" or principle seems to include both pregnance and good figure: "The principle contends that organization of a field tends to be as simple and clear as is compatible with the conditions given in each case" (Köhler, 1938, page 251).

Besides these organizing factors which do not depend on higher mental processes or on past experience, Gestalt theory recognizes two other factors which do so depend: the factor of familiarity and the factor of set or attitude. If some of the dots in a collection make up the outline of a face or of any familiar object, such as a letter of the alphabet, it is easy to see that figure. And if the observer is actively looking for a certain figure he is more likely to find it than if he had no such intention. If you try hard you can force the dots of Figure 1 into three groups instead of the more natural four. The Gestalt psychologists warn us not to overemphasize these traditional factors of familiarity and set, for we are much too prone to explain everything by them and neglect the more direct and primitive factors in organization.

For our own satisfaction we may take the liberty of restating and classifying Wertheimer's factors of organization. We have, then:

1. *Peripheral factors,* present in the given collection of stimuli. Here we have proximity, similarity, continuity, and closed figure.

2. *Central factors,* originating in the organism and imposed on the stimuli: familiarity and set.

3. *Reinforcing factors,* analogous to the reinforcement of a conditioned response, or to the law of effect. Here we would place the factors of pregnance and good figure. If, while you are looking at a mass of dots or lines, some figure begins to emerge that is simple, symmetrical, like an object, or definite in any way, your natural reaction is to emphasize that figure and bring it out as fully as possible. This is a kind of "confirming reaction" (page 66), a reinforcement of the emerging figure, and at the same time a manifestation of Wertheimer's law. If this suggestion should succeed in bridging the gap between two schools as divergent as the Gestalt and neo-associationist, it would be a very desirable closure.

The Dynamic "Field" in Gestalt Theory

To understand the Gestalt theory of organization we must examine more closely the use made of the field concept. Since the work of Faraday and Maxwell the field and its characteristics are very important in the science of physics. The magnetic field and lines of force between and around the poles of a horseshoe magnet are brought out in the familiar figure produced by the use of iron filings. The electric field is demonstrated by experiments on induced currents. When you lead a current of electricity through a circuit of copper wire, you may suppose as the older physicists did that you have confined the electricity to the wire, and you have so confined the actual current, but an electric field surrounds the wire and extends out some distance as shown by the fact that a current is induced in a neighboring circuit whenever the current in your wire starts or stops or is increased or decreased in intensity—the principle utilized in the induction coil and the transformer. The Gestalt psychologists attempt to apply this physical concept of a dynamic field not only figuratively but literally to the visual field, to the organism, and especially to the cerebral cortex.

The contrast between a dynamic field and a machine is brought out clearly by Köhler (1947, pages 100-135). In the action of a machine two factors are operative: the power supplied and the structure of the machine. The power or energy supplied would act in all directions if it were not restricted or "constrained" to produce motion in only one direction prescribed by the structure of the machine. This structure is a system of constraints which determine what effect the energy shall produce. For a very simple example of a machine take a ball rolling along a groove. The energy may be supplied by gravitation if the groove slopes downward or by a thrust given the ball. The groove evidently supplies no energy but it constrains the movement of the ball, making it roll in a certain curve, for example. Or consider what happens in one cylinder of an automobile engine when a spark ignites the explosive mixture. The heated gas tends to expand in all directions, but the rigid wall of the cylinder restricts the motion and only the piston moves to any extent. The still surface of a pond is relatively free from constraints; if you apply energy at a certain point by dropping in a stone, the resulting wave moves in all directions.

The organism is constructed like a machine in some respects. The muscles are attached to the bones by tendons, so that when kinetic energy is generated in a muscle its tendon pulls in one certain direction. The nerves, like insulated wires, constrain the nerve currents to go in certain prescribed directions, as from the retina to the interbrain and thence to the occipital lobe. But in the cortex or any mass of gray matter there would seem to be less constraint, more freedom, more chance for pure field effects. A nerve impulse coming in from the retina, like the stone dropped into the pond, would start a circle of waves in the cortex, but these would be electric waves. A rapid series of nerve impulses, such as comes into the cortex from any stimulated point, would generate a rapid series of waves in the cortex and throw part of the cortex into a specific pattern of electric tensions, a pattern centered at the point which directly receives the nerve impulses from the retina. Just as two stones dropped simultaneously into the pond at different points produce a pattern of interacting waves, so two simultaneously stimulated points of the retina would give a definite pattern of electric tensions in the cortex. We may think of the pattern as analogous to two sharp hills with a valley between, the valley and sloping hillsides being as much a part of the pattern as the hilltops. In seeing the two points, then, the observer gets not merely two points, but rather two points in relation. The relation consists physically in the cortical pattern of electric waves and tensions. If the two retinal stimuli are brought nearer together, the pattern becomes sharper (the slopes steeper). Any factor that flattens the pattern weakens the relation and makes the points look farther apart. Now there is a factor that flattens the pattern: continued stimulation of the same two retinal points, giving continued activation of the same cortical pattern of electric currents, produces increasing "polarization" in the cortex. In effect, resistance is built up to the currents. The pattern flattens out, the two points become physically less closely related and so look farther apart than at first. (This crude sketch is intended to give some idea of the remarkable studies of "figural after-effects" and their physical explanation, reported by Köhler and Wallach, 1944.)

If the cerebral cortex is a free field for dynamic interaction, the old "machine theory" of the nervous system must be given up so far as the cortex is concerned, though it may and probably does hold good of the nerves and of the vast system of nerve-fiber connections in the brain. The older psychologists had thought of each little item of stimulation coming in along the sensory nerves to the brain as remaining an independent unit in the cortex, so that the total sensation at any moment would be a mere collection or "mosaic" of sensory items. This machine theory seems to offer no explanation for the relations and patterns that we have been speaking of and that are so real in actual sensory experience. Each sensory item would have to remain separate from all others, according to the machine theory as viewed by the Gestalt psychologists. They do not do full justice to the possibilities of a machine theory. One pronounced anatomical characteristic of the cortex and other nerve centers is the *convergence* of nerve fibers. Each cell has contact on the receiving side with several or many axons from different regions. So the various items of sensory stimulation, even if they do not interact, certainly *coact* or work together in producing the next phase of the total response. Within the framework of a machine theory, broadly conceived, a psychologist who regarded a pattern as a *response* to a combination of stimuli could perfectly well subscribe to Köhler's conclusion (1947, page 103) :

Our view will be that, instead of reacting to local stimuli by local and mutually independent events, the organism responds to the *pattern* of stimuli to which it is exposed; and that this answer is a unitary process, a functional whole, which gives, in experience, a sensory scene rather than a mosaic of local sensations.

Just because the Gestalt psychologists reject the machine theory we must not assume that they accept the vitalistic rather than the mechanistic view of the organism. They are strongly against vitalism, and that is indeed one reason for their emphasis on field dynamics. The field is a physical reality and at the same time corresponds to the psychological realities of behavior and experience. The dynamic field is a *molar* affair in the same sense as behavior is molar (page 105). Direct experience is molar; a sensory pattern is molar, capable of analysis but possessing distinctive characteristics as a whole. If we wish, as the Gestalt psychologists do wish, to fit the world of behavior and direct experience into the physicochemical world of natural processes, we must look for fields and patterns in the physical world. Especially we must ask what physical patterns of brain processes can correspond with the patterns of behavior and direct experience. Some correspondences are easily found. When we hear a sound grow softer and die away, the cortical process doubtless has the pattern of decreasing intensity. When we see a figure standing out as a unit from its background, the occipital cortex doubtless is active in such a way that a certain physical process is segregated from its surroundings.

In general, Gestalt theory postulates an *isomorphism* between patterns that we see or hear and the corresponding brain processes (Köhler, 1938, pages 185-232; 1947, pages 61-63, 301; Koffka, 1935, pages 53-68). The meaning of isomorphism may be understood by thinking of a map as compared with the country which it represents. The map is very different from the country, just as our conscious experience is very different from any brain process. But certain shapes and relations in the map hold good of the country. What is higher up in the map is farther north in the country. What appears on the map as a wiggly line is present in the country as a river. If we could inspect a person's brain processes as well as we can see a map, and had learned the correspondences, we could read off his experiences as we read a map. Or the person himself could use his own experience as a map of his brain processes. So vague and unrealistic a prospect would have no appeal to the Gestalt psychologists, but as good experimentalists they try to derive from the postulate of isomorphism definite hypotheses which can be tested by psychological experiments, an excellent example being their work on figural after-effects, already mentioned.

Self and Environment in Direct Experience

The Gestalt psychologists object to behaviorism on several counts. They do not object to an emphasis on objective methods and indeed agree that the final test of any hypothesis should be objective. But when the older behaviorists proposed to regard all behavior as composed of reflexes and conditioned reflexes, Gestalt psychologists made the same objection to this proposal as they had made to the brick-and-mortar psychology of Wundt and Titchener and the associationists: behavior no less than sensory experience shows us wholes that are not merely the sums of parts but have their own properties as wholes, and obsession with elements is never going to reveal the essential properties of the wholes.

While both the earlier and the later behaviorists have agreed that conscious experience, even if real, is not a fruitful field for scientific study, the Gestalt psychologists approach the dynamics of behavior from the side of sensory experience, and with some success, as indicated in the preceding sections of this chapter. The sense physiologists had studied such subjective phenomena as color mixture, contrast, and after-images, and had learned a good deal regarding the mechanism of the sense organs and even regarding the brain processes in sensation. The Gestalt psychologists go further by discovering principles of aggregation and segregation operative in sensory experience—which must also be principles of brain activity. Pavlov regarded the conditioned reflex as a window for viewing the higher nervous activity, and motor behavior in general is such a window, but sensory experience is another window affording a view from another side, and perhaps a clearer and more direct view than can be got from the motor side. Apart from brain dynamics, sense perception has proved to be a very fertile field for experimental study even during these years of relative neglect by the behaviorists.

But the principal objection of Gestalt psychology to behaviorism has to do with the stimulus-response or S-R formula. The formula has meant different things to different psychologists, no doubt, but the behaviorists have meant by S the sum of stimuli acting on the sense organs at a given time, and by R the motor response. The dash or arrow between S and R has seemed to imply a direct connection between sensory stimulus and motor response, as if there were no intervening processes of any consequence. Stimulus and response are the objectively observable facts, and behaviorism as originally conceived was not to go beyond them. Watson's "implicit behavior" and the newfangled "intervening variables" (page 107) do of course go beyond the objective data. And Watson really went beyond the objective data when he defined a stimulus as "any object in the general environment or any change in the tissues" (1925, page 6). The object out there is not the stimulus reaching our eyes or other sense organs. To identify the object with the stimulus is to assume in the organism the ability to perceive the object on receiving the stimulus. The behaviorist tacitly assumes in the organism this process of perception intervening between stimulus and response. He takes it for granted and overlooks its importance. As Köhler puts the matter (1947, pages 164, 165, 200):

> The stimulus-response formula, which sounds at first so attractive, is actually quite misleading. In fact, it has so far appeared acceptable solely because Behaviorists use the term "stimulus" in such a loose fashion. . . . When the term is taken in its strict sense, it is not generally "a stimulus" which elicits a response. . . . A man's actions are commonly related to a well-structured field, most often to particular thing-units. The right psychological formula is therefore: *pattern of stimulation—organization—response to the products of organization.* . . . The stimulus-response formula . . . ignores the fact that between the stimuli and the response there occur the processes of organization, particularly the formation of group-units in which parts acquire new characteristics.

The Gestalt psychologists learned their "principles of organization" from the study of sensory experience, but they have gone on to apply these principles to behavior in the broadest sense. Koffka (1935) made a valiant attempt to work out a comprehensive Gestalt theory covering learning, memory, emotion, voluntary and involuntary action, and personality. He tried to be as concrete as possible but could not help being sketchy and very abstract in spots, because some parts of the subject have not been directly studied by the Gestalt school. His painstaking discussions sometimes amount mostly to raising unsolved problems and pointing out inadequacies in the usual "functional" treatment of the subject.

Koffka's approach to behavior is certainly deserving of careful attention. We should regard behavior, he says, not as composed of responses to stimuli but as governed by a field, the organismic field of interacting forces, a field that is self-organized into definite though changing patterns. This organismic field is of course physiological, but as operating in behavior and conscious experience it can be better called psychophysical. Its operations are physicochemical, cellular, or what we have called "molecular" (page 105), but they are at the same time "molar," occurring in patterns corresponding to significant units in experience and behavior. Some of these patterned operations are unconscious (the "unconscious" being part of the molar-physiological field), but some of them are conscious and make up the field of direct experience. There is no sharp, fixed boundary between the field of conscious experience and the rest of the psychophysical field, and conscious experience is open to influences from the rest of the psychophysical field such as unconscious or only vaguely conscious desires. The field of direct experience, along with externally visible behavior, is what the psychologist has to work with, or work from, since it provides his observable facts. And a great deal can be learned from the study of direct experience.

The field of direct experience, as we all know it in adult life, has two poles, the ego and the environment. That is, we are aware of ourselves as surrounded by an environment. These two poles are like the poles of a magnet, with lines of force or stress between them. They are in constant and shifting interaction. Presumably the child does not at first make any distinction between the self and the not-self. But he discovers that his body is a unit distinct from anything else. Some things are in front of him, other things behind him, while he himself is in between. The great qualitative difference between the definite visual and auditory sensations and the background of bodily feelings may play a part in segregating the self from the environment. Tensions develop between himself and persons in the environment and thus the polarity of self and not-self is sharpened. The ego is not a mere pole; it is complex, structured into subsystems. Yet it maintains its identity in the flux of environmental happenings, without ever becoming static. It is never "completely balanced, completely at rest. . . . It is always going somewhere" (Koffka, 1935, page 332). The main point for the Gestalt theory is that there are always tensions within the ego as well as between the ego and the environment.

In a typical experience, I am doing something in the environment. The environment I respond to is of course the environment as it appears to me, and the appearance may not correspond perfectly to the reality. I respond to the apparent environment, which Koffka accordingly calls the "behavioral environment." He introduces this concept with a striking example (1935, pages 27-28):

On a winter evening amidst a driving snowstorm a man on horseback arrives at an inn, happy to have reached a shelter after hours of riding over the wind-swept plain on which the blanket of snow had covered all paths and landmarks. The landlord who came to the door viewed the stranger with surprise and asked him whence he came. The man pointed in the direction straight away from the inn, whereupon the landlord, in a tone of awe and wonder, said: "Do you know that you have ridden across the Lake of Constance?" At which the rider dropped stone dead at his feet.

In what environment, then, did the behavior of the stranger take place? The Lake of Constance. Certainly, because it is a true proposition that he rode across it. And yet, this is not the whole truth, for the fact that there was a frozen lake and not ordinary solid ground did not affect his behavior in the slightest. . . . There is a second sense to the word environment according to which our horseman did not ride across the lake at all, but across an ordinary snow-swept plain. His behavior was a riding-over-a-plain, but not a riding-over-a-lake.

The geographical environment in this case was a lake, while the behavioral environment was a plain. Behavior which is well adjusted to the apparent or behavioral environment does not always fit the physical, real, or geographical environment. The physical situation may be deceptive or at least difficult to grasp, our senses have their limits, and our desires may blind us to the real facts. Persons as well as things are not always what they seem. We may fail to discern their true attitudes and intentions, so that our behavioral social environment differs more or less from the real or geographical social environment. The behavioral environment is different for different individuals even when they are in the same geographical environment. It differs according to their several needs, interests, and abilities. One who is interested in gardening sees a nice garden plot in the spring beckoning him to spade it up and plant things, while to another person the same plot is merely bare ground with no appeal whatever. When a person is dreaming, his behavioral environment is a dream world very different from the room where he is sleeping.

Now *where* is a person's behavioral environment? Is it outside or inside him? From his own point of view it is certainly outside. Here I am with a desk in front of me, a lamp behind me, and somebody playing the piano in the next room. If I fall asleep and seem to hear a military band playing on the parade ground, that environment is still outside me from my own point of view. But you, the psychologist, looking at me, say that my dream is wholly inside me, just as the horseman's plain was present only in his imagination. Even when I wake up and resume writing at my desk, you say that my behavior is governed by my perception of the environment and not by the environment directly. From the geographic environment stimuli reach my sense organs and enable me, if awake, to perceive things more or less correctly. My perceiving (and remembering) process is inside me, and the result of that process, my behavioral environment, is also inside me from your point of view. My motor reaction to the desk is governed by my perception of the desk, and this perception is certainly in me and not in the desk. You as a psychologist are talking about processes, while I am talking about the results of these processes. My processes of perceiving, remembering, desiring take place in my organism, and as a result I perceive my organism surrounded by the environment, quite in accordance with the "geographical" facts. It is easy to become confused here, as Köhler has shown (1938, pages 126 ff.), but one thing is clear enough: stimuli from outside enable the organism to perceive the environment more or less correctly, and the organism's behavior is governed by the environment as perceived.

When anyone is asked to report what he sees, hears, tastes, smells, or touches, he reports things and other environmental facts, as a rule, and not the stimuli received which serve him as indicators. He is reporting his behavioral environment as part of his conscious experience. When an animal's behavior is correctly adjusted to such environmental facts as the direction of a sound or the size and distance of a visible object, that animal is using stimuli as indicators in the same general way as a human being, and the psychologist, without assuming conscious experience in the animal, is still entitled to say that the animal's behavior is governed by a behavorial environment.

All this is familiar and acceptable enough to all psychologists except perhaps the most orthodox behaviorists. What, then, is the Gestalt psychologist's reason for insisting on it so strongly? There are two main reasons. First, the behavioral environment, as contrasted with an assemblage of stimuli, is *organized,* and behavior is governed by this organized field and not directly by the stimuli. This point has already been sufficiently emphasized. Second, the Gestalt principles of organization are held to explain why it is that the behavioral environment corresponds as well as it does with the geographical environment. A bunch of stimuli that are close together and similar gives rise to a segregated whole in the psychophysical brain field. Now such a bunch of stimuli very often comes from a definite object in the environment. Thus the principles of proximity and similarity make us see the environment as containing a multitude of definite objects; and to this extent the behavioral environment corresponds to the geographical. The principles of continuity and closure operate to close accidental gaps in the stimuli received. The "central" factors of set and familiarity certainly are very important—perhaps more important than the Gestalt school is inclined to admit—in exploring the environment and building up an acquaintance with it, part by part. And a great deal could be said for the factors of pregnance and good figure, which we (not the Gestalt psychologists) have regarded as factors of reinforcement (page 131). In spite of many discrepancies between the behavioral and the geographical environments, between appearance and reality, a good measure of agreement is guaranteed, according to the Gestalt theory, by the forces of the psychophysical field within the organism which receives the stimuli from the external world. Many "molar" characteristics of the physical world—patterns and relations— are reproduced in the psychophysical field and in the individual's direct experience and so made available as guides for his behavior in the environment. His motor behavior is determined in the same general way by the field forces; but this side of the theory has not been worked out into very definite form.

Insight and Productive Thinking

Two of the most interesting studies produced by the Gestalt school have to do with problem solving. These are Köhler's book on *The mentality of apes* (1917 in German, 1925 and 1927 in English) and Wertheimer's *Productive thinking* (1945). Other Gestalt studies of problem solving which amply deserve more than this passing notice are those by Duncker (1935, 1945) and by Katona (1940).

Just before the first world war, in 1913, Köhler was made director of an anthropoid station at Teneriffe in the Canary Islands, maintained by the Prussian Academy of Sciences. Köhler proceeded to Teneriffe and began psychological studies of chimpanzees. Marooned there during the war, he had time for the thorough study shown in his book. The problem he undertook was whether the chimpanzee, representing probably the most intelligent group of subhuman animals, showed any genuine intelligence. By intelligence Köhler meant something more than trial and error in the solution of a novel problem. He meant insight, a seeing into the problem. Thorndike had been convinced by his experiments on cats, dogs, and monkeys that these animals attacked a problem by trial and error, i.e., by impulsively trying one thing after another until something succeeded, and that they learned by repetition and the law of effect, the successful reactions being stamped in and the unsuccessful ones stamped out. Though Thorndike's experiments had not extended to the anthropoid apes, the general impression left behind by his work was that trial and error represented the only animal line of attack on a problem. Köhler entertained serious doubts of this conclusion and believed that Thorndike's associationist background had led to ill-conceived experiments and false interpretation of results.

Thorndike had used mazes and puzzle boxes—blind situations, not lying open to the animal's inspection. He did this in order to give the animals something new to be mastered. If he had left a clear, unobstructed path to the goal, the animals would have gone straight to the goal without any problem to solve. Köhler agreed that there must always be some obstacle; the animal must be required to take a roundabout path, a detour, literally or figuratively, to reach the goal. But Köhler held that the animal should nevertheless be able from the start to survey the whole situation, so that if he had the power of insight he could solve the problem without blind trial and error. The pattern or structure of the situation should be visible, and the question should be whether the animal could grasp the pattern and act accordingly.[2]

A very simple example of a detour problem with insightful solution is given by Köhler. A dog was brought into a strange yard containing a length of fence, and when the dog was near the middle of the fence some food was placed directly before him on the far side of the fence. Instead of trying impulsively to squeeze through, the dog almost immediately made a dash around one end of the fence to the food. The dog *saw* the way to the goal even though it was a detour. In a complicated maze, an animal cannot see the entire path to the goal and is bound to show trial and error. Thus the maze does not give the experimenter a chance to see whether insight is possible for the animal. Köhler's chimpanzees solved with ease any problem which consisted literally in a roundabout path to a goal, if only the whole path were in clear view. Other kinds of "detours" gave them more trouble.

While a chimpanzee is confined in a barred cage, a banana is placed on the ground outside at too great a distance to be reached by the hand, but with a string tied to it and laid along the ground to the cage. This single-string problem is easily solved, but if several strings are laid on the ground, all extending in the general direction of the banana but only one being attached to it, a chimpanzee often pulls the wrong string.

---

[2] Köhler was anticipated in this criticism of Thorndike's work by the English scientist, L. T. Hobhouse (1901), who devised a variety of experiments similar to those later used by Köhler, tried them on several kinds of animals, and reached the conclusion that what he called "practical judgment," the ability to respond to patterns and relations, was within the power of animals such as the cat, dog, and monkey.

Prompt insight is prevented by the complexity of the visual pattern and by the animal's haste.

The reaching-stick problem is simple when a suitable stick is laid on the ground between the cage and the banana, but becomes difficult if the stick is placed far away from the banana, especially if it lies at the back of the cage. A compact visual pattern is apparently a great help in gaining quick insight.

The chimpanzees learned rather quickly to use a box as a stool for reaching a suspended banana, but the use of two boxes, one to be piled on the other for reaching a still higher objective, was a difficult problem though solved (with some assistance) by several of the animals. While they evidently appreciated the value of a high stool, they showed no insight in the matter of stability of construction, being content to pile the boxes carelessly and depend on their own agility to reach the objective before the structure collapsed.

The prize performance was the solution by the most intelligent chimpanzee of the jointed-stick problem. He was given two pieces of bamboo which could be fitted together into a long stick—long enough to reach a banana that could not be reached by either stick alone. After an hour spent in fruitless angling with the single sticks and other trial-and-error behavior, he gave up but continued idly playing with the two sticks. Happening to get them jointed together he immediately used the long stick for pulling in the banana and other things as well; and next day he showed almost perfect retention of what he had learned.

The behavioral evidences of insight in these cases are (1) the sudden transition from helplessness to mastery; (2) the good retention; and (3) what psychologists call "transfer." Insight gained in one situation can sometimes be carried over and utilized in another situation which has the same pattern or structure though not the same details. If the idea of piling boxes to reach a banana has been grasped, it should be transferable to a situation where a trunk and a suitcase are available for reaching an apple. Insightful behavior does not consist in separate responses to separate stimuli but in an integrated response to the pattern of the whole situation. A problem amounts to a "gap" in the present situation, insight amounts to perceiving the gap, and insightful behavior closes the gap.

Insight ordinarily means a seeing below the surface of things, but this could not have been Köhler's meaning, since he insisted that the essential structure of the situation should be aboveboard and open to inspection. Insight may of course go much deeper, but it consists essentially in seeing the situation as an organized whole. A rudimentary form of perceptual insight is illustrated by a "transposition experiment," introduced by Lashley and independently by Köhler, and much employed by still other animal psychologists. An animal is first trained to find food in a box marked by a certain shade of gray. Two boxes are always placed before him, A and B, box A being marked with a patch of light gray paper, box B with a medium gray. The two boxes vary in position, but the food is always in B, the darker of the two. When the animal has learned to choose B consistently, box A is removed and a new box C, darker than B, is substituted. Will the animal still choose B, responding to the same specific stimulus as before? As a rule he chooses C, the darker of the two visible boxes. What he has learned, therefore, is to choose the darker of two, not a particular shade of gray. He perceives the lighter-darker pattern or relation, and chooses the darker term of the relation.

This whole experiment does not meet Köhler's requirement that the problem should be openly presented to the animal, for the food is not visible and there is nothing to indicate, at the outset, where the food will be, if anywhere. The animal has to try one box or another and run the chance of making an error. He usually makes many errors before settling down to a consistent choice. But what he learns is response to a relation between stimuli (or objects) and not response to an isolated stimulus. Insight in this rudimentary form consists in perceiving relations, perceiving them well enough to be governed by them in behavior.

In this experiment and many others the animal (or human being) learns by trial and error, or at least *after* some trial and error. Whether the trial-and-error behavior makes any contribution to the solution of a problem, or is simply so much waste motion, is a question for experimental study, and there have been many studies devoted to the question. We cannot pause to discuss this matter thoroughly, but will merely consider the relation of trial and error to Gestalt theory. The Gestalt psychologists speak very disparagingly of trial-and-error behavior and seem to regard it as waste motion for the most part, though they admit that sometimes a blind action of the animal changes the situation in such a way as to give him a clearer view (Köhler, 1927, page 193). It would seem that trial-and-error behavior must *always* be needed whenever it occurs. For the Gestalt theory is not that we *ought* to organize the field but that we always *do* organize it. The field, including the ego and the behavioral environment, organizes itself, and behavior is governed by the resulting organization. If the behavior consists in a false move, that error was dictated by the organized field. The move was an error because the behavioral environment did not conform to the real or geographical environment. The false move makes some change in the environment or in the individual's relation to the environment, resulting in a new organization and a new move. When the successful move occurs, it occurs because the just preceding false move has so altered the behavioral environment as to make it conform to the real environment. Therefore the last of the false moves is necessary for insight. And we could argue back in this vein, step by step, and reach the conclusion that the whole series of false moves is necessary, given the organism and environment as they are at the outset.

Thorndike's cat in the puzzle box, for example, sees the space between two particular bars as a way out, but on trying to squeeze through there finds it not a way out after all. The cat's behavioral environment is changed to that extent, but several other false leads may have to be explored and eliminated before the door button stands out as something to be tried. Even this successful move does not usually clarify the situation completely for a cat, her perception of such a device as a door button being pretty vague.

While the Gestalt psychologists have demonstrated the value of insight, they have not disproved the value of trial and error.

By *trial and error* is meant exploratory or manipulatory behavior that is relatively "blind" in the sense of lacking foresight of the result of a move that is tried. Such blind exploration is inevitable when the situation itself is blind, as it often is in real life, animal or human; and even when the "geographical" situation is completely open to inspection, the "behavioral" situation may be different because of poor observation. By *insight* is meant good observation, perception of the situation as a whole, or perception of those parts of the situation that provide a route to the goal.

If it is true that problem solution depends on perceptual organization and so on the field forces present at the moment—so that errors as well as genuine solutions are bound to occur—is there nothing that can be done to *improve* man's ways of attacking his problems, nothing to make his thinking more productive? A *teacher* can so present problems as to favor insight and can foster in his pupils a genuine problem-solving attitude; and the human individual can be his own teacher, once he grasps the principles of Gestalt psychology. Such was Wertheimer's message in his last book (1945). His case material ranged from the solution of simple geometrical problems by young children up to a personal study with Einstein of the thought processes that produced the theory of relativity. At all levels Wertheimer found examples of "genuine, fine, clean, direct, productive processes," though he also found "factors working against those processes as, e.g., blind habits, certain kinds of school drill, bias, or special interests" (1945, page 189).

Wertheimer's advice for one who would be a productive thinker is to let the whole dominate the parts and never to lose sight of the problem as a whole even while devoting the necessary attention to details. Avoid "piecemeal" thinking, which is sure to be blind. Concentrate on the "structure" of the situation, get that clearly in view and locate the gap in it which constitutes the problem. In scrutinizing details, be always "looking for structural rather than piecemeal truth," asking yourself what role each detail plays in the structure of the whole situation.

The science of logic, as Wertheimer and many others have

pointed out, tests the validity of a conclusion but does not show the actual process of reasoning that leads a thinker to his conclusion. For example, the logical demonstration of a proposition as customarily given in a textbook on geometry enables you to meet the objections of any skeptic and prove to him that the proposition is valid; but if you work out the demonstration as an "original," your own thought process is very different from the formal demonstration given in the book. Other psychologists have emphasized the exploratory, zigzag, trial-and-error process that goes on in actual reasoning; such terms were very distasteful to Wertheimer, who emphasized instead the need for grouping and regrouping, organizing and reorganizing, centering and recentering the data. You may have to change your point of view, but you should always face toward the goal and take no step blindly. Proceed from above downward, from the whole to the parts. The piecemeal attack is sometimes very painstaking and conscientious, but it is blind, stupid, slavish, pedantic.

Wertheimer experimented in teaching children how to find the area of a rectangle by regarding it as divided into little squares—so many rows, each made up a certain number of squares, so that the area could be found by multiplying the number of squares in a row by the number of rows, i.e., by multiplying the base by the altitude. When he was sure that the child had a "structural" understanding of the area of a rectangle he presented an oblique parallelogram, usually a long, slender one, and asked the child how the area of the parallelogram could be found, suggesting that it be compared with a rectangle. Many older children, as well as adults, gave the "associationist" type of answer: "I haven't learned that yet," or, "I used to know that but I've forgotten." But some, even of the younger children, reached a "fine, genuine, original" solution. They saw that the middle portion of the parallelogram was like a rectangle and that only the oblique ends were troublesome; and then they saw that one end could be taken off by a vertical cut and fitted on at the other end so as to make a complete rectangle out of the parallelogram.

Wertheimer (and also Katona, 1940) experimented with a

KURT KOFFKA

MAX WERTHEIMER

WOLFGANG KÖHLER

Photo by Erich Kastan

KURT LEWIN

variety of mathematical and quasi-mathematical problems, seeking methods of leading children to see into the problems and not depend on blind following of rules. [They believe that school teachers tend to depend too much on authority and on blind, repetitious drill in the application of authoritarian rules. They believe that in this way children are "educated" to depend on rules and not on their own intelligence. They believe that the associationist and connectionist psychology, applied to education, supports the traditional emphasis on drill, and that only the Gestalt psychology offers any hope of improvement.]

Some facts, to be sure, like the names of objects, are just facts and have to be learned by association strengthened by repetition. "Repetition is useful, but continuous use of mechanical repetition also has harmful effects. It is dangerous because it easily induces habits of sheer mechanized action, blindness, tendencies to perform slavishly instead of thinking, instead of facing a problem freely" (Wertheimer, 1945, page 112).

Trial and error, in Wertheimer's view, can play no part in productive thinking, except as an interference. He insists that it is possible to move straight toward the solution of a problem, "never losing sight of the deeper issue, never getting lost in petty details, in detours, bypaths" (page 123). Progress may be slow and hesitant at times, but never blind or dependent on chance successes. It is only necessary "to look at the situation freely, open-mindedly, viewing the whole, trying to discover, to realize how the problem and the situation are related" (page 102). Often it will be necessary to take a fresh point of view so as to get a new perspective. Even a "whole-view" may prove to be superficial or one-sided, and even a constant urge toward the goal may blind the thinker to the possibilities of the given situation. Wertheimer reports in some detail two examples of his own solution of mathematical problems, and he insists that trial and error played no part in his thinking, even though many hours or days were required to reach a solution. "There was no trial and error with regard to formulas, no trying of hypotheses. . . . Each step was a step in a consistent line of thinking; there were no arbitrary steps, no blind trial and error" (pages 155, 159). In spite of this strong assertion, there are instances in the reports of his trying a lead that he had to abandon because it was getting nowhere. In his interesting analysis of Einstein's progress toward the theory of relativity, again, there are clear instances of the same sort. "For years Einstein tried to clarify the problem by studying and trying to change the Maxwell equations. He did not succeed. . . . In whatever way he tried to unify the question of mechanical movement with the electromagnetic phenomena, he got into difficulties. . . . But although these attempts did not lead to a solution, they were by no means blind. At that stage it was wholly reasonable to test such possibilities" (pages 171, 188).

No one, certainly, would accuse Einstein of stupidity or of trying leads without some good reason. But he was "blind" in one important respect: he could not see his way through to his goal. Everyone is blind in this respect when confronted by a genuine problem, for if he could see through from the start to the finish there would be no problem. Even in mathematical problems such as Wertheimer used in his experiments, some exploration is necessary; and in concrete matters of fact everyone agrees that exploration is necessary. Now when you explore you do not know in advance what you are going to find. You may find what you want or you may not. Even when you find nothing of positive value, you at least eliminate possibilities that looked promising at the start.

Wertheimer's advice to the would-be productive thinker is all to the good, even though he does not succeed in deriving from Gestalt principles any sure way of being productive all the time. The "field forces" will not always keep you out of blind alleys. On the contrary such factors as proximity and similarity are responsible for many misleading first impressions. The tendency to closure must sometimes be resisted for fear of adopting premature conclusions (pages 110, 195). "Good figure" is something to be found rather than something given in a problematic situation. "Set" is splendid when it takes the form of an "attitude of looking for the objective structural requirements of a situation, . . . facing the issue freely, going ahead with confidence and courage" (page 64). But set is a dangerous handicap when it takes the form of excessive eagerness to reach the goal or the form of a blind reliance on habitual routine procedures (pages 113, 195). The recall of past experience can be a great help in understanding a novel situation, but it is only too likely to lead to a piecemeal attack or to a superficial view based on the apparent familiarity of the present situation. In short the field forces operate to produce errors as well as genuine solutions.

Wertheimer's main contention, after all, is that human beings desire to think clearly and are able to do so. "To live in a fog . . . is for many people an unbearable state of affairs. There is a tendency to structural clearness, surveyability, to truth as against petty views" (page 199). And according to Gestalt theory, as opposed to the skeptical philosophy of Hume and the associationists, truth is attainable if we approach our problems "from above" and resolutely aim at structural understanding. To see evidences of clear thinking in children especially, or in his students, gave Wertheimer great joy. He was, as Köhler assures us (1944), a man of "extraordinary mind" and also "an unusually good man."

Lewin's Field Theory

Kurt Lewin (1890-1947) may be counted either as an adherent of Gestalt psychology or as the founder of a closely related school. He began his career and chose his line of work before the Gestalt debut in 1912, but was later associated with Wertheimer and Köhler at the University of Berlin, where he studied and taught before migrating to the United States in 1933. For ten years he was professor of child psychology at the State University of Iowa, and here, as previously in Berlin, he attracted and trained a considerable number of active adherents.

Lewin began his scientific career as an associationist, but with a particular interest in motives and will. His early work (1917, 1922) convinced him that the association theory required some radical revision. Associations, he said, were not motors, sources of energy, but merely constraints, links, connections, like the couplings between the cars of a railroad train which do nothing except transmit the energy supplied by the locomotive. You have strong associations, for example, between common objects and their names, but these associations do not force you to name every object you see. If you have some motive for naming them, the associations enable you to do so easily; but without some motive the associations have no driving force. Even as passive couplings, associations are nevertheless of great importance, according to Lewin, and in this respect he diverged from the views of the major Gestalt psychologists who sought to get away from the notion of machinelike links or connections and to explain memory as well as perception in terms of dynamics. Lewin said much later (1940, page. 16):

> Psychology cannot try to explain everything with a single construct, such as association, instinct, or gestalt. A variety of constructs has to be used. These should be interrelated, however, in a logically precise manner.

Throughout his three decades of psychological activity Lewin consistently devoted himself to what we may broadly call the motivation of human behavior. Associative machinery and instinctive machinery as well must be activated by driving forces, by needs and quasi-needs, the latter being temporary interests or intentions. This line of investigation differed considerably from the studies of perception and problem solving characteristic of the older Gestalt psychologists, who perhaps felt that the time was not ripe for such an extension, though we find Koffka using Lewin's results in his own attempt to write a comprehensive Gestalt psychology. Again, while Lewin had much to say of psychological forces, he did not attempt to relate them closely to physical forces, nor did he show much interest in the "isomorphism" of direct experience with brain dynamics (see Köhler, 1938, page 357; Koffka, 1935, pages 47-48). His interests led toward social rather than physiological psychology. The "field" of which Lewin had a great deal to say is not the brain field isomorphic with the individual's direct experience, but rather the environment containing one or more individuals. At least that is the general impression one gets from his published work. He does, however, regard the person as a field containing parts in interaction. He says (1940, pages 33, 36) :

The possibilities of a "field theory" in the realm of action, emotion, personality are firmly established. The basic statements of a field theory are that (a) behavior has to be derived from a totality of coexisting facts, (b) these coexisting facts have the character of a "dynamic field" in so far as the state of any part of this field depends on every other part of the field. . . . According to field theory, behavior depends neither on the past nor on the future but on the present field. . . . This is in contrast both to the belief of teleology that the future is the cause of behavior, and that of associationism that the past is the cause of behavior.

Lewin's field is thus the "life space, containing the person and his psychological environment" (1938, page 2). The psychological (or behavioral) environment is of course the environment as perceived and understood by the person; but, more than that, it is the environment as related to his present needs and quasi-needs. Many objects which are perceived are of no present concern to him and so exist only in the background of his psychological environment. Other objects have positive or negative "valence"—positive if they promise to meet his present needs, negative if they threaten injury. Objects of positive valence attract him, while objects of negative valence repel him. The attraction is a force or "vector" directed toward the object, the repulsion a vector directed away from the object. A vector tends to produce "locomotion" in a certain direction. Often two or more vectors are acting on the person at the same time, and then the locomotion is some kind of a "resultant." The locomotion called for by the vectors is often impeded or completely blocked by a "barrier."

Some of these concepts call for a little further explanation. Locomotion includes any sort of approach or withdrawal, as for example turning the eyes toward a beautiful object or away from an ugly one, listening to agreeable music or attending to something else if the music is uninteresting. When you are planning what to do tomorrow, your life space is not the room where you are now sitting but rather the place where you expect to be tomorrow, and your present locomotion in that anticipated environment consists in deciding on one course of action rather than another, according as the resultant of present vectors impels you toward one or the other.

Barriers are very important in the theory. A barrier is a "constraint" which has no valence at the outset and exerts no force until force is exerted on it, when it offers a certain amount of resistance. It may yield when force is applied to it or it may prove to resist your utmost efforts. How rigid it is you can discover only by trying it out, by exploration. A box stands in the way of getting something you want, but how heavy the box may be you have to discover by trying to move it. Some plan of yours may not entirely please your friend, but how much resistance he will put up you have still to discover. (Evidently some trial and error are necessary when an unexplored barrier stands in the way to any goal.) A barrier found to be impassable is likely to acquire a negative valence such as leads to an angry attack or execration.

An awakened need is a state of tension in the person, a readiness for action but so far without any very specific direction. A suitable object, when found, acquires a positive valence. So a vector is set up directing locomotion toward the object. Excessive tension (hunger, for example) may blur the individual's perception of the environment, prevent his finding an object of suitable valence, and so prevent the establishment of a definite vector. Again, frustration by a barrier, by increasing tension, may result in random or ill-directed activity (1938, page 160).

Lewin felt the need of some kind of mathematics to foster exact reasoning on problems of motivation and behavior. Statistics, so much used by psychologists, did not meet his requirements because he wished to deal adequately with the "single case" so as to predict an individual's behavior in a concrete situation (1935, page 68). He needed two things: some means of mapping the life space at a given moment so as to show all the possible goals and routes to the goals; and some means of taking account of the motives determining which one of the possibilities will be chosen by the individual. No existing form of mathematics was exactly suited to Lewin's requirements, but he found he could do fairly well with a combination of topology and vector analysis—topology for mapping the life space, vector analysis for taking care of the motives (1936, 1938, 1940; see also Leeper, 1943). He used only the rudiments of these two branches of mathematics but elaborated his own system both in the form of diagrams and in that of equations. One advantage of mathematical treatment is that the symbols used must be carefully defined. In order to apply mathematics to a concrete problem, we must define our symbols (1) conceptually, by relating one symbol to another, as for example by relating the concepts of need, valence, and vector to each other; and also (2) operationally, by indicating how the facts covered by our concepts are to be observed and measured. The operational definition enables us to secure our data, while the conceptual definition enables us to treat the data mathematically (1938, page 13). The diagrams and equations have some value at least in laying the situation distinctly before the investigator. They should also suggest hypotheses to be tested by experiment, and Lewin found his diagrams useful in this respect, as his pupils have also. One difficulty is that the resultant of two vectors cannot be found in the ordinary way by the parallelogram of forces. If a person sees one desirable goal to the north of him and another equally desirable one to the east, he does not advance eagerly to the northeast. He makes a choice. Probably he "restructures the field," sees it so that the two vectors are no longer equal in force. But about all that can ordinarily be done with divergent vectors is to regard them as directly opposed to each other, so that only their relative strength needs to be considered. Even with this and other limitations, Lewin's mathematics is regarded by many psychologists as a good start toward fertile experimentation in the study of motivation.

However that may be, Lewin was certainly ingenious in devising novel types of experiment in motivation. The following problems, among many others, have been fruitfully attacked by him and his students: tension toward completing a task that has been interrupted; the release of tension by a substitute activity when the original task cannot be resumed; level of aspiration; satiation; anger; frustration; effects of autocratic and democratic atmospheres in work and play groups. (For references and summaries see Lewin, 1935, 1940, 1947.)

CHAPTER 6

PSYCHOANALYSIS AND RELATED SCHOOLS

We come now to a school of psychology which did not, like those we have studied, originate in psychology itself. It originated in medical practice and from the effort to find some cure for the neuroses, some thorough scientific treatment for these baffling conditions. It is a school of psychiatry in the broad sense of that term. But it has built so impressive a theory about its practice as to challenge the attention of all psychologists. It could be called a psychology of behavior, though it is removed very far from behavioristic methods and concepts. It sometimes uses the name "depth psychology," because of its concern with unconscious motives and conflicts. It has sometimes called itself "emotion psychology," so marking its revolt against the intellectualistic emphasis of much nineteenth century psychology. It has little use for the academic psychology of the human or animal laboratory or for the mental tests of the psychologists. Learning, perception, thinking—favorite topics of the psychologists—have appeared to the psychoanalysts as relatively superficial or at least as of little use in their medical practice. Their revolt against the academic psychology, then, has so far consisted mostly in leaving it severely alone.

As a movement within psychiatry, psychoanalysis was a revolt against the dominant "somatic" tendency of the nineteenth century (page 8) and a springing into new life of the "psychic" tendency. Convinced at last that brain lesions could not be found in some mental disorders, psychiatrists were turning to the patient's emotional stress, weakness of will, suggestibility, and irrational habits. The history of this psychiatric development is a story by itself. It is partly the history of hypnotism. Brought to medical and scientific attention by Mesmer in 1780, hypnotism led a checkered career for a century, being associated with a great deal of charlatanism and almost universally rejected by the medical profession until the days of the famous rival schools of Paris and Nancy, along in the sixties, seventies, and eighties of the nineteenth century. The Paris school was dominated by Charcot (1825-1893), the leading neurologist of his day, a striking personality and a great teacher. Charcot made a special study of hysteria. He found that persons subject to hysteric fits could also be put into deep hypnosis, and he used this fact in treating hysteria as well as for interpreting hypnosis, which he inferred to be a peculiar pathological state of the organism. This view was vigorously opposed by the Nancy school, who taught that a mild form of hypnosis could be induced in nearly all normal subjects and regarded it as simply a passive and receptive state produced by suggestion. They used it in the treatment of neurotic conditions. The strife between the two rival French schools was very keen.

Charcot had many pupils who became prominent in the study and treatment of the neuroses. Morton Prince of Boston (1854-1929) used hypnosis and suggestion in the treatment of "double personality," and is well known to psychologists for his experiments on split consciousness and for his theory of the "co-conscious." Pierre Janet of Paris (1859-1947) performed many experiments on automatic writing and similar unconscious or dissociated performances (1889). In the nineties and later he devoted himself intensively to the study and treatment of the neuroses. Following up Charcot's work, he found that hysterical patients were able under hypnosis to recall experiences that seemed in the waking state to be entirely forgotten (1892). Emotional shocks were thus recalled, and particular symptoms such as the hysterical paralysis of one arm were traced back to their source. Moreover, if during hypnosis suggestions were made by the physician to the effect that "that's all past and gone now," the hysterical symptoms connected with the emotional shock disappeared (though the patient was likely to develop other symptoms later, originating in other emotional shocks). Janet went on to investigate other forms of neurosis, the phobias and obsessions, which he grouped under the inclusive name of psychasthenia and treated by re-education rather than by hypnosis and suggestion (1903). He held that the neuroses are due fundamentally to a condition of "low mental tension" or inability to get up enough energy to meet the emergencies and difficulties of life. Given this primary condition of low tension and general feeling of weakness and insufficiency, the individual would react to particular difficulties by developing particular symptoms. Janet's work, slightly antedating psychoanalysis, was beginning to exert considerable influence on both psychology and psychiatry when it was overtaken by the more dramatic conceptions of Freud and rather thrown into the shade.

Sigmund Freud (1856-1939), though a native of what is now Czechoslovakia, lived in Vienna from the age of 4 until the Nazi invasion of 1938. His interest in psychological problems was late in developing. As a young boy he became much absorbed in reading Bible history, and this interest remained with him and came to the fore in some of his last writings. In the classical preparatory school, the "gymnasium," he was a brilliant student, evidently suited to an intellectual career along some line, but what line it should be was not clear to him. Civilization, human culture, and human relationships attracted him most, rather than natural science, but Darwin's theory of evolution, then new and much in the air, opened up a scientific approach to the understanding of the world. After some hesitation, then, Freud registered as a medical student at the University of Vienna, having indeed no desire to be a physician, but aiming at the basic sciences. He found physiology most to his liking and worked for six years in the physiological laboratory. Of the clinical branches, only psychiatry had much appeal for him. Finding that he had no immediate chance of earning his livelihood in pure science, he decided to go into medical practice and in 1882 switched from the physiological laboratory to the hospital, where he specialized as much as possible on the nervous system, its anatomy and organic diseases such as paralyses, aphasia, and the effects of brain injuries in children. The nervous diseases seemed to offer a good field not yet well developed in Vienna. The fame of Charcot was heard from the distance, and Freud in 1885 went over to Paris and studied with the master for a year. He was much impressed by Charcot's use of hypnosis in the treatment of hysteria. Charcot scarcely antici-pated the psychological views regarding hysteria reached by either of his pupils, Freud or Janet, but he had got far away from the old view that it was essentially a woman's disease (the name being derived from the Greek *hystera,* the womb), and he was able to demonstrate the condition in male patients. On returning to Vienna Freud reported to his medical colleagues on Charcot's methods and results, including male hysteria, and was ridiculed by his colleagues for accepting such an absurdity. A few such rebuffs confirmed Freud's already formed convic-tion that his place was bound to be "in the opposition."

It was at this time, in 1886, when Freud was just about 30, that he married and settled down in Vienna as a nerve special-ist engaged in private practice. Since the neuroses were a neglected field in Vienna, he built up his practice in that direc-tion. In hypnosis he had a method of treatment which pro-duced remarkable cures in many hysteric patients. But he soon found difficulties with the method. For one thing, the "cures" were apt to be only temporary, and, for another, many neurotic patients could not be hypnotized. This indifferent success that he was meeting led him to make another pilgrimage over to France, this time to examine the work of the Nancy school, which claimed to hypnotize practically all comers and to have great success in the use of curative suggestions given to hypno-tized patients. He was somewhat disappointed to be informed by the Nancy doctors that their success was not nearly so good with private patients as with the charity patients in the clinic. It seemed that the private patients were too sophisticated to ac-cept the suggestions wholeheartedly. Freud returned to Vienna and continued work on his private patients with the hypnotic method, though with only moderate success. He greatly de-sired to find some more reliable method.

Development of the Psychoanalytic Method

The name *psychoanalysis,* as Freud later insisted, should properly be restricted to the theory and practice developed and named by him. Hypnosis, as he employed it at first after the examples of Charcot and the Nancy school, was a form of mental healing or psychotherapy but could not be called mental analysis since it did not undertake to analyze or investigate the patient's mental condition or the experiences that gave rise to the maladjustment. Janet was beginning to use hypnosis for such analytic purposes, but Freud owed nothing to Janet, whose work he got to know only later. Freud did owe a great deal to his friend Joseph Breuer (1842-1925). Breuer was an eminent physiologist who had made important contributions to the study of respiration and of the semicircular canals, but who was devoting himself mostly to general medical practice. Quite incidentally he had undertaken to treat a severe case of hysteria, a gifted young woman who was incapacitated by a whole swarm of symptoms—paralyses, memory losses, and states of mental confusion. Breuer treated this patient by use of hypnosis, and he found as Janet did that under hypnosis a patient could remember emotional experiences that had given rise to specific symptoms. But Breuer's patient led him one step further toward psychoanalysis: she reported that after remembering an emotional experience and "talking it out" with him while under hypnosis she then found herself free from the particular symptom that dated from this experience. Breuer followed up this suggestion from the patient and succeeded after many such sessions in getting all her symptoms talked out and "abreacted," as he said, so that she was able to resume her normal life. Freud took a keen interest in the new method and tried it out successfully on other patients. Breuer and Freud collaborated in publishing their results in 1893 and 1895. They called their new method one of mental catharsis, because it worked by eliminating sources of disturbance from the patient's emotional system.

In spite of this promising beginning Breuer refused to continue this work or to make any further use of his cathartic method. For one thing, he was fully occupied with his general practice and preferred not to branch out into the treatment of hysteria, and there was apparently another reason which became clear to Freud later. Breuer's patient, when the long series of hypnotic sessions was about to terminate in complete cure, declared that she could not bear to part from him because she had fallen violently in love with him. This unexpected abreaction disconcerted Breuer and led him to conclude that the new method created difficulties for the physician who wished to maintain a strictly professional attitude. Freud soon ran into the same difficulty but was not so easily disturbed. Pondering the psychology of the situation, he concluded that it was not his own personality that was attracting these women but that he was being taken as a substitute for the real and original object of their love. The love was simply transferred to him. If he could continue to treat them while maintaining the professional attitude, he might even make use of this transference as a step toward cure. Besides the loving and dependent attitude of the patient toward the analyst, a hostile, resentful attitude emerged from time to time, but this rebellious attitude also could be regarded as transferred to the analyst from previous authoritative persons such as the patient's parents in childhood. It was years before the theory of transference was fully worked out, but in time the techniques for managing and using it came to have a dominant place in psychoanalytic practice.

Freud believed that the use of hypnosis made the transference difficult to manage, and that was one reason for his decision to give up hypnosis. Another reason was that he desired to extend his practice so as to treat neurotic persons who were not easily or deeply hypnotized. Hypnosis was a great aid in quickly recovering the lost memories, but even in the waking state it should be possible for the patient to get at them if only enough effort were applied. He still had his patients relax physically on a couch while he sat behind them where he could watch without being watched. Then he urged them to search their memory and kept insisting that they could remember the origin of their present troubles if they persisted long enough. This was a strenuous procedure for both doctor and patient, and not always successful.

Freud was then led to take a most important forward step in the development of his method. He got his patients to relax mentally as well as physically. Instead of urging them to search in memory for the source of their trouble, he told them to relax and let ideas come up spontaneously. Borrowing a psychological term he called this the method of "free association," while admitting that the association was not entirely free since it was controlled to some extent by the whole situation of the patient on the couch in the doctor's office. The patient is not making a social call but has come for relief from his neurosis. So the ideas that come up spontaneously will be concerned directly or indirectly with the patient's personal problems. The doctor relaxes his firm hold on the reins and gives the patient his (or her) head. The doctor makes very few comments and tries to interfere as little as possible with the free course of the patient's thoughts. But the patient must accept the "fundamental rule of psychoanalysis"—he must promise to give prompt expression to every idea that comes up, however embarrassing, unimportant, irrelevant, or even foolish the idea may appear.

Freud soon took another step which always seemed to him very important in the development of psychoanalysis. Sometimes it happened during the process of free association that the patient remembered and reported a dream, and Freud found that the dream made an excellent starting point for free association. The patient recounts a dream of the night before and then lets his mind play freely about each item of the dream. The items are followed up remorselessly in the hope of unearthing significant memories which will fit together and reveal the "complex" from which the patient is suffering. Freud believed that the "manifest dream," which the patient could remember, was a mere disguise for the real or "latent dream," and that free association would lead from the manifest toward the latent dream. In dreaming, he believed, one is attempting to find some gratification for unfulfilled wishes. They may be current daytime wishes as when the polar explorer dreams of warm, green fields, or they may be deep-lying but unfulfilled wishes dating from childhood. Believing that an analyst should himself be analyzed, Freud undertook a self-analysis by study of his own dreams through free association, meanwhile working out an elaborate theory of dreams which he published in 1900 as *Die Traumdeutung* (*The interpretation of dreams*) which he always regarded as his greatest work. His most interesting book is perhaps the *Psychopathology of everyday life* (first German edition, 1901) in which he applies the method of free association to the analysis of slips of the tongue and lapses of various kinds and shows how they can reveal hidden wishes and complexes. From that time his work began to awaken the lively if dubious interest of many psychologists.

Equipped with his new technique of free association and dream analysis, Freud proceeded to treat neurotic individuals with considerable success. By reviving forgotten emotional experiences he succeeded in removing hysterical symptoms and neurotic fears and inhibitions. But it often happened that cases dismissed as cured came back later with slightly different complaints. Such has been the experience of all who have attempted to cure the neuroses. Freud, as was usual with him, far from being baffled, remained confident of the value of his method and concluded that he simply had not pushed his analysis deep enough and far enough back in the patient's life—as if he had so far penetrated only the outer layers of the neurosis without reaching its core. Instead of being satisfied when he had recovered recent memories, he felt himself gradually forced back to childhood and even to infancy.

At first Freud believed, with Charcot and Breuer, that the neurosis originated in some particular emotional shock that the patient had experienced. Therefore he probed further and further back in the patient's forgotten memories to find the shocking episode. Many of the neurotic women who consulted him were brought by dream analysis to recall emotional shocks of later childhood. They thought they remembered being sexually attacked or seduced by their fathers, uncles, or older brothers. Shocked himself by the apparent frequency of such occurrences, Freud took occasion to check up on some of these stories and found that they had no basis in fact. This spurious result of his dream analysis really baffled him for a time, but he soon recovered his poise. What the patient had sincerely remembered, he concluded, was some daydream or fantasy of childhood or early youth. Such an imaginary episode might be as important in the patient's life history as if it had been an objective event, because it embodied a childish wish. The daydream of later childhood pointed back to an unfulfilled wish of earlier childhood. If the analysis could be pushed away back to that wish of early childhood, the core of the neurosis would be reached. If dream analysis could enable the adult patient to recover the lost memories of early childhood and to live over again the wishes of that period, a radical cure of the neurosis could be achieved.

Push the analysis back to early childhood? But that is a practical impossibility, if it means that the adult by any amount of free association and dream analysis is to remember the events of his first few years with any approach to completeness. Only a few scraps of the rich experience of those first years are ever recovered. However—perhaps the intellectual recall of those early events is not the essential requirement. What is needed may be, rather, the revival of the emotional attitude of early childhood. Even a very scrappy recall of the early experiences may suffice to bring back that attitude and make the adult a little child again, emotionally. If this childish attitude, this unrealistic desire, is now brought out into the open, the neurosis will be revealed in its true infantile colors and perhaps give way to a better adjustment under the guiding hand of the analyst. Something like this was Freud's view of the psychoanalytic cure of a neurosis.

When the patient thus revives his childish emotional attitudes, without clear memory of the persons and events of his childhood, the door is thrown wide open to transference. He directs his emotions toward the analyst. If the child's father was the object of love and also of defiance, the analyst as a father substitute becomes the object of the transferred emotional attitudes. Sometimes the patient is full of love and enthusiasm for the analyst, but at other times he shows extreme rebellion and even hate. Both the positive and the negative transference reveal phases of the child's attitude toward his father, and both phases must be worked through with the help of the experienced and understanding father substitute, the analyst. As the analysis approaches its goal, positive transference is all to the fore. The patient would be left with a childish dependence on the analyst unless one further step were taken, consisting in the weaning of the patient from the transference. The childish desires, now freed from their original objects, must not be allowed to remain fixed on the analyst but must find an outlet in harmony with the present situation of the adult patient.

Freud laid great stress on the necessity of helping the patient overcome his "resistances." Oftentimes "free association" does not operate freely; it seems to be blocked as if the patient were coming dangerously near to some memory or idea which is too painful or terrible or shameful to be faced—as if some emotional attitude were stirred which he is unwilling to recognize as his own—hatred, for example, toward someone near and dear to him, or unlimited selfishness. As a neurotic patient he admits he is in trouble, but he still has a very good opinion of himself and tends to repel any memory or any insight that would shame him. By degrees, under the guidance of the analyst, he begins to face the facts, though it is a painful process.

The forgotten experiences and unadmitted desires and attitudes that came to light in free association were so often of a sexual nature that Freud early came to emphasize the predominant if not exclusive importance of sexual difficulties and conflicts in the causation of any neurosis. Hostility motives and ambivalence (love and hate for the same person) also came to light but were regarded as arising from frustration of sex desires. From dream analysis he came to believe that certain types of objects in the manifest dream were regular symbols for sexual objects and processes. So there were regular symbols for the male and female genital organs and for copulation, there were father symbols and mother symbols, there were symbols for secret love or hate. Equipped with a knowledge of these symbols, the analyst could quickly penetrate the disguises of a dream and discern the patient's hidden complexes. Having thus reached a diagnosis the physician would, according to customary medical practice, proceed at once to "prescribe." But if he told the patient what he had discovered, he was met with incredulity and resistance. A less authoritarian procedure had to be devised. Apparently Freud quickly went through the three stages which he outlined in a much later book (1920, pages 17-18)[1]:

At first the endeavors of the analytic physician were confined to divining the unconscious of which his patient was unaware, effecting a synthesis of its components and communicating it at the right time. . . .

Since the therapeutic task was not thereby accomplished, the next aim was to compel the patient to confirm the reconstruction through his own memory. In this endeavor the chief emphasis was on the resistances of the patient; the art now lay in unveiling these as soon as possible, in calling the patient's attention to them, and . . . teaching him to abandon the resistances.

It became increasingly clear, however, that the aim in view, the bringing into consciousness of the unconscious, was not fully attainable by this method either. The patient cannot recall all of what lies repressed, perhaps not even the essential part of it. . . . He is obliged rather to *repeat* as a current experience what is repressed. . . . As a rule the physician cannot spare the patient this phase of the cure; he must let him live through a certain fragment of his forgotten life.

Freud's determination to effect a radical cure by penetrating to the core of every neurosis and working back to its origin in early childhood forced him to abandon any hope of expeditious treatment. Three sessions a week for many months or even a couple of years were found to be required. The single analyst could handle only a few cases in the course of a year, and analysts could not be multiplied rapidly, since each analyst must first be analyzed himself and then work for two years under supervision before starting practice on his own account. Thousands and thousands of neurotic persons must be deprived of the benefits of psychoanalysis, not only now but for generations to come. The medical schools teach many difficult subjects of no practical use to the psychoanalyst and they train the student against rather than for psychoanalysis by giving him respect only for physical causes of diseases and objective methods of diagnosis. Freud reached the conclusion that the practice of psychoanalysis should not be limited to the medical profession;

---

[1] Quoted passages are taken from the translations of Freud's works listed in our Bibliography, pages 259-260.

it should rather be a profession on its own account (1926). Most of Freud's followers, being medical themselves, have rejected this one suggestion of the master, no matter how orthodox they are in other respects. As to the expanding group of consulting psychologists, many of them doubtless make some use of Freud's methods, but few are orthodox enough to seek for radical cures by the "classical analysis" such as Freud prescribed. They align themselves more nearly with those medical followers of Freud who seek to simplify the treatment so as to benefit a larger number of more or less neurotic individuals.

Even in the early days before 1913, some of Freud's followers attempted to simplify the psychoanalytic procedure by concentrating on the patient's present problems and maladjustments instead of working back to childhood. Freud vigorously opposed any such attempt, being convinced in his own mind "that the actual conflict of the neurotic becomes comprehensible and solvable only if it can be traced back into the patient's past history" (1914, page 55). The innovators accepted Freud's decree that they were no longer entitled to call themselves psychoanalysts but continued to carry on under other names. Then came the first world war with its large crop of soldiers suffering from "shell shock," soon better named "war neurosis." What could the Army psychiatrists do for these soldiers? There was no time for a classical analysis reaching back into childhood, and yet some of Freud's conceptions and procedures were found useful. In the second world war limited psychoanalysis has been combined with the use of hypnosis, hypnotic drugs, or simple relaxation to get back lost memories of emotional shock in battle (Pascal, 1947).

Of recent years and perhaps especially since Freud's death, those who call themselves psychoanalysts and do all honor to Freud as the father of the movement are showing considerable freedom in modifying his methods. Not always do they analyze dreams or employ the typical free association. Not always do they have the patient recline on a couch; sometimes they face him as man to man, seeking to establish an atmosphere of well-wishing and understanding, though still at the professional level. Instead of aiming at a revival of the experiences and emotional attitudes of childhood, they find it better in many cases to lead the patient's thoughts toward unconscious (unrecognized) motives and attitudes in his present life. They find that many analyses can be brought to a satisfactory termination in much less time than Freud required (Alexander and French, 1946). They may combine psychoanalysis with some use of hypnosis and much use of occupational and recreational therapy (Menninger, 1938). They may even instruct selected patients in methods of self-analysis and depend a good deal on what these patients can do for themselves with rather infrequent consultations with the analyst (Horney, 1942).

Consulting psychologists are naturally much interested in the method called "nondirective therapy" which has arisen within their own ranks. It could claim to be a lineal descendant of psychoanalysis but is so very heretical that no one could call it psychoanalysis, least of all the nondirective therapists themselves. It resembles psychoanalysis in that the client (corresponding to the psychoanalyst's patient) does most of the talking and that his talking helps him to a better adjustment. It differs in that the therapist's remarks do not attempt to lay bare the client's hidden motives but simply show a warm appreciation of the client's expressed feelings with encouragement to go on and express himself further. The therapist's aim is not even to diagnose the client's difficulty, but rather to provide a "warm, permissive psychological atmosphere" over a sufficient time so that the client may achieve some insight into his difficulties and mobilize his constructive forces for a positive advance in his way of life. The technique is more difficult than it sounds in this sketchy description, and also more successful than would be expected (Rogers, 1942). In a sense, nondirective therapy has evolved from psychoanalysis by getting rid of the medical functions of authoritative diagnosis and prescription. It may also be contrasted with the original talking-out or cathartic method by saying that its great concern is not to eliminate disturbing factors but to stimulate the positive, constructive tendencies of the individual.

In the preceding account of the development of psychoanalysis as a method of examining and treating neurotic patients,

Freud's theories have been left to one side. It probably would be possible to use the methods without accepting the theories. Freud's technical terms, standing for his theoretical concepts, have not been introduced as yet, with the exception of *transference* and *resistance*. These two concepts were regarded by Freud as a direct expression of facts observed by him in the behavior of his patients, but they do involve his interpretation of the facts, as will appear in the next section on Freud's psychological theories. It is Freud's theory rather than his method that constitutes a school of psychology.

Freud's Earlier Psychology

Freud's interest in psychoanalytic work was twofold from the start: he needed a practical method for treating the neuroses; and he hoped to make progress in his lifelong quest for insight into the deep, underlying realities of human life. His experience with the neuroses was promptly worked over into psychological concepts which he found intellectually satisfactory and used freely in describing his observations. By 1905 he had worked out what we may call his earlier psychology, and this remained the widely known psychoanalytic doctrine until 1913 and later. About that time he began to develop a more advanced psychology which was not intended to replace the earlier theory except where new observations forced him to revise his earlier views. It was intended, rather, to go deeper and to provide a systematic, even though speculative, conceptualization of the forces operative in individual and social behavior. To many of his adherents, it is safe to say, the earlier theory remains the more significant.

We will first attempt to bring out the main elements in Freud's earlier system. He always insisted that it was not intended to be a complete system. It did not pretend to cover most of the topics usually included in a textbook of psychology, but aimed to explain what all other psychologists were neglecting or leaving unsettled. It dealt almost wholly with motives and their conflicts and with the effects of conflict, especially as found in the neuroses. We shall not need to examine his theories of the neuroses in any detail, for he relates the motivation of the neuroses to that of normal everyday behavior and emotion.

THE UNCONSCIOUS. The earliest of Freud's theories to take shape, according to his autobiography (1946) was his firm belief in unconscious mental or "psychic" processes. Experiments which he witnessed at Nancy in 1889 impressed him strongly. On awaking from a hypnotic trance the subject may be entirely unconscious of what has happened during the trance ("posthypnotic amnesia"), though he remembers it if put back under hypnosis. Breuer's patient and many patients treated by Freud could remember while under hypnosis past experiences which seemed entirely forgotten while the patients were awake. These memories, then, had not been really forgotten but had sunk into the unconscious from which they could not be summoned by the conscious self. So far, Freud's concept of the unconscious did not differ from that formed by earlier students of these phenomena, though some earlier authorities had spoken of "unconscious cerebration" as presumably a physiological process.[2] Freud preferred to stick to psychological terms. He believed that the complex process of planning and deliberating could go on in the unconscious. He even said that the whole psychic life was primarily unconscious, with the quality of consciousness only sometimes superadded (1946, page 41).

UNCONSCIOUS MOTIVES. Freud's conception of the unconscious soon took on a special emphasis that was new and original. It appeared to him that the unconscious consisted essentially of motives. Those memories which his first patients got back while under hypnosis were, to be sure, memories of persons and events, but they were shot through with strong but unfulfilled wishes. A young woman's sense of duty to her sick father forced her to give up her love affair—that was the kind of memory that often came to light. Such a "forgotten" wish might still be very much alive in the unconscious, with queer

---

[2] For example, Carpenter (1876), who also refers to many others holding similar views, among them the elder Oliver Wendell Holmes. A more recent term for unconscious mental work is *incubation*.

effects on conscious behavior. That young woman developed a hysterical paralysis which gave expression to her unadmitted desire to be rid of the duty of nursing her father. In his *Psychopathology of everyday life* Freud assembled hundreds of examples of lapses, errors, and automatisms all of which under his hands were made to reveal more or less hidden motives.

Freud did not spare himself in these analyses. In one instance he had a lapse of memory which certainly appeared remarkable. In going over his account book at the end of one year he was mystified to find the name of a patient occurring repeatedly, though he had no notion who that patient could be —a patient in a sanitarium seen daily for several weeks during the previous summer. Finally he remembered—it was a young girl whom he had treated successfully for a hysterical condition and finally let go though she was still complaining of some abdominal pain. Two months later she was dead of cancer in the abdomen. He had made a regrettable error in diagnosis and his unfulfilled wish was that he had done a better professional job. From such examples, interpreted in his characteristic manner, Freud reached a new theory of forgetting: anything once well known was never forgotten though it might be banished to the unconscious. Without going quite so far as to assert that intentional forgetting accounted for all failures of memory, he did say there was good reason to suspect some motive in any pronounced case.

He said the same thing about any slip of the tongue or any "accident" such as losing or breaking anything. Every such act, he suspected, was intentional, though the intention might be unconscious. A bride loses her wedding ring—a sign that she has a smoldering wish to be free again or at least to be free of her present bridegroom. Freud and his early followers seemed to take a malicious pleasure in pointing out such unadmitted motives in their patients and acquaintances.

In any specific case the hidden motive might be found by means of free association, just as in the analysis of a dream. Freud had also certain guiding principles that seemed to him good leads toward an unconscious motive. One such guiding principle was that what is forbidden must be desired. Unless people desired to do a thing, prohibitions against that thing would not be necessary. What is strongly forbidden must be strongly desired. What is abhorrent and shocking must be very strongly desired. To kill one's own father is an extremely abhorrent deed, and the laws against such conduct have sometimes been exceptionally strict. Therefore there must be a strong and common desire in the unconscious to commit this particular crime. Incest, or sex relations between near relatives, is another extrashocking crime—but why? Freud's guiding principle led him to conclude that the individual must harbor strong unconscious desires for incestuous relations. A similar guiding principle was that what is feared is probably desired, the fear being a mask for the unconscious desire. There is of course a perfectly rational fear in real danger, but the irrational and excessive fears such as the phobias of neurotic persons call for some explanation. The behaviorists would call them conditioned fears, but Freud suspected an unconscious and forbidden wish. In the same way, extreme solicitude for some person's welfare might mask an unconscious desire to do him injury.

PSYCHIC DETERMINISM. An event is "determined" if it has a cause. It is fully determined if it has a sufficient cause so that in every detail its character follows necessarily from the antecedent conditions, nothing being left to chance. Determinism is the belief or scientific postulate that all events in nature have their sufficient causes. As applied to the human organism determinism means that every act or thought or emotion has its sufficient causes, though these may be very complex and difficult to disentangle because of the complexity of the organism and of the environment. Freud believed heartily in determinism. He would not admit that any act "just happened" or that it was due to "free will." He pointed out that important actions and decisions are always ascribed to motives, and that it is only in unimportant matters that we are inclined to say that we could have acted this way or that but just decided arbitrarily to act in this way rather than that. Where there is no conscious motive there must be an unconscious one, he asserted. A slip of the tongue or any sort of "accident" must be motivated by some hidden desire. It is aimed at a certain goal, and though it may not fully reach its goal it interferes with the conscious purpose of the moment and produces unexpected results. A dream is not mere play of imagination but is governed by an unconscious wish and aimed at the fulfillment of that wish.

A "psychic cause," according to Freud, is a wish, motive, intention. Such a cause has to work through the bodily mechanisms, including brain structures and connections, but these belong to physiology rather than psychology. Freud apparently relegated to physiology all studies of conditioned responses and of factors favorable or unfavorable to efficiency of learning and accuracy of perception. For him, motivation was practically the whole field of psychology.

Freud's psychic determinism, as applied to the neuroses, meant that every abnormal symptom has an aim, being driven by an unconscious motive. In a valuable survey of the schools of abnormal psychology, McDougall (1926a, pages 1-19) showed that Freud differed from his predecessors in basing his view of the neuroses on motivation. His predecessors and even his contemporary, Janet, had regarded a neurosis as an expression of the subject's weakness—of "low mental tension." But Freud believed that the neurotic symptoms were more than signs of weakness. He probed for unconscious motives and found them to his own satisfaction and that of his followers. If the neurotic subject did not want his phobia or obsession consciously, he did want it unconsciously, just as the hysteric patient already mentioned wanted her paralysis as a release from the restricting obligation to nurse her sick father. Freud's later followers, even when departing from him on other questions of theory, have clung to psychic determinism. Every symptom, they believe, has a meaning in terms of unconscious motives and unconscious satisfactions. Any symptom, any slip of the tongue, any dream, they assume, points toward an unconscious motive, and if that motive can be brought to light and squarely faced by the patient, there is a chance of dealing with it rationally, and so advancing toward a cure. (The possibility of dealing rationally with a motive, however, implies that the patient's understanding and grasp of the situation and his power to learn new and better ways of managing his life can be potent causative factors. If so, psychic determinism is not limited to motives, and dynamic psychology broadens out to include a vast field of psychological investigation which Freud brushed aside as of no great value.)

RESISTANCE AND REPRESSION. The unconscious motives do not lie dormant. From time to time, at least, they become urgent and seek to emerge into conscious behavior. But they are not pretty, pleasant motives. When they threaten to emerge they awaken anxiety, shame, and a guilty feeling in the conscious self, which therefore resists and tries to hold them down. So Freud interpreted the difficulty often encountered in the attempt to revive old memories. The unconscious motive presses up and outward, and the conscious self exerts a contrary force, pressing down and inward. In sleep the conscious self relaxes its vigilance and allows the unconscious motives to emerge to a certain extent, provided they disguise themselves in the symbolism of the manifest dream. If they emerge too openly, they throw the sleeper into a panic or awaken him altogether.

How did these unconscious motives first become unconscious? There must have been some force resisting them in the first place, equivalent to the force which now resists their emergence. From this reasoning Freud was led to his *theory of repression*. The drives of life are originally unformed and unconscious, but they take shape by becoming attached to objects in the environment. They become a longing for this person, or a hate for that person, or love and hate for the same person. Such wishes may be unacceptable, and then there are two ways of handling them. They may be consciously rejected and deadened, so that they are later remembered as affairs of the past without any present driving force. Or they may be violently thrust down into the unconscious, where they retain their driving force but can no longer be remembered because of the continued resistance of the conscious self. When treated in this second way, they were said by Freud to be repressed.

Because the unconscious motives are sometimes very urgent, the conscious self resorts to various stratagems or "defense mechanisms" to protect itself against them. One of these goes by the rather confusing name of *reaction formation,* which here means about the same as "leaning over backwards," i.e., exaggerating the opposite motive. A person you love and admire may at times arouse in you a feeling of hostility and detestation which is very distressing, and you react by inflating your love and admiration as much as possible. A less obvious mechanism to meet this situation is called *projection,* which means that, refusing to admit your hostility to your friend, you take him to be hostile to you; he and not you is the guilty party, so that your feeling of guilt is transformed into a feeling of being wronged.

These mechanisms were not regarded by Freud as conscious devices, deliberately thought out and adopted. They were "unconscious," and the same was true of resistance and repression. Conscious resistance was present, too, as when a patient in the process of free association came upon something that he preferred not to tell the analyst because it was too personal and embarrassing. But unconscious resistance was shown by the patient's genuine difficulty in following up certain leads and getting back certain memories. Now there is an obvious theoretical incongruity here, since the "conscious self" is unconsciously resisting, unconsciously "projecting," unconsciously "reacting." Some revision was needed either in the concept of the conscious self or in that of the unconscious or in both; and we see here one of the reasons leading Freud to his later system.

PERSISTENCE OF SPECIFIC WISHES. Freud was always looking for hidden wishes, and the wishes he looked for were wishes of the past still alive in the unconscious. The dream, he thought, aims to fulfill not a wish of the present moment but a wish repressed at some time in the past. The neurosis, he thought, is motivated by some repressed wish dating from the past. We have seen how Freud was forced to search further and further back till he reached the patient's early childhood. You may say that everyone accepts the years of childhood as the formative period, but Freud's view went beyond the truism that experience leaves permanent effects on a person's character and personality. He meant something much more definite. He assumed that particular experiences live on in the unconscious and that the specific wishes of childhood, when repressed, remain active in the unconscious and express themselves in dreams, lapses, and neurotic symptoms.

Consider in this connection the matter of transference. The actual fact is the patient's positive or negative emotional attitude toward the analyst. But in Freud's view this attitude is transferred to the analyst from some other person such as the patient's father. In Freud's view the patient's original childhood wishes have persisted and now fasten on the analyst as a father substitute. Suppose that we were interpreting the patient's emotional attitude toward the analyst without assuming the persistence of the specific wishes of childhood. The patient's present situation in relation to the analyst, we should observe, is similar to the child's situation in relation to his father; and free association by bringing back childhood memories has revived the emotional attitude of childhood. Therefore, we would conclude, the patient responds to the analyst as he used to respond to his father. That would not be transference in Freud's sense, because there would be no transferring of a specific wish from childhood to the present. Freud's interpretation may or may not be better, but it is certainly an interpretation rather than a bare statement of fact, and it rests upon the rather bold assumption that the wishes of the past remain unchanged, though they may find new objects as substitutes for the lost objects of the past.

As we shall see, Freud's belief in the persistence of specific wishes and his view of transference are not accepted by some of his followers, nor, indeed, by many other psychologists.

INFANTILE SEXUALITY. The widespread excitement over Freud's early writings was due especially to the fact that he wrote with great freedom and in a very interesting style about the sex life of men and women, making many surprising statements as he went along. The first of these statements was to the effect that neuroses are due to sexual maladjustments. He did not accuse the neurotics of loose living; quite the contrary, he said that they had excessively repressed their sexual desires. Nor, on the other hand, did he advise free sex expression as a cure of the neuroses—this was the "wild psychoanalysis" which he took pains to condemn. What was needed was to get back to the original cause of the repression, and following this trail he seemed always to be led back to early childhood. The second of his surprising statements was that the individual's sex life began in infancy and not at puberty. He ridiculed the sentimental expression, "innocent childhood," for he believed he could demonstrate strong sex desires and malicious tendencies in the young child. He said that his theory of infantile sexuality was "a theoretical extract from very numerous experiences"—experiences, that is, of the analyst in obtaining free associations from his neurotic patients. He continued as follows (1914, page 10):

At first it was only noticed that the . . . actual impressions had to be traced back to the past. . . . The tracks led still further back into childhood and into its earliest years . . . the autoerotic activities of the early years of childhood . . . and now the whole sexual life of the child made its appearance. . . . Years later, my discoveries were successfully confirmed for the greater part by direct observation and analyses of children of very early years.

The sex drive of the infant has not nearly the intensity that it will have in adolescence when the sex glands and hormones have matured, and it does not yet have the definite aim of the sexually excited adult. It is diffuse rather than sharply focused, Freud said. It aims simply at bodily pleasure from any organ, from the mouth, from the anus, from the genitals. It is autoerotic, not yet being directed toward any other person as a love object. It first gains satisfaction from the mouth in sucking. The sucking of a hungry baby, to be sure, is driven by hunger and not by the sex urge, but when a baby who is not hungry sucks his thumb or a pacifier with apparent pleasure, he cannot be motivated by hunger but must be driven by the pleasure-seeking motive, the rudimentary sex motive in Freud's conception. Somewhat later the young child gets pleasure from his bowel movements and may delay evacuation so as to obtain stronger sensation. Still later he obtains pleasure from manipulating the genital organs. At each of these stages—oral, anal, genital—his erotic activity is likely to encounter restriction and frustration from the social environment. He may adjust himself adequately to the social demands, or he may react by first intensifying and then repressing the particular activity. When he represses, he "fixates" this particular urge in the unconscious where it persists unchanged, though it may obtain partial satisfaction through some form of "sublimation" which is socially tolerated or even approved. So the oral-erotic individual is acquisitive, the anal-erotic thrifty and orderly, the repressed genital-erotic ultraconscientious.

Still other pleasurable activities of the child were regarded by Freud as belonging under the general head of sexuality: biting things and putting them in the mouth; rhythmical movements of the arms and legs in the baby, swinging and seesaw in the older child; tearing things apart and throwing things down; showing off and looking at things—especially, of course, exposing one's own naked body or looking at that of another person; and, in short, any activity which seems to afford the young child sensuous and natural pleasure. At a higher level Freud included under sex gratification all affectionate behavior and comradeship originating in the infant's attachment to the nursing mother. Love for art or music, too, he included under the sex impulse. Whatever we say in ordinary language that we love or love to do is classed by Freud as sexual. Well, you say, that is simply his use of terms; he chose to define sexuality as equivalent to love and pleasure-seeking in the broadest sense. But we must notice, on the other side, that Freud objected strenuously to anyone who attempted to "dilute" his theory by desexualizing it. He insisted that affection was truly sexual and that thumb-sucking gave the baby genuine though rudimentary sexual pleasure. He insisted that his conception of sexuality was strict as well as broad (1905, 1916).

THE EGO AND LIBIDO MOTIVES. One of Freud's basic assumptions was that of a polarity of motives. There must be, he felt, two main opposed trends of motivation—two great forces acting in opposite directions. If an unconscious wish striving to emerge into conscious behavior is resisted, there must be some resisting force. In the earlier theory which we are now considering he adopted as his two main motives the traditional biological instincts of self-preservation and repro-duction. Self-preservation is represented by hunger, fear of danger, self-assertion, which he called ego motives. Reproduc-tion is represented by the fully fledged sex desire of the adult, but also by any kind of pleasure-seeking which cannot be brought under the head of self-preservation. Hence his broad-strict conception of the libido or sex motive.

The ego was also regarded as the conscious self and in touch with the environment. While libido seeks for immediate and uninhibited pleasure, ego is confronted by the realities of the physical and social environment which often make it dangerous to gratify a desire. Ego can learn and does learn to avoid pleas-ures which will result in punishment. In daydreams and in the unconscious a person follows the "pleasure principle," but in waking life he is subservient to the "reality principle."

THE OEDIPUS COMPLEX. Though the child's libido is at first autoerotic and not focused on any external love-object, in the course of the first few years it begins to attach itself to some person or persons. Usually the boy's libido fastens on the mother, the girl's on the father. This is an instinctive hetero-sexual tendency, Freud believed, and it is usually helped along by the preference of the mother for her son, and of the father for his daughter. The boy, in demanding sexual love from his mother, comes into rivalry with his father, and the girl becomes a rival of the mother for the father's love. So arises the "fam-ily romance" or "Oedipus situation" which is most clear-cut in the case of the boy.

Oedipus, the lame hero of Greek legend, as will be recalled, was exposed to the elements by his father, the king of Thebes, with a spike through his feet, because an oracle had predicted that this child would slay his father and marry his mother. He was rescued by a shepherd and adopted by the king of a neigh-boring state, where he grew to early manhood in ignorance of his true parentage and of his predicted fate. On one occasion, however, when he visited the oracle, he was told that he would slay his father and wed his mother. To avoid such a calamity he remained away from his adopted home, but in his wanderings he encountered his true father, quarreled with him, and slew him. As he continued his wanderings he arrived at Thebes, where by solving the riddle of the Sphinx he freed this city from a long-standing pest and was consequently proclaimed king and given the widowed queen to wife. Years later, after four children had been born to the innocently guilty pair, the truth came out and poor Oedipus, in despair, put out his eyes. He lived miserably ever after.

Of this legend Freud needed only the bare outline. Oedipus unwittingly killed his father and married his mother—just what the little boy of four or five years desires. But the boy does not merely hate his father; he loves him as well, admires him, and has long taken him as the model to be imitated. His adored ideal has become his hated rival, and his chosen love-object spurns him. Terrible conflict rages within him, and there is nothing left for him but renunciation and repression. This heroic feat the normal boy accomplishes. He puts the past behind him so thoroughly that the vivid experiences of early childhood are forgotten (Freud's theory of the loss of childhood memories). And, what is more important, the boy identifies himself with his father, takes him into himself, and adopts as his own both the positive precept, "Thou shalt be like thy father," and the prohibitions, "Thou shalt not hate thy father nor covet his wife." These laws of conduct and feeling become the basis of the boy's conscience which Freud in his later system renamed the "superego." When the boy has successfully solved the Oedipus problem, he is freed from the urgency of his infantile libido and can enter upon the relatively calm and educative period of sexual latency which lasts until puberty.

The girl meets a similar problem at about the same age, but it is more complicated and less dramatic, as far as Freud could make out. Usually, too, the drama is complicated by an admixture of homosexual tendency in either boy or girl. As Freud saw the matter much later (1923, pages 42-43) :

SIGMUND FREUD

ALFRED ADLER

CARL G. JUNG

KAREN HORNEY

One gets the impression that the simple Oedipus complex is by no means its commonest form, but rather represents a simplification or schematization which, to be sure, is often enough adequate for practical purposes. ... A boy has not merely an ambivalent attitude towards his father and an affectionate object-relation towards his mother, but at the same time he also behaves like a girl and displays an affectionate feminine attitude to his father and a corresponding hostility and jealousy towards his mother. It is this complicating element introduced by bisexuality that makes it so difficult to obtain a clear view of the facts.

To the practicing psychoanalyst the simpler form of the Oedipus problem is more useful because it can more readily be understood by the neurotic patient. The patient who accepts this theory finds it possible to overcome his resistances and take a calm view of his present conflicts. If a conflict can be seen as one dating from infancy it will be approached more objectively by the patient. Perhaps not so useful to the psychoanalyst but more likely to square with the facts is Fromm's view (1947, page 157) that the child's hostility to the like-sexed parent stems from rebellion against authority and not from sexual rivalry. Certainly rebellion against parental authority and jealousy among siblings are observable facts, but they need not arise from frustrated infantile sexuality or bisexuality unless these terms are used in a very broad sense indeed. Freud himself recognized some such possibility in the passage just cited, when he went on to say, "It may even be that the ambivalence ... is not ... developed ... in consequence of rivalry." But the more mystical idea has an appeal for the neurotic patient.

Freud's Later Psychology

Freud was not contented to leave his theory as it stood in 1905. He continued to mull over it and modify it year after year for the next two decades. His life quest, we remember, was not so much to cure the neuroses as through the study of his patients to reach an understanding of the deep forces of human life, social as well as individual. He had other reasons, too, for seeking to make his theory more comprehensive. Some of his earlier followers, especially Jung and Adler, who will be considered later in this chapter, began to diverge so much from his own views as to eliminate themselves, he held, from the psychoanalytic movement. Yet they had some good ideas which he wished to incorporate in his own system. Jung wished to expand the concept of libido and have it include all the motives of life, and Adler believed that the ego motives rather than the sex motives were responsible for the neuroses. Such views amounted to an abandonment of the psychoanalytic theory, so Freud believed, and yet he saw some merit in them and believed that his own theory could cover them if it were perfected. Another motive was to make psychoanalysis adequate for treatment or at least interpretation of the psychoses as well as the neuroses. Dementia precox (or schizophrenia) was a special challenge. Analysis was not successful with schizophrenic patients, but it did seem that their trouble, their withdrawal from reality, indicated a disturbance of ego rather than of libido. So from 1914 on we find important changes beginning to take shape in Freud's theoretical writings.

NARCISSISM. In the old Greek tale of Narcissus, this handsome youth, untouched by the charms of a beautiful maiden, falls in love with his own reflection in a glassy pool and is transformed into a flower that bends over the water. A narcissist, accordingly, would be a person in love with himself, and the term had been applied to a person, male or female, who obtained his sexual satisfaction from admiring himself in a mirror and caressing his body as if it were that of another person. Much more common than this frank, naïve narcissism, Freud believed, were less conscious forms of self-love which he chose to call by the same name (1914a). The schizophrenic is withdrawn from the world, has lost his interest in persons and objects, and seems to be wholly absorbed in his own self. Freud said that the schizophrenic has withdrawn his libido from the external world, probably because of disappointment or disillusionment in love, and has centered his love life on himself. Because of this extreme narcissism he is distinctly abnormal, psychotic. But an individual may be narcissistic to a degree without being deranged. Just as a lover "sees with eyes of love" instead of viewing the loved person objectively, so the moderately narcissistic individual will view himself lovingly rather than coolly and objectively, overrating his charms and merits and underrating his faults. By this standard everyone is somewhat narcissistic, Freud was quite willing to believe, but some much more than others. One who always craves love and admiration, without feeling love and admiration in return, is strongly narcissistic.

PRIMARY NARCISSISM. Self-love, Freud argued, must precede object love, since the infant has at first no perception of objects but only a vague (unconscious?) awareness of himself. But why should the infant love at all before he has found an object to awaken his libido? Freud conceived of libido as a form of instinctive energy or excitation arising in the organism from biological sources like the action of sex hormones. It is generated from within, seeks an outlet but at first finds no outlet, and is dammed up within as self-love. When the child has begun to explore the environment and find suitable objects (persons), his libido goes out to them. It goes out to the mother especially. It is sure to encounter some rebuffs and frustrations and then is drawn back, partially at least, into the self. The more object-libido, the less self-libido, and vice versa. The normal condition after early childhood is for part of the libido to be directed toward external objects (persons) while part remains attached to the self, the proportions varying from time to time and from individual to individual.

The concept of narcissism was evidently very congenial to Freud and yet it caused him considerable embarrassment on the theoretical side. Here he had self-love, or ego-libido, combining the two major instincts which he had regarded all along as polar opposites. How was he now to account for the conflict of motives which was basic to his whole theory of the neuroses? He could not go along with Jung and regard the libido as a unitary and all-inclusive instinct. He still had the polarity of self-libido versus object-libido, but he needed some sharper and more drastic conflict of motives. So it seemed to him, and he apparently labored several years before reaching an acceptable solution.

LIFE AND DEATH INSTINCTS—EROS AND THANATOS. Finally (1920) Freud took the bull by the horns and said to himself, in effect: "Very well. The instincts of self-preservation and propagation of the species, though having different immediate goals, are ultimately alike in being aimed at growth and increase of life. Let them be combined into an inclusive life instinct, and what have we got left to oppose them? What, indeed, except a death instinct!" The assumption of a basic death instinct was not absurd to a thoroughgoing motivationist like Freud. Since death is the matter-of-fact goal of life, there must be inherent in living matter an urge or tendency toward that goal. There must be a primal, unconscious drive toward death, and it must be present in every individual from the beginning to the end of his life. Polarity enough! Eros and Thanatos—Eros the principle of life and growth, Thanatos the principle of decay and death; Eros the loving and constructive, Thanatos the hateful and destructive.

If, however, there is a death instinct, it must somehow manifest itself in the feelings and behavior of human beings. Here Freud could reason as he did in the case of narcissism. Just as the libido is generated within the organism but attaches itself to external objects, so also with the death instinct. It manifests itself for the most part not as a desire to die but as a desire to kill. Turned outward it is the urge to destroy, injure, conquer. It is the hostility motive, the aggressive tendency, which certainly manifests itself abundantly. Finding something outside to destroy, it does not need to destroy the self. But when frustrated in an external aggression it is likely to turn back upon the self as a suicidal tendency. Its scope, like that of libido, must be very wide. It is not limited to homicide and suicide but covers the milder forms of aggressiveness, whether directed toward the self or toward external objects. Self-punishment and self-condemnation are included, and so are jealousy among rivals and rebellion against authority.

INCREASING EMPHASIS ON HOSTILITY AND AGGRESSIVE-NESS. From the viewpoint of this later theory of motives, it seems strange that Freud did not accept the basic role of hostility much earlier. He had much to say of hostility even in his early writings. The unconscious wishes that were fulfilled in dreams were often spiteful wishes such as the childish desire for the death of a brother or sister. In the Oedipus complex the boy becomes hostile to his father as the one who is frustrating his love demands on his mother. But in the earlier theory Freud was satisfied to regard hostility as merely a self-evident corollary of frustrated libido. The libido was energy which could be displaced from one object to another and even from one emotion to another or from one kind of behavior to another. So the transformation of love for the mother into hostility for the father seemed possible without any new drive coming into play. The love-hate ambivalence manifested in the feelings and actions of friends and lovers all came from the libido drive. And the cruelty of the sadist who obtains sexual satisfaction only when subjecting his love mate to torture could also, so it seemed at first, be merely a distortion of the libido. But with the death instinct accepted, Freud's view of sadism changed. "How can the sadistic drive which aims at injury to the loved one be derived from the life-sustaining Eros? Must it not stem from the death instinct?" (1920) And the love-hate ambivalence must be a fusion or alloy of the two basic drives rather than a mere distortion of libido alone. Any concrete motive is a fusion of love and hate, of constructiveness and destructiveness.

Man's constructive activities are at the same time destructive. To build a house he chops down trees. Any action on the environment destroys or at least disturbs the existing state of affairs. The muscles are primarily the agents of aggression, and in any dealing with the environment aggression leads the way, with Eros joining forces later. Such statements are found in Freud's later works.

In his earlier thinking on social psychology Freud emphasized the conflict between the sexual demands of the individual and the restrictions made necessary by social life. In his later

works he laid at least equal emphasis on the natural hostility of
man to man as the great obstacle to civilization (1930). The
individual's demand for justice and fair play arises from jealousy. Each child in a family wants to be the favorite but
finally backs down to the extent of saying, "If I cannot be the
favorite, neither shall you. We will all be equals" (1921).
Eros tends to bind men together in families, clans, and ever
larger groups, always with love and justice within the group but
with hostility and aggression for outsiders. Civilization develops through the conflict and fusion of these two major
drives.

The difference between Freud's earlier and later theories of
motivation can be brought out by reference to family life.
Since the family is based on the reproductive function and centers in the sex act, the earlier theory regarded family life as
wholly motivated by the sex instinct. Freud ridiculed anyone
who failed to see a woman's behavior in childbirth as a clear
example of sex behavior driven by libido. Since the mammary
glands are sex organs, nursing the baby is sex behavior, and by
extension all care of the child is sex behavior. The child, being
born into this sexually motivated milieu and participating in its
activities, is necessarily sex-motivated when he nurses, when he
is bathed, when he is loved and protected in any way. His demands on the family are sex demands, and even his jealousy
and rebellion when his demands are not fully met are direct
derivatives of the sex motive that dominates his entire life in
the family circle. So far the earlier theory. But with the recognition of a primary destructive tendency the picture changes.
Now the baby comes into the world with a primary tendency to
fight his environment. This aggressive tendency accounts for
his rebellion and jealousy. By itself it would make life impossible in the family group, but the erotic tendencies come to the
rescue and by fusing with the destructive tendencies lead to behavior which is a workable balance between love and hate.

The death instinct was a bitter pill for many of Freud's
loyal followers, nurtured as they had been on the libido theory.
It gave a harsher picture of human life. To Freud it was more
and more convincing in his old age (1932, pages 124-143;

1940), passed in a period of wars and persecutions. He became more conscious of an aggressive tendency in himself. He had always been a "good hater" according to the testimony of his most devoted disciples (as Reik, 1940, page 6; Sachs, 1944, page 116). His early "debunking" of so-called "innocent childhood" was followed late in life by works tending to "debunk" religion (1927, 1937). Though he believed these efforts to be only what was demanded by his loyalty to the truth as he saw it, psychoanalysis itself would indicate that the aggressive motive must have furnished the fundamental drive.

In Freud's earlier theory maladjustments were traced to the repression of libido, and a considerable change would be revealed by any emphasis on the repression of the aggressive tendency. Without going quite so far himself, Freud certainly came near it in such statements as these:

What we have recognized as true of the sexual instincts holds to the same extent, and perhaps to an even greater extent, for the other instincts, for those of aggression. . . . The limitation of aggression is the first and perhaps the hardest sacrifice which society demands from each individual [1932, p. 143].

The holding back of aggression is unhealthy, creates illness [1940, p. 14].

Some of Freud's relatively orthodox followers of the present day speak confidently of repressed aggression as the source of neuroses. Franz Alexander (1942, pages 167, 232), while defending the general theory of the Oedipus complex, believes its essence is not the boy's sexual demand for the mother, but rather "a possessive attachment to the person on whom the child depends for satisfaction and security, and jealousy and hostility against competitors." These hostile impulses, if carried out, bring quick punishment and have to be repressed. "The repression of hostile impulses thus becomes the most significant fact in the domestication of the human animal and is, in conjunction with anxiety, the core of every neurosis."

No one has been more confident of the hostility motive than Karl Menninger (1938, pages, 81, 427; 1942, pages 128, 134, 167). He regards Freud's death instinct as an important theory but not so well established as the wish to kill or destroy and the wish to be punished for wrongdoing. The suicidal tendency springs from the wish to be punished rather than from any demonstrable wish to die. In normal behavior the erotic and destructive tendencies are fused, as Freud said, with destructiveness taking the lead. The newborn child "begins to respond to the irritations of the outside world, meeting them first with hostility, then with tolerance, finally with affection. . . . In the normal course of development, the constructive energies begin to assume dominance." It is the aggressive tendency rather than libido that undergoes sublimation, as it does in both work and play, and psychotherapy consists very largely in finding suitable outlets for aggression.

An orthodox and yet discriminating presentation of Freud's theories, both early and late, is found in the work of Otto Fenichel. He did not accept the polarity of life and death instincts and argued that no basic polarity of motives is necessary. "Of course, the existence and importance of aggressive drives cannot be denied. However, there is no proof that they always and necessarily come into being by a turning outward of more primary self-destructive drives." Aggressiveness is rather a mode of responding to environmental conditions, and conflict of motives also can result from environmental conditions rather than from any basic internal polarity (1945, pages 54, 59).

EGO, ID, AND SUPEREGO AS PARTS OF THE PSYCHE. Another major alteration in Freud's theory, made at about the same time as his shift from the ego-libido polarity of motives to the life and death instincts, had to do with his doctrine of the unconscious. A belief in the reality and importance of unconscious mental processes was fundamental in Freud's thinking throughout his life. At first he regarded the unconscious and the conscious as the two component parts of the mind (or soul). There was, indeed, a "preconscious," consisting of memories and wishes that could easily be summoned into full consciousness, but the conscious and preconscious belonged to one system as opposed to the unconscious material which lay beyond the reach of the conscious mind. The conscious self was in touch with the environment through the senses and acted on the environment by use of the muscles. It was engaged in perceiving, thinking, remembering, and acting. The unconscious was constantly striving to emerge into conscious behavior but was held down by the conscious self. The conscious self was also called the ego, and the ego had the task of resisting the unconscious.

But this simple scheme ran into the difficulty already mentioned (page 175). It was found that patients under analysis were not aware of their own resistances. Consciously they were trying to recall certain experiences or to engage in "free association," but unconsciously they were resisting. The ego, as the resister, was therefore acting unconsciously. It must be partly conscious and partly unconscious. The ego is the manager, the executive, but it exerts its control unconsciously in large measure. If we picture the whole psyche as a sphere—like the earth—the outer crust is the ego which makes contact with the external surroundings and also with the interior. It is conscious externally and unconscious internally. The interior of the psyche, which Freud now named the id, is wholly unconscious (1923).

The id consists primarily of drives, inherited instincts, or urges. These are not quiescent but continually strive outward toward satisfaction in behavior. But the id has no direct access to the environment; it has no sense organs or muscles. It does not know anything, it cannot do anything of itself. It is unorganized, unstructured, like a boiling cauldron of mixed desires, libido and destructiveness seeking an outlet. The only outlet is through the ego, which at first is little developed and offers little resistance to the surging of the id. But the ego learns from experience. It gets to know the dangers of the environment and the necessity of restraining the id. Its job is to take over the instincts from the id, as far as it can, and make them conform to the reality principle. But when it "represses" a desire of the id, this repressed desire and its associated objects and experiences are driven down and added to the id, so making it even more troublesome than before. When the ego is strong enough to master a desire, making it bide its time and take its humble place in a rational plan of life, then the ego is performing its own proper function. Psychoanalysis helps maladjusted persons to substitute rational control for frightened repression and so to build up the ego at the expense of the id. "Where id was, there shall ego be" (1932, page 106).

As if the ego's task of controlling the id were not enough, a third part of the psyche emerges in early childhood to complicate the problem. Because the child is made to feel his weakness and inferiority in comparison with his parents and other adults, he takes these superior beings as models, "identifies" with them and builds up an ego-ideal, which is himself as he aspires to be. But these superior beings are not simply admired; they are feared. They punish him; they tell him he is naughty; they have rules of right and wrong which he must obey. Finally he adopts these external commands as his own internal laws of conduct and keeps watch over himself to make sure he does not disobey. So the ego is split into two: the doer or executive which remains the ego proper, and the watcher and moral critic which is the superego.

The superego corresponds to what we ordinarily call conscience, so far as conscience means a blind feeling of right and wrong rather than a knowledge of what is good for us and socially valuable. The superego says "Thou shalt" and "Thou shalt not" without saying why. It cannot explain its commands because the source of its authority is buried in the unconscious. Freud believed that the rudiments of the superego were inherited from primitive mankind and that it took shape largely in each child's struggle with the Oedipus complex (page 179). Some neurotic patients are excessively conscientious. They are never satisfied with their own behavior but always accuse themselves of sins of omission and commission. They feel guilty for acts which they have not performed if they have merely thought of doing them, and they may go through elaborate rituals of self-punishment, making life miserable for themselves and their friends. They admit that their guilty feeling is irrational, but they cannot get away from it. Their superego is fierce and relentless. In general Freud held that the superego is motivated by the aggressive tendency turned inward against the ego.

All the instinctive motives, except fear, belong primarily to the id. The superego appropriates some of the aggressive tendency for use against the ego. The ego, so far as it succeeds in mastering the instincts and making them contribute to organized living, has all the motives at its disposal, while its own peculiar motive is the need for security, revealed by its fears and anxieties.

The proverb tells us that one cannot serve two masters. The poor ego has a still harder time of it; it has to serve three harsh masters, and has to do its best to reconcile the demands and claims of all three. These demands are always divergent and often seem quite incompatible; no wonder that the ego so frequently gives way under its task. The three tyrants are the external world, the superego, and the id. . . . The ego . . . feels itself hemmed in on three sides and threatened by three kinds of danger, towards which it reacts by developing anxiety when it is too hard pressed. . . . I must add a warning. When you think of this dividing up of the personality into ego, superego and id, you must not imagine sharp dividing lines . . . we must allow what we have separated to merge again [1932, p. 103].

As to the merits of Freud's later system, he himself points out one difficulty in the last words quoted. This dividing of the individual into distinct entities which are always warring against each other gives an unreal picture of what actually goes on in thought, feeling, and behavior. For scientific purposes, to be sure, we require not so much a realistic picture as a working model, a conceptual framework in which we can think clearly and predict what behavior will occur under given circumstances. Did Freud himself in his later works find his system of scientific value? In some passages he indicates that it was of definite value, while in other passages he seems to be struggling with its complexities. The ego remains a somewhat ambiguous concept. In contrast with the id or superego it is the active, executive function. In contrast with the libido it is still the instinct of self-preservation. In contrast with the external world it is the entire individual, as it must be in narcissism, for the ego that is loved is not the executive function but the self as a whole. One must say, too, that if Freud overdid the libido in his early theory, he overdoes hostile aggression in the later theory. *Aggression* is an ambiguous word, sometimes implying anger and hostility, sometimes vigor and initiative. It must be a mistake, so we feel, to regard all human activity as either erotic or destructive, in any reasonable sense, or as combining the two in some kind of fusion. There must be outgoing, constructive motives that are not erotic, and energetic, enterprising motives that are not belligerent. A sculptor and a mineralogist stand before a block of marble. The sculptor says: "I love that stone; I want to hug it to my heart. I hate it; I want to smash it into powder. So I will compromise by carving it into the form of a beautiful girl." The mineralogist says: "I love it, I hate it, so I will compromise by cutting a thin section of it which I can examine through a microscope to bring out its inner structure." Must not other motives be present to govern the devoted attention which these two people will give to a block of stone?

Freud himself was a man of marvellous energy and enterprise, a man of intense devotion to his work—a keen observer, a fearless and original thinker. However his motives may be psychoanalyzed, and however his theories may be finally evaluated, he was a stimulating pioneer whose important place in the history of psychology is amply assured. And we must not forget that his primary contribution was to the understanding and treatment of the neuroses. His invention of the psychoanalytic method and his recognition of motives and their conflict as important factors in the causation of neuroses, and probably also of psychoses, are acclaimed by psychiatrists of all schools though they may differ from him considerably on many matters of theory and practice.

The psychoanalysts of today vary among themselves in theory and practice and feel free to differ from Freud more than was the case two or three decades ago. Yet they all honor Freud as the founder and master. Since we cannot hope to do any sort of justice to the many who deserve our attention, we must content ourselves with brief accounts of a few, beginning with Jung and Adler, already mentioned as being early dissenters. These two men were not pupils of Freud in the full sense, for they had both embarked on their careers before coming under his influence. For a few years they were contented to accept his leadership, especially in such matters of technique as free association and dream analysis, but their ideas soon showed so much divergence from Freud's that he was unwilling to have them call themselves psychoanalysts. Freud found it possible to incorporate some of their ideas in his later system, and some of their ideas have been revived by later psychoanalysts. Neither Adler nor Jung has had anything like Freud's great following, and the same can be said of several other early adherents of Freud who broke away because of more or less serious theoretical heresies.

Alfred Adler and the School of "Individual Psychology"

It was about 1912, ten years after psychoanalysis had begun to attract some medical adherents, that cleavages first appeared in the group that had gathered around Freud in Vienna and in the young international association of psychoanalysts. Alfred Adler (1870-1937) of Vienna differed from Freud in several respects, most noticeably at first by his emphasis on ego rather than libido as the great motivating force in life and the source of neurotic difficulties. On separating, or being separated, from Freud's group, Adler started a rival school of "individual psychology," so named to emphasize the importance of individual differences in personality, dependent on differences in early environment, which were relatively uninteresting to Freud.

The "infantile sexuality" which was so much stressed by Freud seemed to Adler a strained interpretation of the little child's behavior. Much more obvious and fundamental in Adler's view were the child's resistance to domination and eagerness to dominate. The child is actually weak and inferior in many ways to those around him and at times feels inferior, but he combats this feeling by asserting himself as far as possible and by aspiring to grow up and be superior. Everyone, Adler said, has a fundamental will for power, an urge toward dominance and superiority. If an individual feels himself inferior in some respect, he is driven by this feeling of inferiority toward a goal of superiority. He strives to make himself superior or at least to put up a pretense of superiority. He is driven toward *compensation* of one kind or another. He may genuinely compensate for an inferiority by well-directed effort, as Demosthenes overcame stuttering by practice in speaking on the seashore with pebbles in his mouth and became the greatest orator of Greece, or as Theodore Roosevelt overcame his frail physique by ranch life and became a "rough rider" and an explorer. Or the individual may compensate for inferiority in one respect by achievement in some other direction, as the boy who is muscularly weak may find he can shine in school. Many a man whose success in life makes us suppose him proud and perfectly sure of himself turns out, if we come to know him intimately, to have suffered from strong feelings of inferiority which he has not wholly overcome. In short, Adler regarded the self-assertive impulse rather than the sex impulse as the major drive, and as the drive most likely to be frustrated by the environment. It was likely to generate hostility toward competitors, antisocial attitudes, and the maladjustments of neurosis and psychosis.

But how can this individualistic, aggressive tendency be held in check so that community life may be at all possible? Adler, no less than Freud, was forced to provide a polarity of motives, though disinclined to appeal to heredity and innate drives. The child has at least a native capacity for friendly, loving response, and this germ will develop into a loyal cooperative spirit if the child is properly treated in the first few years. The mother, as the young child's closest associate, has the task of developing this spirit by establishing a genuine human relationship with her child. She makes a mistake if she pampers the child and allows him to dominate over her without limit, or she may make the contrary mistake by dominating over him at every point and seeking to break his independent spirit. What he needs is to get the spirit of give-and-take, cooperation, interest in people. With this basic social attitude established, the child is prepared to meet the problems of life with confidence and without hostility.

Of course the mother cannot be held solely responsible. The entire family situation with which the child has to cope in his first few years stimulates him to develop a certain attitude toward life—a certain "style of life" in Adler's well-known phrase. The pampered child expects always to command and let somebody else do the work. The bullied child takes the attitude of trying to escape to a safe distance. The oldest child in a family tends toward a conservative attitude, seeking to keep what he has and not be displaced by the second child, who tends to adopt the radical attitude of changing things in his favor. These attitudes or styles of life, formed in the first few years, are extremely persistent. Each individual adopts his style early in life and maintains it as he meets the problems of youth and adult life. Thus Adler, no less than Freud but in a very different way, laid great stress on the family situation as formative of the individual's character.

While not questioning the importance of the sex impulse, Adler did not allow it the fundamental role assigned to sex in Freud's earlier theory. The first problems of life are not sexual, and by the time the urgent problems of sex are encountered the individual's style of life is already formed. The sex life has to find its place in a total style of life with its goal either of selfish or of socialized superiority. When psychoanalysis attempts to center everything about sex it gives a distorted picture of the individual's activities. Sexual impotence or frigidity, for example, may be merely an unconscious stratagem enabling a person who lacks social feeling to get the better of the partner. Of the three typical problems of life—community living, occupation, sexual love—it is the social task that the child meets first, and his social adjustment sets the pattern for his approach to the other problems as they arise. If the child's social attitude is one of courage and cooperation, ready both to give and to receive, he can later take up the sex interest into this style of life and succeed in love and marriage. But if the child's social attitude is an anxious seeking to outdo his associates, sexuality will later be used as a means to this same end.

The neurotic, according to Adler, instead of suffering from repressed sex complexes, is hampered by a style of life that lacks a proper balance between the individualistic and the social drives. His goal of superiority is not realistic for community living, and he has to substitute pretense for genuine achievement. His unconscious aim is to score a fictitious superiority by evading difficulties instead of conquering them. In Adler's words (1930, pages 41, 46, 47) :

The problem of every neurosis is, for the patient, the difficult maintenance of a style of acting, thinking and perceiving which distorts and denies the demands of reality. . . . As the work of Individual Psychologists has abundantly proved, an individual goal of superiority is the determining factor in every neurosis, but the goal itself always originates in . . . the actual experiences of inferiority. . . . 'If I were not so anxious, if I were not so ill, I should be able to do as well as the others. If my life were not full of terrible difficulties, I should be the first.' By this attitude a person is able still to feel superior. . . . His chief occupation in life is to look for difficulties. . . . He does this more to impress himself than others, but naturally other people take his burdens into account and . . . he wins his way to a privileged life, judged by a more lenient standard than others. At the same time, he pays the cost of it with his neurosis.

In examining a patient the Adlerian psychologist seeks to discover the patient's style of life and the peculiar goal of superiority adopted in childhood and still followed in some way or other. His position in the family and the general family situation in childhood, his early memories, his likes and dislikes, his "heroes" from history or fiction, his occupational choices in childhood and later, all provide clues. His present manner of standing, walking, and sitting may reveal his "style." His way of shaking hands may be revealing, and even the posture he takes in sleeping. "When we see a person sleeping upon the back, stretched out like a soldier at attention, it is a sign that he wishes to appear as great as possible. One who lies curled up like a hedgehog with the sheet drawn over his head is not likely to be a striving or courageous character. . . . A person who sleeps on his stomach betrays stubbornness and negativity" (1930, page 215). Such sweeping statements, of which Adler made an enormous number, give the impression that he must have trusted a great deal to his own intuition and experience without being able to convey his methods, in writing anyway, to those who might wish to follow them. In practice, the "individual psychologist" bases his conclusions on a comprehensive view of the patient's behavior traits (Wexberg, 1929).

Dream analysis was accepted by Adler as one of Freud's major contributions to psychotherapy. But the dream should not be regarded merely as a fulfillment of old wishes; rather, it can serve to reveal the patient's emotional attitude toward his present problems. It is a symbolic rehearsal of an act that the patient must soon perform in real life and indicates his personal attitude toward this act. A man whose style of life was characterized by doubt and hesitation, being on the point of getting married, dreamed that he was halted at the boundary between two countries and threatened with imprisonment—a comparatively easy dream to interpret in Adler's way. Adler interpreted the plot of an entire dream rather than the associations obtained from the separate items. He discarded the reclining couch of the Freudian technique, preferring a more direct, conversational approach, free of constraint and with a "good human relationship" of social feeling between patient and therapist, both cooperating in the task of understanding the patient. Tact must be employed by the therapist to avoid the appearance of preaching or moralizing. The patient cannot be forced; no demands must be made on him, but he can be led gently to the point of seeing how he has been trying to achieve superiority "on the useless side of life" while missing his opportunities "on the useful side." The whole treatment takes much less time than is required for the "classical" psychoanalysis.

Adler's theory and practice have been generally condemned by psychoanalysts as being hasty and superficial. Yet they are tending to utilize his methods in certain types of cases. Not all patients require the same kind of treatment (page 167). Especially in assisting children to overcome their maladjustments, Adler's approach has proved its value. His theory, while certainly not a "depth psychology," does contain much common-sense truth that is applicable to daily life, and his conception of a "style of life" is a valuable contribution to the still embryonic psychology of character and personality.

Carl Gustav Jung and the School of "Analytical Psychology"

Outside of Vienna the chief early center of psychoanalysis was at Zurich in Switzerland, where Eugen Bleuler (1857-1939), the eminent psychiatrist who developed the concept of schizophrenia, became interested in Freud's work. His young assistant, C. G. Jung (born 1870), began using Freud's methods along with a method developed at Zurich of employing the already familiar "free association test" of the psychologists for the new purpose of detecting hidden "complexes" in psychiatric patients. Jung and Freud became personally acquainted and together founded in 1911 an international psychoanalytic society with Jung as the first president. But by 1913 it was clear that Jung's ideas were deviating considerably from Freud's, and at Freud's insistence Jung ceased to call himself a psychoanalyst. Instead he began to call himself an analytical psychologist and proceeded to develop an active school at Zurich and elsewhere.

Jung's innovations had to do with the neuroses and with the libido. Freud, by tracing the adult's neurosis back to the Oedipus complex of the small child, had revealed the "predisposing cause" of the neurosis but not the "exciting cause." Many a person harbors unadjusted complexes left behind from childhood and still does not fall victim to a neurosis until he is blocked by some new problem in adult life. Therefore, urged Jung, the exciting cause of a neurosis is some problem demanding for its solution a greater output of psychic energy than the individual can muster. (Here Jung was following Janet, whose lectures he had attended in Paris.) Failing to solve his present problem, the individual takes refuge in earlier ways of trying to handle difficulties. He regresses to the line he took as a child in meeting the Oedipus situation; and, his childish adjustment having been poor, reviving it now does no good. If his childish reaction was to withdraw from the real situation into fantasy life, he now tends to do the same—an obviously poor adjustment to his present situation. But now let his present problem "solve itself" without him—immediately his infantile behavior ceases, his neurosis disappears because its exciting cause is no longer present. Free association and dream analysis are used first to discover the patient's present problem.

Take away the obstacle in the path of life and this whole system of infantile phantasies at once breaks down and becomes again as inactive and ineffective as before. But do not let us forget that, to a certain extent, it is at work influencing us always and everywhere. . . . Therefore I no longer find the cause of the neurosis in the past, but in the present. I ask, what is the necessary task which the patient will not accomplish? [2]

Jung used the term *libido* in an even broader sense than Freud, stripping it of its distinctively sexual character. He made it include both Freud's libido and Adler's will for power, and in short the whole range of motives. He made it equivalent to Schopenhauer's will to live or to Bergson's *élan vital*. For Jung, then, libido was the total vital energy of the individual which finds its outlets in growth, in reproduction, and in all kinds of activity. Its first outlet in the infant is by way of nutrition and growth. It is the source of the child's pleasures, which are not sexual pleasures because the sex drive has not yet emerged out of the total urge to live. Jung expressed himself quite forcibly on Freud's conception of infantile sexuality (1928, pages 339, 340):

A strictly Freudian analysis . . . is exclusively a sex-analysis, based upon the dogma that the relation of mother and child is necessarily sexual. Of course any Freudian will assure you that he does not mean coarse sexuality, but "psycho-sexuality"—an unscientific and logically unjustifiable extension. . . . A child's regressive tendency can be designated an "incestuous craving for the mother" only figuratively. . . . The word "incest" has a definite meaning. . . . To apply the same term to the child's difficulties . . . is worse than absurd.

Freud still insisted that the libido was genuinely sexual even in childhood. Jung's effort to "purify" it seemed to Freud to betray the cause of psychoanalysis by discarding the great gains that Freud himself had achieved in sex psychology. A little later, however, as we have seen (page 184), Freud's study of

---

[2] Jung, 1920, p. 232. The quotation dates from a paper of 1913.

narcissism led him to combine libido and the other life instincts under the name of Eros, which is essentially the same as Jung's libido, except of course that Freud then postulated a death instinct or destructive tendency as the polar opposite of Eros.

Without accepting the death instinct, Jung was himself fully convinced of the necessity of postulating opposed forces, not only to account for conflicts and maladjustments, but still more to account for synthesis and normal development (Fordham, 1945). Jung's complicated theoretical system demands several polarities (Jacobi, 1943, 1945). The best known is that between *introversion* and *extroversion.* Jung believed it possible to distinguish two types of individuals, those whose interest and attention were centered on what went on in themselves (the introverts) and those whose interest and attention went out to the physical and social environment (the extroverts). The extrovert is "set" for dealing with the external world, the introvert for dealing with the inner world of ideas and feelings. The extrovert finds the values of life in the objects (and persons) he perceives and manages, while the introvert finds his values in thoughts, feelings, and ideals. The libido, as Jung would say, has an outward thrust in extroversion, an inward thrust in introversion.[3]

Individuals differ in the *direction* of their interest and activity according as they are introverts or extroverts; but they also differ in the *kind* of mental activity to which they are most inclined. Jung distinguished four main kinds of mental activity: thinking, sense perception, intuition, and feeling. Of these four, thinking and feeling are polar opposites, for so far as a man is thinking in logical concepts he is not valuing things in terms of likes and dislikes, pleasantness and unpleasantness. The extrovert thinker deals logically with external things, while the extrovert feeler is engaged in liking and disliking external things. Sense perception and intuition are regarded as another pair of opposites, sense perception being attentive to de-

[3] Following Jung's lead, many psychologists have attempted to work out the introversion-extroversion dimension of personality in detail, but are coming to the conclusion that more than a single factor is involved (Guilford, 1936).

tails, intuition to broad general effects and configurations. Combining the four kinds of mental activity with the two directions of interest, Jung has eight main types of individuals besides intermediate types which he also recognizes.

And this is not all, for there is still the great polarity of conscious and unconscious to be considered. Jung makes even more use than Freud of the concept of the unconscious. For Jung there are deeper and deeper layers of the unconscious. The least deep layer is the *personal unconscious,* which is composed in part of material repressed by the individual, as Freud pointed out, but also contains material that has been simply forgotten and material that has been learned unconsciously. Deeper than the personal unconscious lies the racial or *collective unconscious,* the common groundwork of humanity out of which each individual develops his personal conscious and unconscious life. The collective unconscious is inherited, coming down to us from our primitive ancestors. It is inherited in the structure of the organism, including the native brain structure, which predisposes the individual to think and act as the human race has thought and acted through countless generations. The collective unconscious includes the *instincts* (the "id" of Freud's later system) and it also includes what Jung calls *archetypes.* The instincts are primitive ways of acting, the archetypes primitive ways of thinking, and the two are not entirely separate, since thinking and acting go on together, especially at the primitive level. An archetype becomes an idea when it is made conscious, but in the collective unconscious it is more like a tacit assumption, such as the primitive belief in magic and action at a distance. While almost entirely submerged in the normal waking life of civilized adults, archetypes crop up in dreams, in the fantasies of children, in the delusions of the insane, and in the myths and fairy stories which have come down to us from distant ages and still make a mystic appeal to our inner nature.

The total psychic individual, in Jung's theory, is composed of the conscious and the unconscious, the two being complementary. What the individual is not consciously, that he is unconsciously. If he is an extrovert consciously, he is an introvert unconsciously; if he is of the thinking type consciously, he is of the feeling type unconsciously. All the capacities and potential interests which he has not developed and employed in his conscious life remain as latent tendencies in the unconscious. Success in practical life calls for specialization and leads to one-sided development. This is all very well in the first half of life, but in the second half of life, say from the age of forty on, the one-sided individual is likely to be oppressed by a sense of the emptiness and futility of it all and to long in a confused way for something deeper. Jung's theory and practice were aimed largely at such persons in the second half of life. Tap the unconscious, bring out and develop some of its latent potentialities, integrate them into the conscious life and so round out the individual's personality. First get at the personal unconscious, as was done by the psychoanalysts, and then advance gradually into the collective unconscious. Help the patient to become aware of his "shadow" or darker self, which comprises the tendencies that are rejected from the "ego ideal"—no easy task. Help the man to recognize the "eternal feminine" in himself, the woman to recognize her "eternal masculine." Recognize the deeply human religious instinct, which goes beyond Freud's pleasure-seeking instinct and Adler's will for power; without dictating the patient's theological beliefs, lead him through direct acquaintance with his own collective unconscious to a sense of oneness with mankind and indeed with the universe. And do not be disturbed as a scientist if your patient comes out with a rather mystical viewpoint, so long as life for him becomes once more meaningful and worth while.

In his treatment Jung encouraged his patients to immerse themselves in mythology and to give free expression to their unconscious in some form of artistic activity. He also made much use of dreams as indicators not only of disturbing complexes left over from the past, but also of constructive stirrings of the unconscious looking toward the future. He once contrasted his own and Freud's line of interpretation in the instance of a dream reported by a young man who had just finished his university studies but was unable to decide on an occupation and had become neurotic. The dream was (1920, page 219):

I was going up a flight of stairs with my mother and sister. When we reached the top I was told that my sister was soon to have a child.

This would be an easy one for a Freudian analyst, climbing stairs being accepted as a regular symbol for sex behavior, and mother and sister being the regular objects of infantile sex desires. (Adler could easily see a dependent style of life in this dream, since the dreamer did not climb the stairs alone.) Not satisfied with such a ready-made interpretation, Jung proceeded to obtain his patient's free associations suggested by the dream. The mother suggested neglect of duties, since he had long neglected his mother. The sister suggested true love for a woman. Climbing stairs suggested making a success of life, and the prospective baby suggested new birth or regeneration for himself—an archetype. Jung concluded that this dream revealed unconscious energies beginning to work on the young man's present problem.

Neo-Freudian Psychology

Since old controversies lose their sharp personal edge in the course of time with the disappearance of the original protagonists from the scene, it is natural that many who now call themselves Freudian psychoanalysts should feel free to deviate from the master to some extent. We have already noticed certain deviations in respect to short therapy (page 167), the Oedipus complex (page 181), and the death instinct (page 188). Rigid adherence to all of Freud's ideas is no longer considered necessary by those who use Freud's methods, perhaps with some freedom, and who certainly deserve the name of psychoanalysts. Some of them, however, who wish to differentiate their theories and even their techniques quite sharply from those laid down by Freud, are sometimes spoken of as forming a neo-Freudian school of psychoanalysis.

The neo-Freudians urge that psychoanalysis should shift its "orientation" from biology to sociology. It should regard itself as one of the social rather than one of the biological sciences. Instead of tracing human motives to the inherited instincts of self-preservation and sexual reproduction (with or without the death instinct), psychoanalysis should seek the source of human motives in the requirements of the human situation, which is always a social one. Instead of regarding the child's emotional development as being closely bound to his slow bodily growth and delayed sexual maturity, psychoanalysis should focus on the influences reaching the child from the family, the school, the culture. And since the family, the school, and the culture differ in different countries and change in the course of time, we have to expect corresponding differences and changes in child development, in human motives, and in the frustrations and maladjustments of the emotional life. What Freud so keenly observed in Vienna about 1900 might not hold good in other times and places. Then, it might be, the sex desire was most frustrated, but now the aggressive tendency or the need for security. Times change, and neuroses change with them.

The cultural point of view is forcefully presented by Abram Kardiner (1939, 1945) and by Erich Fromm (1941, 1947). Kardiner has opened up a promising lead for cooperation with social anthropology in studying the interaction of social institutions and individual personality. He believes it possible by use of the psychoanalytic approach to reveal a basic personality characterizing each culture. Fromm brings out the social psychoanalyst's divergence from Freud in such statements as this one: "We believe that man is *primarily* a social being, and not, as Freud assumes, primarily self-sufficient and only secondarily in need of others to satisfy his instinctual needs." Freud's oral and anal characters are not primarily due to fixation at these levels of sexual development but result from the way a child is treated by his parents. An attitude of dependence (oral) or of self-sufficiency (anal) is built up by the child in dealing with his whole social environment, and not simply in relation to feeding and defecation, though these important infantile problems certainly play their parts in his development.

Karen Horney in her interesting books has set forth the theory and practice of a neo-Freudian school, which she is actively engaged in developing by training young psychoanalysts in her methods. After fifteen years of work by Freud's methods, largely in Europe, she became convinced that they were not suited to many neurotic patients that she treated, both over there and in her new location in New York. Her dissatisfaction with Freud's theories was confined at first to his death instinct and his very unflattering conception of the feminine personality, but as she reconsidered Freud's whole system of theory and therapy she found that it hung together but that its major premises were highly debatable. Her thinking, she says, was influenced by the work of Fromm. Finally she found it possible, by abandoning Freud's biological premises and giving due weight to the social environment in individual development, to work out a revised psychoanalytic theory which freed the therapeutic practice from certain hampering restrictions imposed by the strict Freudian theory.

These "biological premises" had to do with Freud's "instincts" and with the process of child development. Freud thought of the instincts as internal sources of energy—which, by the way, is not a very biological conception, since no sources of energy are known except the general source in metabolism. We may better say, biologically, that he regarded them as tensions built up by internal processes. Hunger and the sex drive, at least, would fit this biological conception. Freud went on, not very biologically, to think of these tensions as dammed up and directed toward the organism itself until some external outlet was found, and turning back upon the self when frustrated externally—as if, for example, the organism tended to eat itself if it could find nothing else to eat, or to fear itself if it could find nothing else to fear. The safety motive evidently did not fit very well into this scheme. But when the death instinct was brought into the picture, that, too, was conceived as an inner energy or tension seeking something to destroy and turning back upon the self when blocked externally. These instincts could fuse and find perverted or sublimated outlets, but that was about all that the system would allow in the way of derived human motives. Now hungry behavior, sexual behavior, safety-seeking behavior, and even hostile behavior are certainly observed facts at a primitive level, so that the individual must have the native capacity to *respond* in these ways to certain stimulating conditions. If we substitute native responsiveness to environmental conditions for instinctive energies seeking outlet, we are on quite different ground and can allow much more scope to the environment in the formation of particular human motives. Something like this is the argument of Fromm and Horney with regard to the instincts.

With regard to the process of development Freud had a sound biological basis for emphasizing the importance of the prolonged human growth period, but he had no biological reason for dividing childhood into two periods, a sexually active period up to about five years and a latency period from then to puberty. This and other details in his theory of sexual development were based on his psychoanalytic data. No doubt Freud thought of the emergence of the Oedipus complex and the superego at about five years of age as a predetermined necessity in the growth process, while Horney would say that this whole development depends on the way the child is treated. But it is not good biology to neglect the influence of the environment, so that the new sociological orientation is not truly unbiological.

But the point in Freud's theory of development which Horney finds most objectionable is related to his conception of the unconscious. He taught that a repressed wish or experience remains isolated and unchanged in the unconscious to crop up from time to time in dreams, lapses, or neurotic disturbances of conscious behavior. The adult's maladjustment is due to the persistence of such impossible childish goals. What Horney has to say on this matter is fundamental in her theory and in her practice as well:

Freud tends to regard later peculiarities as almost direct repetitions of infantile drives or reactions; hence he expects later disturbances to vanish if the underlying infantile complexes are elucidated. . . . We recognize that the connection between later peculiarities and earlier experiences is more complicated than Freud assumed: there is no such thing as an isolated repetition of isolated experiences; but the entirety of infantile experiences combines to form a certain character structure, and it is this structure from which later difficulties emanate [1939, p. 9].

The character structure, first established by the child's experiences and reactions, is evidently about the same as Adler's "style of life," but the idea is more fully worked out by Horney. She does not regard it as absolutely fixed and unchangeable by later experiences and reactions. In opposition to Freud, she credits the individual with "constructive forces" that "strive toward growth and development," a forward-moving tendency that aims at a better self and the realization of one's latent potentialities, though it has to combat inertia and a fear of venturing forward into the unknown (1942, pages 21, 269). In the psychoanalysis of an adult, then, the great problem is to get the patient to see his present character structure, how it operates in his personal relations, and how it could be improved. To dig in memory for its origins in childhood may help or may prove to be a blind alley.

It is the neurotic character structure of her patients, rather than the normal personality, that Horney has been able to work out with great thoroughness. Whether the child shall develop a normal or a neurotic character structure depends primarily on his home environment and the way he is treated by his parents. With unfavorable treatment he is oppressed by a "basic anxiety," from which he seeks to escape by developing "neurotic trends." These, however, are ineffective and mutually conflicting, so that the child is left with an unintegrated personality and is incapable of putting his whole heart into any kind of personal relationship.

Basic anxiety is the child's feeling that the social environment is hostile and dangerous. It seems to him "unreliable, mendacious, unappreciative, unfair, unjust, begrudging and merciless . . . a menace to his entire development and to his most legitimate wishes and strivings" (1939, page 75). He is openly or subtly intimidated and given to understand that he does not "belong," his spontaneous expansiveness is throttled, and he is made to feel guilty if he dares to rebel or show any independence. Naturally the child tries to contrive some defense against such conditions, and when one line of defense fails he tries another, but none of them is really successful. If a rebellious boy runs away from home, he is forced back by his need for a home; the dilemma between his hostility and his dependence seems insoluble. To repeat, in Horney's words, basic anxiety is

... the feeling a child has of being isolated and helpless in a potentially hostile world. A wide range of adverse factors in the environment can produce this insecurity in a child. ... The child gropes for ways to keep going, ways to cope with this menacing world. ... He develops not only *ad hoc* strategies but lasting character trends which become part of his personality. I have called these "neurotic trends." If we ... take a panoramic view of the main directions in which a child can and does move under these circumstances ... three main lines crystallize: a child can move *toward* people, *against* them, or *away* from them [1945, pp. 41-42].

The moving-toward, compliant trend expresses the child's helpless dependence; the moving-against, hostile trend expresses his rebellion; the moving-away, withdrawing trend expresses his sense of isolation and not-belonging. To shift from one of these attitudes to another according to the circumstances would be normal (though none of them is the true social feeling), but if each attitude is compulsive and also ineffective, the outcome is a neurosis with severe conflict between the trends. Freud was right in regarding neuroses as the result of conflicts, but the conflicts are not between the ego on one side and the id, environment, and superego on the other, as Freud held, but between the individual's divergent trends in his struggle to cope somehow with the environment. This conflict of trends is not directly conscious but manifests itself to the subject in feelings of anxiety and fatigue, and to the trained observer by a curious inconsistency and ambiguity of behavior.

The goal of psychoanalytic therapy, then, is not to unearth and uproot the repressed desires of early childhood, but to enable the patient to see the conflicting trends that make up his shaky character structure and to awaken his constructive desire for a more adequate personality and better personal relationships. To trace the trends back to childhood may be helpful, but it is not enough. The patient must come to grips with his present trends and conflicts and see his present half-hearted and inconsistent behavior in relation to the trends. Such a therapeutic goal calls for prolonged psychoanalysis, though mild cases are much helped by brief treatment, and some patients can be trusted to do a good share of the analytical work for themselves, with only occasional guidance from the professional analyst (1942). The therapist takes a more active, directive part in the analysis than Freud recommended.

The sex drive and its social frustrations are no longer regarded by Horney as the prime factors in neurotic maladjustment. "Sexual difficulties are the effect rather than the cause of the neurotic character structure." Consequently the analysis and elimination of a sex problem often fails to reach the fundamental difficulty or to put the patient squarely on his feet (1939, pages 10, 55). The obstacles to harmonious social life, which Freud in his earlier theory located in the excessive demands of the sex instinct, and in his later theory in the instinctive hostility of every man toward his neighbor, are attributed by Horney to the competitive structure of our western civilization. Competitiveness is accused of "carrying the germs of destructive rivalry, disparagement, suspicion, begrudging envy into every human relationship" (1939, page 173). She seems not to take account of the elements of good sportsmanship and fair play that are present in well-organized competition.

With all these rejections and innovations, what is left of Freud's psychoanalysis that is acceptable to the neo-Freudians? Much rather than little, according to Horney, who lists the following as "fundamentals of psychoanalysis" (1939, pages 17-36):

1. *Psychic determinism,* without qualification
2. The *importance of emotional forces,* as contrasted with "rational motivations, conditioned reflexes and habit formations"
3. *Unconscious motivations,* the point being that while a motive may not be entirely unconscious, its role in the individual's personal relationships is hidden by rationalization, projection, and other such ways of distorting and concealing the truth
4. *Repression and resistance,* and the importance of analyzing the resistances during therapy

5. *Inner conflicts,* though the conflicting forces are differently conceived
6. The *persistent influence of childhood experiences,* though this influence is carried by the character structure rather than by separate unconscious memories
7. The *essential techniques of free association, dream interpretation, and the utilization of transference*

The "academic psychologist" certainly finds it much easier to go along with Horney than with Freud. It is interesting to observe that the elements in Freud's theories which aroused the greatest "academic" skepticism have been subjected to radical revision by psychoanalysts themselves. We must not leave the impression that the neo-Freudians have won the day and that practical unanimity now prevails in the whole body of psychoanalysts. Rather, the present seems to be a time of free experimentation with new ideas and procedures, and of active dissension, though less rancorous than formerly, within the total psychoanalytic school. "Psychoanalytic theory today, then, is far from an accepted body of dogma; on the contrary, a great deal of it is fluid, ambiguous, unintegrated and exceedingly polemic" (Masserman, 1946, page 92).

To what extent have the results and theories of psychoanalysis been taken up into general psychology? The field of motivation and personality in which psychoanalysis works is recognized by all psychologists as a very important though difficult field. They should welcome any enlightenment offered by the psychoanalysts; and in a general way much enlightenment has come to psychologists from their study of psychoanalysis. But the clinical experience and therapeutic success on which the psychoanalysts rely as evidence for their views seem to many and probably most psychologists rather a shaky foundation for scientific laws and theories. Simpler explanations can be offered for the same facts. When an experimental psychologist has undergone psychoanalysis, he may be able to verify the major phenomena of an analysis—the emotional upheaval with its anxiety and hostility, the revival of some childhood memories and attitudes, the new insights into one's motives and behavior—and still he may "see no need to speak of unconscious motivation or of unconscious dynamics" (Landis, 1940). He may wish that psychoanalysis would employ "operational" concepts, less steeped in Freudian theory. Freud's quest for the "deep" things of life, along with his flair for sensational ideas that would surely command attention, loaded psychoanalysis with a host of terms and concepts that do not fit readily into a sober scientific framework.

Besides his general theory Freud offered a large number of more particular laws or hypotheses which, it would seem, could be tested by psychological experiments and direct observation of children. There have indeed been not a few attempts by psychologists to do so, as can be seen from the critical survey of such work by Sears (1943). The net result, so far, is that Freud's statements regarding child life and development are overgeneralized, to say the least, while some of his dynamic laws can be verified or paralleled in relatively simple laboratory situations. Young children do show some of the sex interest that Freud assumed (though whether it is genuine libido or a liking for what is hidden and forbidden is not so clear). Some children do pass through a phase much like Freud's Oedipus situation, though it is the exception rather than the rule. Freud's idea that the memories of early childhood are lost because of repression occurring at the close of the early sexual period seems to be pretty well disproved, and the existence of a clear-cut "latency period" of sex interest in later childhood is very doubtful. On the other side of the ledger, it has been found possible to set up laboratory experiments demonstrating the tendency to *repress* and forget experiences that were humiliating to the individual, the tendency to *project* or attribute to other people those characteristics of the self which one is unwilling to admit, and the tendency when frustrated to *regress* to earlier and perhaps more infantile ways of acting. It is freely admitted that the laboratory situations are mild affairs in comparison with the emotional difficulties that sometimes entangle a person in real life. For that reason the experimenters may never succeed in putting some of Freud's dynamic principles to the test, but it is reassuring to have some of them verified in a small way and so brought down out of the clouds and made available, along with the experimenter's abundant material on the processes of learning and perception, for incorporation into the growing science of dynamic psychology.

The preliminary report (1948) of Kinsey and his associates on their statistical survey of sex behavior in the human male population of the United States contains much material that should have a bearing on the Freudian theories. The mere fact that sexual behavior is prevalent in the male adult and adolescent population has no particular bearing, unless perhaps as indicating that the restriction of sex behavior is not so marked as Freud seemed to assume. The great variety of common sex practices seems inconsistent with the tendency of psychiatrists to regard as pathological any but the strictly normal form of sex behavior. The question of "sublimation" is a slippery one, but if the meaning is that intellectual or artistic activity necessarily reduces the amount of sex activity, demonstrative cases of such sublimation were not found in the Kinsey sample. One definite result is that individuals differ enormously in the amount of their sexual activity—a fact to be borne in mind in any generalizing theory. Some young boys, even in the first year of age, were found to be capable of orgasm, and the reported incidence of such manifestation increased gradually up to adolescence. There was no statistical indication of Freud's latency period. Actually it is hard to find in such data any clear-cut proof or disproof of Freud's theories.

CHAPTER 7

HORMIC AND HOLISTIC PSYCHOLOGIES

Without forming any compact school, quite a number of psychologists during the past fifty years have started rebellions of some importance against what they consider the dominant intellectualistic and analytic trends in psychology. Some of them have objected mostly to any emphasis on intelligence, perception, learning, and thinking, to the neglect of emotion, motivation, and personality. Others have been most critical of the emphasis on any such separate functions of the organism, to the neglect of the organism as a whole. Those who insist that the most important part of psychology has to do with motives, purposes, and urges have called themselves purposive or hormic psychologists (*hormic* from the Greek *hormé*, "an urge"). Those who insist on considering the individual as a whole have called themselves self-psychologists, personalistic psychologists, organismic psychologists; because of their emphasis on the whole person or organism we may label them all *holistic*. Those who belong under the one head usually belong secondarily under the other also.

The most militant of these rebels was William McDougall with his purposivism or hormism, which we shall examine first.

Purposivism or Hormic Psychology

Just as structuralism finds the fundamental fact of psychology in sensation, behaviorism in bodily movement, and Gestalt psychology in the perception of patterns, so there is a school that starts from the fact of purpose. Human activity has these various aspects, if not more besides, and any aspect may excite the interest of a psychologist and lead him to build a psychological system upon the kind of activity that appeals to him as most significant.

THE FACT OF PURPOSE. In the older "arm-chair" psychology, will and purpose came in for a lot of discussion and good moral advice to the student, but when psychologists started to be scientific they found it difficult to handle this topic either from the purely introspective side or behaviorally. What is the experience of willing and purposing? There is a sensation of muscular tension, and an "I will" experience, but little more could be reported. Purpose seemed to belong under the head of meaning or value, which Titchener ruled out of an existential psychology. To Watson, purpose belonged decidedly among the outworn introspective fantasies which he threw overboard. Yet anyone who got acquainted with either Titchener or Watson soon felt that he was in the hands of a very purposeful individual. And both of them said as much in their writings. Titchener wrote freely of his *aim* to steer psychology into pure existential channels. "The psychologist seeks, first of all, to analyze experience into its simplest components. . . . Then he proceeds to the task of synthesis" (1909-1910, pages 37-38). And Watson is equally frank (1924-1925, pages 6, 11): "In 1912 the behaviorists . . . decided either to give up psychology or else make it a natural science. . . . The behaviorist . . . dropped from his scientific vocabulary all subjective terms such as sensation, perception, image, desire, purpose. . . . He wants to control man's reactions as physical scientists want to control and manipulate other natural phenomena." Now you should not accuse these men of inconsistency. They are lapsing in these passages into the language of common sense, abandoning for the moment their scientific vocabulary because they are not really talking psychology but only talking about psychology. They reveal as anyone else would the *prima facie,* commonsense fact of human purpose. Whether this fact is to be explained away or made fundamental in psychology is another question.

The purposive school makes purpose fundamental, while the early behaviorists sought to explain it away. No one has expressed this behavioristic attitude more clearly than Z. Y. Kuo (1928), an eminent Chinese adherent of the group.

> The concept of purpose is a lazy substitute for . . . careful and detailed analysis. . . . With better understanding of the . . . elementary stimuli and the stimulus pattern, with more knowledge of physiological facts, and with clearer insight into the behavior history, the concept of purpose of whatever form will eventually disappear. . . . The duty of a behaviorist is to describe behavior in exactly the same way as the physicist describes the movement of a machine. . . . This human machine behaves in a certain way because environmental stimulation has forced him to do so. . . .
> The rejection of the concept of purpose implies a repudiation of the current view of trial and error learning in animals. For this view is based on the notion that . . . the animal has a purpose, or is making some effort to solve a problem. . . . The purpose is preconceived or created by the experimenter—the animal itself has no aim or goal. . . . Whether an act is successful or unsuccessful depends on the purpose of the experimenter. From the objective standpoint, one act is just as successful or just as unsuccessful as any other one.

Surely these are the words of a purposeful individual! His purpose is to eliminate purpose from the behaviorist's scientific vocabulary and way of thinking. What to common sense is a purposive act must be analyzed into simpler processes. But suppose the analysis is successfully accomplished—does it prove the unreality of that which is analyzed? Has the chemist, by his successful analysis of water into hydrogen and oxygen, shown that water is unreal or that the property of water to dissolve salt, for example, and the immense role of water in the life of plants and animals, are only illusions? Water, the chemist will reply, functions in the world as a compound and not a mere mixture of hydrogen and oxygen. Purpose, we may well believe, is as real as water and plays an immense role in behavior —in human behavior at least—a role for psychology to investigate. Purpose is a "molar" fact (page 105), a distinctly psychological fact.

Purposive behavior is the same as goal seeking. In a fullfledged purposive act, as we know it in ourselves, two factors are combined: desire and foresight. We foresee the goal and we desire to reach it. Foresight and desire do not always go together. The aviator in a certain predicament may clearly foresee that he is going to strike a tree—without desiring that result. The hungry infant desires a full stomach—without knowing what he desires. In the primitive kind of goal seeking there is a striving without any clear foresight of the goal. Purposivism asserts the prime role of striving in all behavior; it emphasizes striving rather than foresight, though inclined to place much emphasis on foresight as well, even in animal behavior. It is because of its major emphasis on striving that it has adopted the name of hormic psychology.

McDougall Champions a Hormic Psychology. William McDougall (1871-1938), an Englishman by birth and education and for the larger part of his active career, was a distinguished student of biology and medicine and an active anthropological field worker before settling down in 1900 to the work of a psychologist, first at London and then at Oxford. During the first world war he was a medical officer in the British Army in charge of cases of war neurosis. After that war he became professor at Harvard and later at Duke University.

We have already noticed that McDougall was one of the first to define psychology as the science of behavior (page 73). A mere science of consciousness seemed to him "sterile and narrow." The behavior of men and animals under all conditions of health and disease was the proper field for psychological study. McDougall himself was trained in physiological methods. He was fond of animals and from time to time used animal subjects in his psychological experiments. Accordingly he stressed the importance of objective methods, but he was by no means inclined to reject introspection. If we limit ourselves rigidly to objective observation, we are apt to get a mechanical view of an animal's behavior and even a human being appears like a machine, as Kuo said in the quotation given. But we know our own behavior from inside and know it to be purposive and not mechanical; and there is no point in forgetting what we know by introspection when we turn our attention to animal behavior. McDougall was not afraid of anthropomorphism.

What, then, is behavior? As we look around in the world we find some things that are inert and mechanical, moved by external forces, and other things that *behave,* that "seem to have an intrinsic power of self-determination, and to pursue actively . . . their own ends and purposes. . . . The striving to achieve an end is, then, the mark of behavior; and behavior is the characteristic of living things" (1912, page 20). If anyone objects that we cannot observe the "striving," McDougall counters by pointing to several objective characteristics of goal-seeking behavior, as follows (1923, pages 43-46) :

1. It *persists.* An activity may start in response to a stimulus but continue after the stimulus has ceased. A rabbit scurrying to its hole after a momentary noise is an example.
2. With all the persistence there is considerable *variation* of the activity. An obstacle is by-passed and the same goal is reached as if there had been no obstacle.
3. The activity *terminates* when the goal is reached, and some other activity takes its place. The cat makes a dash for a tree and up the trunk, but then sits down on a branch and calmly watches the dog.
4. The activity *improves* with repetition. Useless movements are eliminated, and the whole performance becomes smoother and quicker. In short the animal learns to reach the goal more efficiently.

These objective criteria of purposive behavior, first formulated by McDougall in 1912 [1], are about the same as those later adopted by Tolman and other recent behaviorists. Although most of McDougall's work was not well received by the behaviorists, we must credit him with considerable influence in this respect (page 105).

If behavior, both human and animal, is characterized by goal seeking, a very important problem for psychology is to discover what goals are sought. The particular goals vary enormously, but they may fall into a few natural classes. The tree for the cat and the hole in the ground for the rabbit fall into the class of places of safety; they have the same fundamental

---

[1] In the fifth edition of his *Introduction to social psychology,* pages 354-355.

appeal. What are the fundamental appeals or motives that lead to goal-seeking behavior? This is the question raised by McDougall in 1908 in his *Introduction to social psychology,* on the whole the most important of his many books. It was an effort to provide a psychological foundation for the social sciences. Up to that time the psychologists had made no serious attempt to provide such a foundation but had left each historian or economist or sociologist to improvise a psychology for his own use. The experimental psychologists had made good progress in the study of such intellectual processes as sensation, perception, learning, memory, and thinking, but what the social sciences seemed to need was knowledge of human motives, thus far almost neglected by the psychologists. Why do men live in groups, why do they follow leaders and submit to governmental regulation—through mutual fear, mutual helpfulness, or simply inertia and imitation? Is religion the result of a religious instinct, and political life the working of a political instinct? Is all conduct motivated by a desire to obtain pleasure and avoid pain? The social thinker who required an answer to these questions adopted the best answer that suggested itself to him, while psychology offered no solution.

McDougall's revolt against the existing state of affairs was twofold. He objected to the rough-and-ready psychology that he found in the social sciences, and he objected to the one-sided intellectualism of psychology. This intellectualizing tendency had led to the assumption that all human conduct was rational and dependent on foresight of consequences. But why should some consequences be chosen rather than others unless there were some basic needs and preferences? Or consider the doctrine of "psychological hedonism," that all desire is necessarily a desire for pleasure. This "axiom" puts the cart before the horse, at least in many cases. For when is eating pleasant? Only when you are hungry, i.e., have a desire for food. The pleasure depends on the desire, and the desire is more fundamental than the pleasure; and so it is with other appetites. To get down to fundamentals we must find the natural desires and goals of men, some of which like hunger and sex desire may be common to men and animals.

McDougall set to work in earnest in the hope of developing a systematic psychology of motives for the use of the social sciences. His general assumption was that there must be a number of fundamental motives which are natural and hereditary and that all other motives must be derived from these primaries in the course of the individual's experience. He chose to call the primaries by the old name of "instincts"—a choice which he later regretted. An instinct for him was not a mechanical affair like a reflex or chain of reflexes. It was, rather, a motive, a striving toward some type of goal. There was emotion in it— the emotion of fear, for example, in striving to escape from danger. And there was a cognitive element in it, a perception of danger in the case of fear. He regarded an instinct as a complete mental process at the primitive level, capable of analysis into three parts: (1) On the receptive side, it is a predisposition to notice significant stimuli—like food odors when one is hungry. (2) On the executive side, it is a predisposition to make certain movements or to approach a certain goal. (3) In between is the emotional impulse or striving, the core of the whole instinct. Sometimes a distinction can be made between the striving and the emotion, but on the whole McDougall later concluded that the two were scarcely distinguishable.

It was necessary for McDougall to work out a fairly adequate list of human instincts or *propensities,* as he later preferred to call them (1932). If any important ones were omitted, the motivation of human behavior would not be sufficiently explained. But he had to take care not to admit any secondary, learned motives into his list of primaries, and not to fall into the absurdity of "explaining" each human activity by assuming an instinct for it—a political instinct to explain politics, a religious instinct to account for religion, an instinct of workmanship to account for the high standards of the expert workman, etc., etc. In 1908 McDougall listed twelve major human instincts. He reviewed this list from time to time without making any radical changes and by 1932 had a list of seventeen besides a number of minor ones such as the breathing instinct or desire to breathe when out of breath, and similar desires to sneeze, cough, etc. He included in this later list laughing, crying, sleeping, avoiding discomfort, and the somewhat questionable migratory tendency. His main list of instincts or native propensities remained as follows. It is instinctive:

1. To desire food periodically (hunger)
2. To reject certain substances (disgust)
3. To explore new places and things (curiosity)
4. To try to escape from danger (fear)
5. To fight when frustrated (anger)
6. To have sex desire (mating propensity)
7. To care tenderly for the young (mothering propensity)
8. To seek company (gregarious propensity)
9. To seek to dominate (self-assertive propensity)
10. To accept obvious inferiority (submissive propensity)
11. To make things (constructive propensity)
12. To collect things (acquisitive tendency)

Each of these instincts or propensities is to be regarded as a natural inclination or motive. The self-assertive and submissive propensities might be called the "pecking order" instincts, with reference to behavior observed in a henyard. The hens quickly establish a relatively permanent order of dominance, each one asserting her claim to any morsel of food as against certain other hens but yielding without resistance to certain others. Any particular pecking order is of course learned and not instinctive, what is instinctive being the tendencies to dominate as far as possible but submit as far as necessary. McDougall argued that submitting gracefully, following a leader happily, and being suggestible and imitative toward prestige persons were sufficient indications of a true native tendency to submit.

How seriously McDougall regarded his list of instincts or propensities can be seen from these words from the *Introduction to social psychology* (1908, page 44):

Directly or indirectly the instincts are the prime movers of all human activity . . . determine the ends of all activities and supply the driving power . . . and all the complex intellectual apparatus of the most highly developed mind is . . . but the instrument by which these impulses seek their satisfactions.

This quotation, however, tends to create a false impression of McDougall's system of motives, for he goes on to show how the instincts become modified by learning and experience. The fighting instinct, for example, is modified in two principal ways. On the sensory side it becomes attached to new stimuli; it becomes conditioned, as Pavlov would say. The stimulus arousing angry behavior in an infant consists of physical restraint and interference with the infant's movements. Later, restraint or interference of a more subtle sort, exerted by an adult's verbal commands, will arouse the child's anger. On the motor or executive side, too, much modification occurs through learning. The infant's slashing and kicking give place to biting and scratching, to hair pulling and striking with the fist, to angry talk and various indirect ways of injuring the adversary. In spite of all these sensory and motor modifications the instinct remains the same at its core, the core being the angry impulse to fight. The infant who reacts to some one holding his elbows by movements of slashing and kicking, and the adult who reacts to an offensive letter by devising some scheme that will damage the offender's reputation, appear on the surface to be performing entirely different acts, and yet the angry impulse to hurt the enemy is there in both cases. When to fight and how to fight are learned, but the primary motive of fighting back against interference remains the same from infancy to old age.

With only so much modification of the instincts as already described, the infant would scarcely become a humanized adult. McDougall recognizes another modification. The instinctive tendencies become combined into what he calls *sentiments*. They become combined by being attached to the same object. A man's love for a certain woman includes sex desire and also some of the tender, protective tendency that we called the mothering propensity. These two natural tendencies and probably others as well are attached to that one love object and are thus combined into the sentiment of love, which is a powerful adult motive. Patriotism is a sentiment. There is no single instinct of patriotism, but a man's native land becomes the object of several instincts. His country in danger awakens fear in him; an attack on his country awakens his anger; his country in rivalry with another country awakens his self-assertive tendency; and as his home it awakens loving emotions. Thus his country becomes the object of his complex sentiment of patriotism which can be a powerful motivating force in his behavior.

Your sentiment for a person is what the person means to you emotionally. Your sentiment for any object is what the object means to you emotionally. The object may be your family or another family, your school or another school, your religion or another religion, your ideology or another ideology. The self-assertive instinct is likely to be an important factor in any sentiment. You identify yourself with your school, for instance, feel that it is your school, boast of its triumphs, feel personally humiliated by its defeats.

McDougall did not say, as he is sometimes supposed to have said, that adult human behavior is directly motivated by the instincts. What he said was that human behavior is motivated by sentiments derived from the instincts and still possessing the emotional striving of the instincts. Behavior, he said, is not driven by purely rational considerations, but by loves and hates, interests, zeals, rivalries, enthusiasms, all of which have an emotional and impulsive character derived ultimately from the native propensities of mankind. Social behavior, then, while not based on a single social instinct, is based on loyalties and interests resulting from the instincts combined into sentiments. The gregarious propensity, by itself alone, would simply keep men together in groups; but group life gives a chance for all the instincts to become conditioned to social situations and combined into social sentiments.

EARLY AND LATER REACTIONS TO THE HORMIC PSYCHOLOGY. Such was the type of psychology which McDougall gave to the world in 1908. It was received with enthusiasm by psychologists—by many though not all of them—and quickly led to books and university courses on social psychology by psychologists. It created social psychology as a branch of psychology, where previously it had been treated almost exclusively by sociologists. By the social scientists, too, it was received with great interest and accepted for a few years as just what they needed. How social institutions are based on human instincts became the theme of a succession of books by sociologists and economists. Society, it was said, has to meet the instinctive demands of the individual. An industrialized society may get so far away from the primitive conditions of life to which the instincts were adapted that it can no longer satisfy the instinctive cravings of the individual. Mechanized industry may allow the workman too little play for his self-assertive impulse, and the now-common delay of marriage tends to thwart the sex instinct. Frustrated instincts tend to produce restless, neurotic behavior. Society may have to be remodeled so as to afford scope for the instincts. Such was the line of thought of Graham Wallas, the English economist, in his *Human nature and politics* (1908) and *The great society* (1914), and much the same line was taken by Ordway Tead in his *Instincts in industry* (1918) and by Carleton Parker in *The casual laborer and other essays* (1920).

McDougall's doctrine of instincts, though well received at first, ran counter to what may be called the professional bias of the sociologists. With their eyes fixed on the social group as the important object of study, they were less impressed with the natural demands of the individual than with another line of facts suggesting that the individual was molded by society. The individual derives his language, his manners and customs, and to a large extent his beliefs from the social environment. All that the anthropologists call the culture of the group appears to be imposed upon the individual and not demanded by him. While to the psychologist it may be self-evident that society is composed of individuals and must meet their demands, to the sociologist the main fact is that society is there before any given individual and imposes on him its demands and standards. We behave alike and "behave like human beings," not in the main because of our instincts, but because of the culture we all receive. Such is the characteristic approach of a sociologist or social anthropologist.

Among the sociologists, then, a long-smoldering discontent with the instinct doctrine broke into flame about 1920. The greatest single conflagration was a book by L. L. Bernard, in 1924, entitled *Instinct, a study of social psychology,* which sought to show up the silliness of much of the current talk about instinct and to demonstrate the unimportance of instinct in society. One part of the author's task was easy enough. No two psychologists gave the same list of instincts. Some allowed over a hundred, while others by pruning and combining brought the number down to two or even one. Such disagreement argued against the validity of the whole conception.

Bernard's more serious criticism was that what were called instincts in common speech and even in the psychology books were far from being purely instinctive. They were complex activities, differing from culture to culture and acquired by the individual from the social environment. Mating behavior with its forms of courtship and marriage was an obvious example. The human mother's care of her baby is not instinctive mothering behavior but a complex activity acquired largely from older women or from the doctors. And so with self-assertion, acquisitiveness, and constructiveness—as we see them among men they cannot be hereditary units. McDougall's belief in an emotional "core" of an instinct, present as the driving force in all its varied activities, seemed to Bernard a touch of mysticism. No doubt there were many biological instincts, like breathing and sneezing, but they were small affairs of little social importance. They could not be allowed the important role that McDougall assigned to the instincts; they did not determine the goals and provide the motive force for man's social behavior.

What does determine the goals and provide the motive force, in Bernard's opinion, is the social environment. This supplies the formative factors in the development of intelligence and character. Man's environment is very different from the natural environment in which biological instincts would be appropriate. Mankind, in the course of many generations, has built up a highly artificial environment of houses, roads, and manifold material objects, and also of customs and institutions. No doubt society has to meet the individual's biological needs, but in the main the individual is plastic and is molded by environmental pressures. A few sentences from Bernard will illustrate his point of view (1924, pages 26, 54) :

> There are two well-defined viewpoints in the social sciences regarding the importance of a theory of the instincts as a basis for the development of social theory. . . . The instinctivists, fairly represented by McDougall, maintain that the acquired elements in character or control are formed under the dominance of the instincts. The environmentalists maintain the opposite and look to the environment, especially to the psychosocial environment, for the formative factors.

Bernard counts himself decidedly as an environmentalist. For the most part, he speaks of environmental pressures determining the individual's behavior. He admits that the individual is not exactly putty, and that environmental pressures are really stimuli arousing the individual to respond. He would apparently agree with Kuo, who said (page 215) that the "human machine behaves in a certain way because environmental stimulation has forced him to do so," except that Bernard stresses the social environment. He appears to have little more respect than Kuo for the individual's purposes and motives. But you will find Bernard lapsing occasionally into a way of speaking that seems to give away his whole case. Notice what he says of "environmental dominance" (1926, pages 138-139) :

> Civilization is itself in large part a system of sublimations and repressions. We do not give our pugnacious, sexual, gustatory, fear, and gregarious impulses free rein. . . . The best method of control . . . is by what we call sublimation. This involves the turning of the impulses into derivative and substitute channels. . . . Our formative institutions . . . should be able to devise a system which will bend the native impulses to the service of the best abstract ideals of a cultural civilization.

If this last quotation fairly represents Bernard's views, there is no fundamental difference between him and McDougall. Both speak of native impulses which can be redirected or find new outlets in social life. Besides his theory of the sentiments, McDougall attempted to show in some detail how the instincts operate in society. For example (1908, page 279) :

> The instinct of pugnacity has played a role second to none in the evolution of social organization. . . . But its modes of expression have

changed with the growth of civilization; as the development of law and custom discourages and renders unnecessary the bodily combat of individuals, this gives place to the collective combat of communities and to the more refined forms of combat within communities.

Bernard could have quoted this passage to illustrate his "control by sublimation." Both men would seem to agree that there are native impulses that motivate social behavior, though Bernard would probably not agree that all social behavior can be traced back to native impulses and their combinations.

We have distorted the historical course of events by considering the sociological reaction against McDougall before the psychological. The psychologists had never accepted McDougall's treatment of the instincts with anything like unanimity. Both Thorndike and Watson soon criticized these broad instincts as poorly established and did not see much promise in the idea of native driving forces operating throughout life. But the main question for the psychologists was how far any complex behavior patterns were inherited rather than built up by the processes of learning. Doubts began to be raised whether complex actions were ever provided by heredity; it might be that only simple movements were so provided, while all complex behavior patterns, in man at least, had to be learned. At any rate, the native and the acquired elements in behavior were so interwoven as to make separation impossible (Dunlap, 1919). The outcome of this discussion was to make psychologists more critical of instincts and more inclined to lay all their emphasis on learning. In very recent years the pendulum has swung back a little, and the reality of some unlearned complex behavior has been admitted, at least in animals such as the much-studied white rat (Lashley, 1938).

This critical revision of the doctrine of instincts, however, has nothing to do with the essential doctrine of purposivism. Two different problems were mixed together in this debate on instinct. How far are behavior patterns native rather than learned? That is the question which has most interested the psychologists, and their answer has been the critical attitude of demanding proof before they will admit that a behavior pattern is native. The other problem has to do with native impulses or primary motives. It would not seriously damage McDougall's theory if he were forced to admit that almost all the behavior patterns of fear, anger, love, curiosity, self-assertion, and the other instincts are acquired by learning. What his theory demands of the fighting instinct is not a skillful fighting performance but an innate tendency to combat any interference by an angry reaction. If that tendency exists in human nature, operating in different patterns at different levels of behavior, we are justified in accepting a primary pugnacious motive.

This distinction between motive and behavior pattern had been recognized by McDougall from the start. The emotional-impulsive "core" of the instinct, which was native and remained unchanged by experience and learning, was evidently the motive. The sensory and motor parts of the instinct, which were modified by learning, made up the behavior pattern. In speaking of instincts as being combined into sentiments he was evidently referring to their "cores" and not to their behavior patterns. Thus he used the word *instinct* in two senses: to refer to a native behavior pattern with its emotional-impulsive core, and to refer to the core alone. In his latest statement of the theory (1932, page 78) he recognized this source of confusion and needless controversy and dropped the use of *instinct* in referring to human motives and behavior. A typical instinct, such as the nest-building of a wasp, includes a native ability "geared to" a native propensity. The native ability is shown by the fact that the wasp builds the characteristic nest of her species without ever having a chance to learn the use or form of the nest. The native propensity is shown by the fact that when she has matured to the egg-laying stage she devotes all her energy to building and stocking the nest. The human being has many native abilities (or capacities) and quite a number of native propensities, but the abilities are not innately geared to the propensities. So the human being has no full-fledged instincts (except the "minor" ones like breathing and sneezing). If his self-assertive propensity is aroused, he draws upon any ability that is convenient ("See what I can do!"), not upon one particular preordained ability; or if it is the sex propensity that is aroused, he may utilize any ability that seems likely to "make a hit." The abilities (in McDougall's view) do not have any driving force in themselves, but must be driven by the propensities, either by the native propensities or by sentiments derived from the propensities. We may indeed acquire "tastes" for certain activities, like music or bridge, i.e., we learn to like to exercise certain abilities for their own sake, but such likes (and dislikes) have no strong motivating force. "Broadly speaking . . . we may say that, while our sentiments determine the major goals toward which we strive, our tastes determine our choice of means, the kinds of activities and instruments we use" (1932, page 239). Another recent qualification of the theory is that an immediate goal has a strong pull, no matter what the ultimate motive may be. "If from any motive you set yourself to attain the goal"—the exit, for example, in a maze puzzle— "from that moment the exit becomes your goal, you foresee and desire the passing out through the exit. . . . It is the same whenever we solve a problem. . . . The solution is the goal towards which we look forward" (1932, page 348). In thus recognizing the motivating power of tastes, of which there are many, and of immediate goals, of which there are an indefinite number, McDougall seems to some of us to have modified his theory quite seriously (and desirably).

PRESENT STANDING OF THE HORMIC THEORY. Though McDougall laid great stress on native propensities and also on native capacities and individual differences, this emphasis on the native and hereditary was after all not the mainspring of his system. He wished above all things to win general acceptance of the fundamental importance of goal-seeking, of purposive striving. The older structuralists and behaviorists, as we saw, were averse to any such principle in scientific psychology, and many other psychologists regarded his idea of "driving forces" or "sources of energy" as a sort of mythology. By 1930, however, it seemed to him that his crusade had made noticeable progress. He wrote (1930, pages 3-4):

Fifteen years ago American psychologists displayed almost without exception a complete blindness to the most peculiar, characteristic, and important feature of human and animal activity, namely, its goal-seeking. All bodily actions and all phases of experience were mechanical reactions to stimuli. . . . Now, happily, all is changed; the animal psychologists . . . are busy with the study of 'drives,' 'sets,' and 'incentives.' . . . Much the same state of affairs prevails in current American writings on human psychology. . . . American psychology has become purposive . . . in the vague sense. . . . My task is the more difficult one of justifying the far more radical purposive psychology denoted by the adjective 'hormic,' a psychology . . . which asserts that active striving towards a goal . . . cannot be mechanistically explained or resolved into mechanistic sequences.

What he objected to was the tendency of psychologists, while finally admitting the fact of goal-seeking, to reduce it to some form of "mechanistic" process. Hunger, drowsiness, and perhaps sex craving were regarded by the mechanists as "tissue needs," chemical conditions of the organism predisposing to activity or inactivity. A "set" toward a certain goal could be conceived as a response to suitable stimuli and as operating like the setting of an adjustable machine which determines what the machine shall do. Thus purposes would arise as effects in the stream of natural processes and would produce effects in the same stream. Some psychologists, indeed, after going to great pains to show how purposes could be natural behavior events, were still afraid to allow them any causal efficacy—which was rather absurd, for if a purpose occurs as a natural effect, it must also be a natural cause of further effects. McDougall was deeply dissatisfied with all such schemes. If purposive striving toward a goal has any real influence on the course of events, it must operate by "teleological causation," he held, and not by "mechanical causation." He was not a complete teleologist, it would seem, for he did not go so far as to say that the future event exerts a pull on the present event. It is not, he admitted, the future goal-reaching, but the present goal-seeking that influences the present course of events. But it appeared to him that the goal-seeking must operate in some entirely different way from other causes, for it is energy directed *toward* a result. But is not all energy directed toward a change of state, just as all motion is motion toward as well as motion away from?

Most of us psychologists feel out of our depth in such speculations.

While McDougall exerted considerable influence on psychology in directing attention to the reality and importance of goal-seeking, he did not convert many to his hormic philosophy or even to the doctrine of "mental energies" corresponding to the native propensities. In this doctrine of energies he evidently stood rather close to Freud. His original 1908 book was written without knowledge of Freud's work, and his list of instincts is very different from Freud's polarity of two great instincts and, we must say, much closer to the facts of behavior. As he got to know Freud's work he was much impressed by its rich, deep appreciation "of the range of subconscious activities, of the wide and subtle influences of conflict, of repression, of sublimation, of symbolism, of the genesis of symptoms, errors, myths and dreams" (1936, page 103). And here is his general characterization of Freud's work (1936, pages 17-18) :

In my opinion Freud has, quite unquestionably, done more for the advancement of our understanding of human nature than any other man since Aristotle. . . . This judgment implies, of course, that there is much that is of value and relatively true in Freud's teaching. And yet I hold that every bit of such truth is mixed almost inextricably with error; or embedded in masses of obscure implications and highly questionable and misleading propositions.

McDougall expressed his opinions of the other schools with similar candor and picturesqueness. For example:

As to Wundt's *Outline of psychology*: "A quagmire of pedantry, a mass of confusion and error, lacking even the modest merit of internal consistency. . . . Experimental psychology of the strict Wundtian type may be said to have died of pernicious anemia under the too drastic purgative treatment of Dr. Titchener" (1932-1933, pages 197-198).

As to Gestalt: "The name is a novelty; but the principle has long been recognized" (1932, page 46).

As to Watson: "By repudiating one half of the methods of psychology and resolutely shutting his eyes to three quarters of its problems, he laid down the program of Behaviorism and rallied to its standard all those who have a natural distaste for difficult problems and a preference for short, easy, and fictitious solutions" (1926, pages 277-278).

Or again: "I regard Dr. Watson as a good man gone wrong . . . a bold pioneer whose enthusiasm, in the cause of reform in psychology, has carried him too far . . . and landed him in a ditch. . . . And, so long as his followers continue to jump into the ditch after him, shouting loud songs of triumph as they go, he does need great moral courage in order to climb back and brush off the mud" (1924, page 14).

As to the "middle of the road": "A deplorable influence in almost all parts of the world . . . largely responsible for the disappointing state of psychology . . . sterilizing for research and paralyzing for the teacher" (1936, page 11).

Such blandishments failed to win votes. Yet McDougall in his autobiography (1930a) reveals himself as a man desirous of approval from his colleagues as well as from the general public, and despondent over what he regarded as his small measure of success. His influence was probably greater than he thought, but it was limited by his insistence that psychologists should follow him beyond the proper bounds of psychology into regions that seem to us the province of philosophy.

Holistic Psychologies

The individual is a unit, a whole. Every psychologist would be willing to assent to this statement, and it would seem to offer no basis for any rebellion or controversy or for the formation of any school. Did not Titchener say that psychology was concerned with experience considered as dependent on the individual? And did not Watson say that behavior, as contrasted with the action of muscles, glands, and other separate organs, was the activity of the organism as a whole in relation to its environment? But perhaps these statements have not been taken seriously enough in the actual work of these psychologists or of psychologists in general. Such has been the complaint of quite a number of critics. We cannot speak of a holistic school, however, for these rebels have not spread out from a single center nor shown any tendency to come together and agree on a program. They would agree, and others with them, that the individual is a unitary organism, and that the human individual is a whole person. But with that as a starting point the question is where to go next, how to proceed on some distinctive line of investigation. What new holistic knowledge shall be sought, or how shall our existing knowledge be organized into an organismic or personalistic system? The answers given to these questions are rather divergent but still interesting and valuable.

Of all the holistic psychologists only a few of the most outspoken will be cited here, and these will be classified under the heads of organismic and personalistic psychology. The organismic group take a more biological, the personalistic a more social point of view.

ORGANISMIC PSYCHOLOGY. Let us notice first two main lines of attack against tradition that are suggested by the concept of the organism as a whole. The great enemy is sometimes the old mind-body dualism, and sometimes the still-prevalent tendency of psychologists to speak of separate functions and motives of the organism.

Adolf Meyer (born 1866, long professor at Johns Hopkins), who soon became the acknowledged leader of American psychiatry, rebelled as a young man against the mind-body distinction current in nineteenth century psychiatry. The cleavage between the somatic and psychic theories (page 8) seemed to him wholly unrealistic and unprofitable. As he pointed out in 1897, the organism in its development from the one-celled egg begins and continues as a unit. "In this unit the development of the mind goes hand in hand with the anatomical and physiological development, not merely as a parallelism, but as a oneness with several aspects." And in 1908 he wrote: "It is unfortunate that science still adheres to an effete and impossible contrast between mental and physical. . . . Mind . . . is a sufficiently organized living being in action; and not a peculiar form of mind-stuff." He found this "psychobiological" concept a better working hypothesis for psychiatric work than the materialistic and mentalistic approaches that were customary. If somatic disorders are found, well and good—diagnose and treat the patient accordingly—but if none are demonstrable, it is futile to imagine some brain disorder underlying the symptoms; it is better to utilize the available facts of the patient's behavior and life history. He should be seen as a person confronted with a situation that is too much for him, rather than merely as a "case" to be classified under some one of the recognized psychoses. His trouble can sometimes be traced in the Freudian manner to an unsolved problem of childhood, but often it has a more gradual development and amounts to a faulty habitual attitude toward social situations—a growing tendency, for example, to retreat from the real situation into the realm of fantasy. While not a prolific writer, Adolf Meyer was a great teacher and therapist and he built up in the Henry Phipps Psychiatric Clinic in Baltimore an outstanding and influential institution. His psychobiology has been found a very useful basis for psychiatric work. His point of view has recently found expression in "psychosomatic medicine," which looks for mental or emotional factors operating in such organic conditions as stomach ulcer and also for organic factors possibly present in cases of behavior disorder. (For Meyer's teachings, see Rennie, 1943; Richards, 1941.)

George Ellett Coghill (1872-1941) was led by a primary interest in psychology to a study of the nervous system and finally to a combined study of the early development of the nervous system and of behavior in the same animals. This he was able to accomplish by working with salamander tadpoles. The eggs of the salamander *Amblystoma* develop in fresh water, first into little motionless tadpoles, then into swimmers and finally into land walkers. Swimming occurs by a wavelike wriggling of the trunk and tail, before the legs make their appearance. When the legs do appear, their first movements are not separate and independent but occur only with the trunk movement as integral parts of the swimming action. As development proceeds, the leg movements become "individuated," in Coghill's terminology, so that the legs can move separately as in walking. Total organismic movement precedes partial movement. The total movement is not built up by the combination of originally separate movements, but the development proceeds from the whole to the parts. When this significant work first came to the attention of psychologists, they were inclined to suppose that the animal *learned* to isolate part movements out of the total movement—just as the beginner in piano playing learns to move his fingers separately instead of together as is more natural. But Coghill's anatomical studies showed that the individuation of leg and other movements was due to maturation and not primarily to learning. It is due to the growth of new nerve fibers into the legs, etc., and this neural growth precedes the emergence of the separate movements.

At any rate Coghill's view that the more general movements of the organism are primary and not built up by combination of smaller, local reflexes—as seemed to be the view of some older theorists—had much influence on later thinking in regard to child development. It led to work on the earliest movements of young organisms, including those of the human child before the normal time of birth, with a persistent effort to make sure whether general body movements always appeared before smaller movements of the arms, legs, fingers, mouth, eyes. The results are not quite the same in all species of animals. Not all local movements are individuated out of total bodily movements, even though Coghill's proposed law holds good to a considerable extent. The human infant at birth (i.e., after several months of motor development) certainly possesses many specific movements—sucking, vocalizing, grasping, eye movements, etc.—but also a large fund of movements that are relatively diffuse and non-specific, at least so far as any definite environmental effects are concerned; and it is mostly out of this fund that specific learned movements are formed (Carmichael and Pratt, in Carmichael, 1946).

In this line of active investigation we have an instance of an organismic theory leading somewhere. And yet, in a broad sense, it seems unimportant to a general organismic psychology whether motor development proceeds from the general to the specific or vice versa. For suppose that local movements did appear first and were later combined into the larger movements

WILLIAM McDOUGALL

WILLIAM STERN   MARY W. CALKINS

International News Photo

Photo by Sargent Studio

ADOLPH MEYER   GORDON ALLPORT

Photo by Lotte Jacobi

KURT GOLDSTEIN

—it would still remain true that the organism was a unit composed of interacting parts. How otherwise could the part activities combine? Sherrington, whose classic analytical work on reflex action has made him appear to the organismic biologists and psychologists as the archenemy, was actually the one who said, "The nervous system functions as a whole. Physiological and histological analysis finds it connected throughout its whole extent. . . . Are there in the body no reflexes absolutely neutral and indifferent one to another? . . . Two reflexes may be neutral to each other when both are weak, but may interfere when either or both are strong. . . . Correlation of the reflexes . . . is the crowning contribution of the brain towards the nervous integration of the individual" (Sherrington, 1906, pages 114, 146-147). Such statements can certainly be regarded as "organismic."

Kurt Goldstein (born 1878, now in New York), one of the strongest defenders of the organismic point of view, believes that the study of reflexes makes a poor and misleading approach to any true understanding of the organism's behavior. The reflex is supposed to be a constant, uniform response to a constant stimulus, but such constancy of the single reflex cannot be obtained except under constant conditions in the rest of the organism. Even the knee jerk, that typical local reflex, cannot be obtained in regular, uniform strength unless the leg is in a certain position and "isolated" from the rest of the organism by instructions to the subject to think of something else. And the knee jerk can be made exceptionally strong if the subject clenches his fists or is exposed at the proper instant to a sudden noise. Therefore "the reflex cannot be properly understood in terms of the isolated mechanism alone" (1939, page 69). A reflex is really an act of the whole organism and can be understood only as a particular manifestation of the nature of the whole organism. How absurd, then, to expect to understand the organism's behavior as a combination of reflexes! "There do not exist discrete, individual reactions of parts, as combinations of which the behavior of the organism can be understood. On the contrary, only knowledge of the whole organism leads us to understand the various reactions we observe in isolated parts" (1940, page 123). We must start with a true impression of the organism's unitary action; then we can see the reflex playing its part in this organismic action and so make our view of the whole organism more detailed and more diversified. We must proceed from the whole to the parts, not from the parts to the whole.

Isolation of pieces of the organism's behavior is characteristic not only of the physiologist's investigation of reflexes but also of the psychologist's study of habits, thoughts, motives, feelings, sensations, and perceptions. Every experiment demands constant conditions so as to isolate the particular phenomenon to be observed. Only by this isolating, analytic procedure can any scientific data be obtained. The organismic approach finds itself in a dilemma, since it wishes to see the organism in its behavioral wholeness and yet must resort to isolating observation in order to secure any dependable facts. It rejects the analytic-synthetic method of first examining the parts and then trying to piece them together. Instead it adopts the holistic-analytic method. First must come a holistic view of the behaving organism; then follows isolating observation which yields data for correcting and amplifying the first impression. The holistic or global impression plays the role of a working hypothesis which almost certainly can be improved in face of the particular facts as they are discovered. Or, the global view provides a framework for holding the facts, a framework that is not too rigid to accommodate itself to the growing mass of data. Or again, in Goldstein's words: "We do not try to construct the architecture of the organism by a mere addition of brick to brick; rather we try to discover the actual *Gestalt* . . . through which some phenomena may become intelligible. . . . We sketch a picture of the whole organism, which in turn, so long as we encounter discrepancies between this picture and factual experience, stimulates further questions and investigations" (1940, pages 23, 26).

The global picture or Gestalt shows an organism endowed with certain capacities and needs, continually challenged by the environment and seeking always to "come to terms with the environment" so as to achieve optimal performance. If the challenge is too severe, the organism is thrown into a "catastrophic" state of anxiety, a feeling of inability to perform its chosen tasks. Brain-injured men, closely studied by Goldstein in his medical capacity in Germany during and after the first world war, are especially subject to this feeling of "catastrophe," and their reaction is to get rid of the tensions so produced. But the normal tendency is not, as Freud and others have theorized, to get rid of tension, but rather to maintain an optimum of tension such as is necessary for accomplishment and progress. "Freud fails to do justice to the positive aspects of life. He fails to recognize that the basic phenomenon of life is an incessant process of coming to terms with the environment; he only sees escape and craving for release. He only knows the lust of release, not the *pleasure of tension*" (1939, page 333).

The behavior of neurotic and of brain-injured people manifests certain traits very strikingly,. but we have to be on our guard here against the isolation error. A sick person's behavior is dominated by isolated needs, such as the need for self-preservation. Seen in isolation these needs appear unduly strong and rigid; in the normal person under normal conditions, such needs are not isolated from the general tendency to come to terms with the environment. The same error of isolation is likely to vitiate the experimental study of animal drives and even the much overvalued study of children, for the young child is still uncentered or unintegrated. Only the normal adult responding normally to a favorable environment gives the holistic picture, and he is animated by a single comprehensive motive, which Goldstein calls the urge toward self-actualization or self-realization, "the tendency to achieve the optimal performance of the total organism" (1947, page 228). Nevertheless, though the organism has this one holistic motive, it engages in various activities and seems to be seeking various goals. This is because it has various capacities and tends to actualize its potentialities. "The traditional view assumes various drives. . . . We assume only one drive, the drive of self-actualization, but are compelled to concede that under certain conditions the tendency to actualize one potentiality is so strong that the organism is governed by it. . . . The organism has definite potentialities, and because it has them it has the need to actualize or realize them. The fulfillment of these needs represents the self-actualization of the organism" (1940, pages 144, 146). Taken literally, these statements could apply only to an extremely self-conscious organism whose interests were wholly centered in the self and not in the environment.

We have spoken of "isolation" as a necessary though risky procedure of the scientific investigator, and we should also notice that isolation is an inevitable characteristic of the behavior of an organism, at least of a higher organism possessing various capacities. Though, in a sense, the organism always acts as a whole, it cannot actualize all its potentialities at the same time. Its behavior is governed by one need or capacity at a time. Here there are two extreme possibilities. The organism may yield itself passively to the configuration of the present environment, this being the "concrete attitude"; or, being self-conscious and aware of its own many capacities, the organism may analyze the situation and choose for itself which capacity to actualize, this being the "abstract attitude." The concrete attitude is rigid and cannot shift from one capacity to another so long as the concrete situation remains unchanged; but as soon as the situation changes, the response passively follows suit. The abstract attitude, on the contrary, can shift from one line of attack to another upon an unchanging situation, and it can maintain a persistent line of attack upon a changing situation. The normal human adult can adopt either attitude; in planning, choosing goals, and selecting ways and means, he takes the abstract attitude, while in carrying out a specific manipulation of the environment he necessarily acts concretely. Goldstein's study of brain-injury cases convinced him that their essential defect was the loss of the abstract attitude. They were unable "to break up a given whole into parts, to isolate and to synthesize them . . . to abstract common properties reflectively . . . to plan ahead ideationally" (Goldstein and Scheerer, 1941, page 4). With his several collaborators he has designed and adapted a number of tests for the abstract attitude and has found that schizophrenics and the feeble-minded, as well as young children, are more or less deficient in this ability. Here, then, we find organismic psychology of a productive sort, though it is not quite clear how the productive research depends upon the organismic viewpoint. Goldstein would claim, however, that his discovery of the abstract and concrete attitudes was due to his firm determination to view the patient's symptoms and test results from the standpoint of the personality as a whole.

Is Goldstein to be counted as a member of the Gestalt school? The leading Gestalt psychologists have claimed him, but he himself is inclined to make a distinction. He thinks primarily as a biologist rather than a psychologist. "Our basic view agrees in many respects with Gestalt psychology. . . . Yet my guiding principle has been a different one, inasmuch as the 'whole,' the 'Gestalt,' has always meant to me the whole organism and not the phenomena in one field, or merely the 'introspective experiences.' . . . Certain differences arise between the views advanced by Gestalt psychologists and by myself" (1939, page 369). For him a "good gestalt" is not merely an organization of the perceptual field; rather, it is a performance of the organism, a way of coming to terms with the environment as well and economically as possible. Gestalt psychology has undervalued the central factors, the "field forces" supplied by the organism itself and not by the stimulus configuration. And the existing Gestalt theory does not allow sufficiently for the "abstract attitude." Indeed, Goldstein's emphasis on the abstract attitude as a prime necessity in science and in normal adult behavior seems exactly opposed to Wertheimer's abhorrence of any "piecemeal attitude."

Jacob Robert Kantor (born 1888, professor at Indiana) has been advocating an "organismic psychology" since 1924 or earlier, having in view both of the reforms already mentioned (page 232). He wishes to rid psychology of the old mind-body dualism, and he insists that the organism always acts as a whole and never part by part. "It is always the whole person who reacts. . . . It is a biological and psychological impossibility for the organism to act unless it acts as a whole" (1924, pages 56, 133). The real whole, however, is not the organism but the organism in its effective environment, the organism in active relations with certain objects at a given time. Psychological observation, whether objective or introspective, always reveals an organism interacting with objects present or thought of, and nothing less than this complete statement can give us genuine psychological data. "The data of psychology can only be the concrete interactions of organisms and the things to which they respond" (1924, page xiv). Or again, "Psychology has its own subject-matter—specific interactions between organisms and stimulating objects" (1933, page vii). This "organismic" psychology, then, is primarily concerned not with what goes on in the organism but rather with what goes on in the field including the organism and its objects. Accordingly Kantor regards it as inaccurate to speak of perceiving, learning, and thinking as functions of the organism; they are functions of the organism-object field, just as the function of batting a ball involves the ball and the bat as well as the batter. All psychological functions depend on the organism-object situation and not on the organism alone.

If psychological functions cannot be localized in the organism, still less can they be localized in the brain. The brain undoubtedly has its functions, but they are physiological functions on a par with the contraction of a muscle or the conduction of a nerve. The muscles, nerves, sense organs, and brain all perform their physiological functions and so play their parts in a psychological act such as batting a ball, but the psychological act is the total event, which does not occur in any of these organs. Psychological events, being interactions between the organism and the relevant objects, must not "in any manner be regarded as functions of particular structures or of the total organism. . . . Obviously no psychological event is lacking in muscular action. . . . But surely the most elaborate description of such participating biological factors cannot cover the essential features of the psychological event" (1947, pages 307, 337). Kantor is especially concerned to combat the proneness of psychologists to attribute functions like learning and perceiving to the brain. He will not even allow that the brain is modified in learning (1947, page 103), though he does not indicate where else in the total organism-environment field the modification can possibly occur. Again, though he insists on the importance of preparatory set (1924, page 58), he rejects the idea that this set occurs in the brain, an idea which he says "certainly stems from a mind-body source" (1947, page 195).

It is somewhat surprising, then, to find Kantor devoting a whole book to problems of physiological psychology (1947). The tone of the book, however, is severely critical and even negativistic. Its aim is to discredit false conceptions of physiological psychology and so clear the decks for an "authentic physiological psychology." But the critical part occupies all but the last three of the 345 pages in his text. He keenly ferrets out any lingering trace of the old mind-body dualism and any heedless localization of psychological functions in the brain. No psychologist, not even the most organismic, is found to be free of these defects. Adolf Meyer's psychobiology had indeed "the great merit of dealing with the activities of the whole organism . . . operating in a distinctive human environment. . . . Nevertheless, the psychobiology of Meyer and his followers . . . leaves us with the old dualism" (1947, pages 316-317). Goldstein's organismic psychology provides "a fine orientation toward an objective physiological psychology. . . . This writer does not, however, give up symptoms as . . . correlated with particular areas. In a definite sense, then, the holistic idea is not consistently maintained. . . . Goldstein persistently posits an association between higher mental functions and the frontal lobes. . . . Goldstein [stresses] the organism as the central feature in a psychological situation, with a deplorable disregard of the essential place of the other items in any psychological field" (1947, pages 318-319). Kantor's other books are less negative than this one, though they all contain a large element of criticism of the errors of psychologists. The positive and constructive discussions are less stimulating and give an outsider the impression that this approach to psychology may be relatively sterile. It is reported, however, that Kantor's students find him an inspiring teacher and guide in research.

PERSONALISTIC PSYCHOLOGY. The reality of the self is as obvious to the introspectionist as the reality of the organism is

to the behaviorist. We should have to go far back in the history
of psychology to find the beginnings of the personalistic view.
With the coming of empirical and experimental study of psychology the person tended to drop out of the picture because
attention was focused on analytic data, separate sensations,
images, and feelings. This way of approaching psychology was
criticized by William James in his famous chapter on "The
stream of thought" (1890, I, 224-225). On the contrary, he
said,

> The first fact for us . . . as psychologists, is that thinking of some
> sort goes on. I use the word thinking . . . for every form of conscious-
> ness. . . . How does it go on? We notice immediately five important
> characters in the process . . . :
> 1) Every thought tends to be part of a personal consciousness.
> 2) Within each personal consciousness thought is always changing.
> 3) Within each personal consciousness thought is sensibly con-
>   tinuous.
> 4) It always appears to deal with objects independent of itself.
> 5) It is interested in some . . . objects to the exclusion of others.

Mary Whiton Calkins (1863-1930), a pupil of James beginning in 1890, was for a decade the active head of the psychological laboratory at Wellesley, though she later switched mostly
to philosophy. She invented the important "method of paired
associates" for the study of memory. During the 1890's she
became more and more dissatisfied with the Wundt-Titchener
psychology and more and more impressed with the importance
of the self as the integrating factor in conscious experience.
In 1900 she came out strongly for "psychology as a science of
selves," and in 1901 she embodied this view in her first book,
An introduction to psychology. In this book she endeavored
to do justice to both the atomistic and the personalistic views of
psychology. She came to believe, however, that the atomistic
data were significant only in relation to the self, and in 1909 her
revised textbook, called *A first book in psychology,* made a radical innovation "by its abandonment of the duplex conception
of psychology, as science alike of succeeding mental events and
of the conscious self, in favor of a single-track self-psychology"
(1930, page 40). She argued that the self, far from being

merely a metaphysical concept, was an ever-present fact of immediate experience and fully worthy to be made the central fact in a system of scientific psychology.

The conscious self of each one of us . . . is immediately experienced as possessed of at least four fundamental characters. I immediately experience myself as (1) relatively persistent—in other words, I am in some sense the same as my childhood self; as (2) complex—I am a perceiving, remembering, feeling, willing self; as (3) a unique, an irreplaceable self—I am closely like father, brother, or friend, but I am, after all, only myself: there is only one of me. I experience myself (4) as related to (or conscious of) objects either personal or impersonal [1914, p. 3].

The self is consciously related to its objects in various ways. It takes a receptive attitude toward an object in observing it, but a dominating attitude in managing it; it has the attitude of liking certain objects but of disliking others. To speak of pleasantness and unpleasantness as impersonal conscious states is as absurd as to speak of them as unrelated to objects, for the real datum is the self being pleased or displeased by an object. Among the "objects" of the self the most important are other selves. The self is consciously a social being. Only a self-psychology can provide the basis for a genuine social psychology. Behaviorism cannot make a start on social psychology without sneaking in assumptions contrary to its major principle of regarding individuals as not having conscious experience; for, no matter what the behaviorist may say, the individuals he is considering certainly treat each other as conscious beings. Aside from this fanatical negative doctrine of behaviorism, its positive research findings can be welcomed and assimilated by self-psychology.

Calkins was distinctly an introspectionist and approached the self from this point of view. In her textbook she constantly appealed to the student to introspect for himself and to see the personal significance of the different topics in psychology. But she was eager also to bring the schools together and hoped to accomplish this by securing general acceptance of the fundamental importance of the self or person in all the psychologies. Though she herself much preferred "the strictly psychological conception of the self-which-has-a-body" to that of the conscious organism, she became convinced that the "biological form of personalistic psychology provides a middle ground in which most schools of contemporary psychology may meet" (1930, page 50). She noted that the "psychosomatic personalists," such as Stern whom we have soon to consider, attributed to the "person" the same fundamental characteristics as she attributed to the "self," and that "nothing forbids the self-psychologists from enriching their doctrine by distinctions stressed by these biological personalists." And nothing prevents the self-psychologist from utilizing the "atomistic" data of the structural or existential school. "Only the great negation of existential psychology, its outlawry of the self, its insistence on contents or ideas or experiences as the one concern of scientific psychology, is inconsistent with personalistic theory." She found herself in substantial agreement with Gestalt psychology except in its neglect of the "supreme illustration of the *Gestalt*"—that "integrated complex whole inclusive of parts" which is the self. And in psychoanalysis, which she regarded with a critical eye, she found the self appearing again and again in different guises —as the censor, for example, of Freud's earlier period and as the superego of his later theory (1930, pages 52-53). In fact it would be almost impossible to write psychology without lapsing, even against one's theoretical preconceptions, into the language of self-psychology. Why, then, should not all the schools unite in a personalistic psychology? Her plea seemed to fall on deaf ears, probably because most psychologists felt there was little to be gained by continually reiterating the truism of the reality and unity of the self or organism. Yet, looking back over the past fifty years, one can see that psychology has been moving in the direction she desired.

William Stern (1871-1938) offered his personalistic psychology to the world in 1906, just a few years after the self-psychology of Calkins made its appearance. Stern was apparently unacquainted with the work of Calkins; the Germans of 1900 or even of 1920 paid little attention to the American output in psychology. The two authors were alike in having a predominant interest in philosophy, as well as in making substantial contributions to experimental psychology. Stern was an exceptionally enterprising and inventive psychologist, a pioneer in the psychology of testimony and an active contributor to applied, differential, child, and clinical psychology. It was he who invented the IQ for use in connection with the Binet tests. His most important position was at Hamburg (1916-1933) where he was professor of psychology and director of the many-sided Hamburg Psychological Institute, devoted largely to clinical and guidance work in connection with the public schools.

Stern's great ambition throughout his career was to develop a philosophy that should reconcile the atomistic tendency of science with the human demand for real values in the world—that should integrate mechanism and teleology; and, like Calkins again, he believed that the concept of *person* made this reconciliation and integration possible. The person has unity, value, and purpose. The person is a whole of many parts, *unitas multiplex*. Taken part by part he (the person) can and should be studied mechanistically, i.e., in terms of cause and effect and the interaction of different factors; but taken as a whole he can be understood only in terms of purposes, goals, and values. The typical person is an adult human being; but a child is a person; an animal or any living organism is a person under Stern's definition; and there are superindividual "persons," organized social groups having their own goals and composed of individuals as the individual is composed of cells.

Each person has an environment selected by himself to some extent, and it is characteristic of a person to be in active relations with his environment. There are three levels of relations between the individual and his environment: the biological level of nutrition, etc.; the psychological level of conscious experience; and the valuational level which Stern regards as the province of philosophy. Psychology is concerned with conscious experience. Its data are the "phenomena" which the individual reports. But psychology goes behind the phenomena and recognizes "acts" of the person which are revealed by the phenomena, such as the acts of seeing, remembering, desiring. Psychology goes behind the momentary acts and recognizes enduring "dispositions" such as abilities and propensities, which are potentialities of the organism needing only to be awakened by stimulation from the environment. And finally psychology attempts to go behind the manifold dispositions and envisage the unitary person; but psychology cannot by itself reach this goal, because the unitary person is not purely mental but biological as well and also related to the world in a system of values which have to be approached from the philosophical angle (Stern, 1938, pages 70-84).

The true conception of the person dawned on Stern during his intensive studies of his own children in the home.

Here I became aware of the fundamental personalistic fact of *unitas multiplex;* the wealth of phenomena concomitantly or successively observable arrayed themselves in a unified life-line of the developing individual. ... Here I discovered the fundamental form of personal causality: the convergence of the stirring character-traits in the developing child, with the totality of environmental influences [1930, pp. 350-351].

This concept of *convergence* is important in Stern's system. The child's development is not due to heredity alone, nor to environment alone, nor to a mere sum of heredity and environment, but to the convergence (or synergy) of the two, convergence being possible because of the unity of the person. In the same way the person has a multiplicity of traits, but these converge in his unitary personality. He has a multiplicity of drives, but these converge in his unitary purposive behavior. Freud grossly underestimated the multiplicity of the individual's drives and motives, and he also failed to take due account of the unity of the person (1938, page 37).

Yet Freud's idea of a "depth psychology" is important, for there are depths in the person beneath the level of conscious experience. These depths are biological rather than psychological, but they have their influence on behavior. The unconscious cannot be rightly conceived in the categories of conscious activities such as ideas, memories, and definite desires. There is a gradation in depth extending from wholly unconscious biological activity of the organism, up through the various degrees of vaguely conscious feelings and activities, to the most sharply conscious and attentive perceptions and voluntary acts.

Whatever is sharply conscious is said by Stern to be *salient;* and whatever is salient is at the same time *embedded* in the deeper layers of the person. When you are closely observing a certain object, that observation is salient; but at the same time there is a background of feeling in which the specific observation is embedded; and the feeling itself is embedded in the unconscious life of the organism. "Everything that 'stands forth' from the whole nevertheless remains 'embedded' in it, despite its isolation, and receives from this relationship its sense and order" (1930, page 380). Stern suggests the analogy of a mountain range.

The peaks (cognition and acts of will) appear to stand out from the earth as sharply defined separate structures; but they are not separate from it, being held up by the mountainous mass (feeling) which, while visible itself, displays no shape of its own nor any sharp edge above and below; it is very near to the earth and is rooted, along with the peaks, in the invisible ground common to them all (sphere of the so-called "unconscious") [1938, p. 531].

Feeling, regarded not in isolation but as personal background experience, is not limited to pleasantness and unpleasantness but has a great variety of shades and tones. It can be mapped in many dimensions, including excitement-tranquillity, activity-passivity, attraction-avoidance. It is "shapeless" but still has much influence on behavior.

Gestalt psychology, in its emphasis on shape or configuration, has neglected the important role of the non-Gestalt, the shapeless. It has said much of figure and ground but devoted all its attention to the figure and regarded the ground as a minor matter. But the ground is not simply the spatial background of a visual figure; it is, rather, the personal feeling in which the act of perceiving the figure is embedded. Visual figures, so much used by the Gestalt psychologists, are not suited to bring out the whole range of psychological dynamics. They are too much like the old isolated elements. A whiff of odor, a sunset, a breeze blowing on the skin, have a degree of salience though they are shapeless non-Gestalts rather than Gestalts. Such sensory experiences, along with the feelings, must have their place in our psychology. Salience and embedding are a more comprehensive and useful pair of concepts than figure and ground. Such is Stern's contention (1938, page 112).

Stern made practical application of his personalistic psychology in the clinical and guidance work of his Hamburg institute. The "total procedure" used there has been described by a colleague (Bogen, 1931). The mere accumulation of tests in the hope of sampling the individual on all sides is not entitled to be called a "total procedure," because limitations of time would not allow for a complete survey, and also because the totality principle would be neglected. The real requirement is to see the individual as a unity in his multiplicity. The focal question must be, "What goal is this person seeking—what situation is he trying to make real?" Each person is regarded as having two goals: (1) an intrinsic goal bound up with his individual nature, and (2) an adopted goal representing his adjustment to his social environment. The adopted goal is the resultant of the converging influences of the intrinsic goal and the environment. The psychologist's task is to discover the intrinsic as well as the adopted goal of the individual. Achievement and aptitude tests are given, also the Rorschach with some freedom of interpretation, and a typological questionnaire based partly on Kretschmer. But the main thing is to get the subject to tell the story of his life beginning as far back as he can remember. Freud's rule, to keep back nothing, is followed, but nothing like a full psychoanalysis is attempted, nor are the Freudian concepts used. The psychologist is on the watch for resistances, conflicts, and the subject's childhood feelings toward his environment. Special attention is given to what the subject can tell of his childhood play. Did he have his own favorite kinds of play, or did he follow the season and the crowd? Sometimes it is desirable to obtain from the subject an account of his relatives, especially of those whom he "takes after" to his own knowledge. From all these indications an opinion and recommendation are offered and discussed with the subject before being regarded as final.

THE "UNDERSTANDING" PSYCHOLOGY—A PSYCHOLOGY THAT SEEKS TO UNDERSTAND RATHER THAN TO EXPLAIN. This is one of the oldest of still-contemporary schools. No sooner had the infant experimental psychology begun to show its hand than philosophers who were impressed with the richness of mental life and with the need for a broad, deep psychology as a basis for the social sciences began to utter wails of disappointment. Wilhelm Dilthey (1833-1911) if not the first was about the most outspoken and influential. In 1894 he urged that there should be developed a "descriptive and analytic psychology" very different from the "explanatory psychology" that was imitating the natural sciences and attempting to discover the elements of conscious experience and the laws of their combination. This explanatory psychology seemed doomed to depend on unverifiable hypotheses, while a direct appeal to consciousness would reveal a living unity calling for no such artificial constructions. The explanatory psychology had no means of approaching the motives of men or the achievements of great minds, and its natural-science techniques broke down altogether before the problems of social institutions and cultural history. The method of descriptive psychology, as applied to the individual, would start with the integrated totality of mental life and then examine parts of this totality in their intimate relation to the whole. "Understanding" cannot be purely intellectual but must be appreciative, sympathetic, feelingful. Values as well as facts are directly given in the inner life. The component parts discovered by true psychological analysis are seen in their relations to the whole. But the full scope of mental life cannot be gained from this introspective study; it is revealed in the achievements of great men and in human history and culture, envisaged as living processes. Dilthey's unremitting emphasis on the integrated whole *(Zusammenhang)* and on its articulated structure sounded a note that is common to many of his successors in Germany, such as Stern, Goldstein, and the Gestalt school. We should include here the *Ganzheit* ("wholeness") psychology of Felix Krueger, Wundt's successor at Leipzig. (Fuller accounts of this general movement are given by Hartmann, 1935, and by Klüver, 1929.) What

Dilthey had to offer was a project and not a descriptive psychology worked out to any extent, but he did offer the suggestion (1895-1896) that types of men, men with distinctive aims in life, would well repay psychological study.

This lead has been followed by Edouard Spranger (born 1882, professor of philosophy at Berlin). Spranger's interest in the problems and aspirations of young people, along with his interest in philosophy and the history of culture, led him to take up Dilthey's demand for an "understanding" psychology (1928). While the "explanatory" psychology was occupied with elements and physiological processes, understanding psychology must proceed at the higher level of meaningful acts and attitudes. A meaningful act has some goal, some value. What are the goals and values of really meaningful human activity? They are not limited to the biological goals of self-preservation and reproduction, for we find mankind seeking other values. Mankind finds value in knowledge, and one of its goals is the advancement of knowledge. Another is seen in the love for beauty and the age-long devotion to artistic production and enjoyment. By keeping in view both the living individual and the history of mankind we can develop a psychology of values and understand the individual's attitude toward life. After prolonged attention to the problem Spranger believed he could identify six typical human goals—six dimensions of human value, we might say—aside from the biological goals mentioned. Here is his list of goals, values or attitudes:

> The theoretical, knowledge-seeking
> The esthetic
> The economic or practical
> The religious
> The social or sympathetic
> The political or managerial

Spranger speaks of "types of men": the practical man, the religious man, and so on. He does not mean that people can be cleanly grouped under these heads, for every individual will appreciate more than a single value. As a type, the "practical man" is idealized; and the same thing is true of the other types. Yet actual individuals differ in their interests, some inclining more toward the practical, others more toward the theoretical, others more toward the political. This is not only common observation, but it has also been demonstrated by the use of questionnaires based on Spranger's types, so that his system has found use in studies of personality.

Interest in "types" is not confined to the personalists. Jung, we remember, introduced the famous distinction between introverts and extroverts (page 200). Freud and his direct followers distinguished several types which they believed to originate in the fixation of early stages of psychosexual development: the oral-erotic, dependent type; the sadistic or "biting" type; the anal-erotic, characterized by parsimony, obstinacy, and orderliness; and the more mature genital type (page 178). Adler distinguished several "styles of life" (page 195). Horney's character trends are much like Freud's: the moving-toward-people, compliant character; the moving-against, hostile character; and the moving-away, withdrawing character (page 208). Fromm has now worked over the psychoanalytic types, which he calls orientations toward the world and life, and added a new one. He speaks of the receptive-dependent type; the exploiting-sadistic type; the hoarding-remote type; the self-marketing type, always seeking to adjust to the current fashion and demand; and finally the only truly productive, creative, and maturely loving type (Fromm, 1947, page 111). These types, like Spranger's, are not separate classes of actual individuals so much as "ideal types" combined and blended in any individual's orientation.

Gordon W. Allport (born 1897, professor at Harvard) may be cited as an outstanding representative of a large group of contemporary psychologists who are endeavoring to build up a science of personality. They do not attach themselves to any of the schools we have mentioned, preferring a fresh approach though with free use of their predecessors' methods. They do not despise the "explanatory" psychology of the experimentalists and factor analysts, and make use of it to some extent, but their feeling is that the individual as a living whole is being neglected in all this attention to perception, learning, and abilities. The individual as a unique organized whole, Allport says (1937), does not come into focus when serving as a subject in an experiment on perception or memory. The experimenter is seeking for general laws, using the individual only as a specimen. Even the student of individual differences is not really concerned with the individual except as he occupies a certain position in the distribution curve of one or another ability. Psychoanalysis neglects the unique individual in its preoccupation with universal causes. "The properties of the unconscious, it holds, are . . . the same for all people. The desires of the infant . . . and the stages of development through which he passes are prescribed; the three-fold division of the self: the super-ego, the ego, and the id permit no variation" (1937, page 12). Gestalt psychology and the "understanding" psychology have opened up lines of attack on the problem of personality, but much remains to be done. Stern introduces unnecessary metaphysics on one side and on the other overlooks the possible uses of general experimental psychology. A psychology of personality does not need to discard the laws of general psychology but it demands laws "that tell how uniqueness comes about" (1937, page 558). Presumably these will be laws of organization. For another serious attempt to discover such laws see Murphy, 1947.

CHAPTER 8

THE MIDDLE OF THE ROAD

In view of all the divergent movements that we have surveyed, all these "warring schools" of contemporary psychology, the reader may easily carry away the impression that we psychologists are anything but a harmonious body of scientific workers. Looked at from outside, our fraternity has seemed to be a house divided against itself. Other scientists and philosophers have sometimes said that "until psychologists can put their own house in order, they have no claim on the attention and respect of other groups," and that "a meeting of psychologists must be a perfect bear den." You would get a very different impression from attending one of the International Congresses of Psychology or a meeting of one of the national societies such as the American Psychological Association. You would hear papers read on various psychological topics, with very little mention of any of the schools and with discussions of the usual scientific type, free from acrimony though not of course from the give and take of doubt and criticism. Outside of the meeting rooms you would see friendly groups engaged in animated conversation and you would find that a single group often contained members of different schools. If you attended the business meeting or looked into the business enterprises of the society, you would find members of different schools serving together on committees and editorial boards and evidently able to cooperate in advancing the general interests of psychology. You might query how they could conscientiously cooperate when their views are so different as to what psychology ought to be doing, and perhaps you would conclude that these psychologists liked and respected each other personally and left really serious questions out of their public affairs. But then you would probably reflect that after all there is something common to all the schools. All psychologists are interested in psychology, and though their definitions of the subject appear to differ, there is something common to all underlying the definitions. Whether they speak of behavior or of conscious experience or of activity in general, they all have before them the individual in his relation to the environment.

The total field of psychology is very wide and diversified, and the possible applications of the science to human welfare are numerous. Some psychologists are drawn into one part of the field and some into another. Their diverse lines of work do not usually result in the formation of "schools," as was said in the introductory chapter, but to quite an extent the schools do represent different lines of work. The behaviorists are more interested in problems of learning, the Gestalt group more in problems of perception, the psychoanalysts more in motivation. The human individual, enmeshed in all the problems, is what holds the specializing groups of psychologists together, and we may hope that the interrelations of the problems will become increasingly evident with the general advance of the science. Already *rapprochements* are becoming visible (Dashiell, 1939).

Another reason for the continued unity of psychology is found in the fact that only a minority of psychologists have become active adherents of any of the schools. Some may lean toward one school and some toward another, but on the whole the psychologists of the present time are proceeding on their way in the middle of the road. After all there was a great deal in the psychology of 1900 against which there has been no revolt. Many of the results of the earlier research still hold good, and fresh research during the past half century has added many new results that have no direct connection with any of the schools. The psychologists of 1900 were on their way, and their way is our way, but we seem to be farther ahead.

No worldwide census of psychologists has been attempted for fifteen years and more, and we do not know how numerous we are. Probably 10,000 would be a conservative estimate, a very large number in comparison with 1900, though very small in comparison with some contemporary scientific groups, as for example the chemists. If we could assemble all these psychologists in a convention hall and ask the members of each school to stand and show themselves, a very large proportion of the entire group would remain seated. If, instead of mentioning the schools, we should ask the experimental psychologists to rise, the clinical psychologists, the social psychologists, the child psychologists, the educational psychologists, the industrial psychologists, and a few more such groups, we should soon have the entire convention on its feet. Anything like a cleavage into separate "psychologies" seems much more likely along such lines than along "school" lines. But for the present there seems to be a determination among psychologists to stick together in one inclusive group.

Finally we may raise a question which has been hinted at more than once, especially in the early discussion of functional psychology. A broadly defined functional psychology starts with the question "What man *does*" and proceeds to the questions "How?" and "Why?" This we thought to be the underlying conception of psychology, coming down from the old days and persisting underneath even when the formal definitions were quite different. So broadly defined, we have said more than once, functional psychology scarcely deserves the name of a school because it would include so many psychologists who have not professed themselves. Now the question is whether our middle-of-the-roaders are not after all members of this broadly conceived functional school. If we had our convention assembled we could put the question to a vote. But if the middle-of-the-roaders are really functionalists, the question is then whether the same would not be true of all the schools. Are they not all functionalists at heart? Without calling them up one by one and pressing the question home, we can at least say that they have all made contributions to the solution of functional problems. Every school is good, though no one is good enough. No one of them has the full vision of the psychology of the future. One points to one alluring prospect, another to another. Every one has elements of vitality and is probably here to stay for a long time. Their negative pronouncements we can discount while we accept their positive contributions to psychology as a whole.

BIBLIOGRAPHY

ADLER, A. 1930. *Problems of neurosis.* New York: Cosmopolitan Book Co.

ALEXANDER, F. 1942. *Our age of unreason.* Philadelphia: J. B. Lippincott Co.

ALEXANDER, F., and FRENCH, T. 1946. *Psychoanalytic therapy.* New York: The Ronald Press Co.

ALLPORT, G. W. 1937. *Personality, a psychological interpretation.* New York: Henry Holt & Co.

ANGELL, J. R. 1904. *Psychology, an introductory study of the structure and function of human consciousness.* New York: Henry Holt & Co.

——— 1907. The province of functional psychology. *Psychol. Rev.,* 1907, **14**, 61-91.

——— 1936. Autobiography. In C. Murchison, *History of psychology in autobiography.* Worcester, Mass.: Clark University Press, 1936, Vol. III, 1-38.

BAIN, A. 1855. *The senses and the intellect.* London: Edwin S. Parker, Ltd.

——— 1859. *The emotions and the will.* London: Parker & Son.

——— 1868. *Mental science; a compendium of psychology, and the history of philosophy.* New York: D. Appleton & Co.

BEKHTEREV, V. M. 1913. *Objektive Psychologie; oder, Psychoreflexologie, die Lehre von den Assoziationsreflexen.* Leipzig: B. G. Teubner.

——— 1933. *General principles of human reflexology.* Trans. from 4th (1928) Russian edition. London: Jarrolds.

BENTLEY, M. 1926. The psychologies called "structural": historical derivation; the work of the structuralists. In C. Murchison, *Psychologies of 1925.* Worcester, Mass.: Clark University Press, 1926, 383-412.

——— 1930. A psychology for psychologists. In C. Murchison, *Psychologies of 1930.* Worcester, Mass.: Clark University Press, 1930, 95-114.

BERKELEY, G. 1709. *An essay towards a new theory of vision.* Dublin: N. P.

BERNARD, L. L. 1924. *Instinct, a study of social psychology.* New York: Henry Holt & Co.

——— 1926. *An introduction to social psychology.* New York: Henry Holt & Co.

BINET, A. 1903. *Étude expérimentale de l'intelligence.* Paris: Schleicher.

BOGEN, H. 1931. Zur Methodik des "Totalverfahrens" in der berufseignungspsychologischen Begutachtung. *Z. angew. Psychol., Beihefte,* 1931, **59**, 15-32.

BORING, E. G. 1929. *A history of experimental psychology.* New York: Century Co.

1930. Psychology for eclectics. In C. Murchison, *Psychologies of 1930*. Worcester, Mass.: Clark University Press, 1930, 115-127.

1942. *Sensation and perception in the history of experimental psychology*. New York: D. Appleton-Century Co.

1945. The use of operational definitions in science. *Psychol. Rev.*, 1945, **52**, 243-245, 278-281.

BORING, E. G., and STEVENS, S. S. 1936. The nature of tonal brightness. *Proc. Nat. Acad. Sci.*, 1936, **22**, 514-521.

BREUER, J. and FREUD, S. 1895. *Studien über Hysterie*. Leipzig: Franz Deuticke.

1936. *Studies in hysteria*. Trans. by A. A. Brill. New York: Nervous & Mental Disease Publishing Co.

BRIDGMAN, P. W. 1927. *The logic of modern physics*. New York: The Macmillan Co.

BROWN, T. 1820. *Lectures on the philosophy of the human mind*. Edinburgh: Tait, Longman.

CALKINS, M. W. 1900. Psychology as a science of selves. *Philos. Rev.*, 1900, **9**, 490-501.

1901. *An introduction to psychology*. New York: The Macmillan Co.

1909, 1914. *A first book in psychology*. New York: The Macmillan Co.

1926. Converging lines in contemporary psychology. *Brit. J. Psychol., Gen. Sec.*, 1926, **16**, 171-179.

1930. Autobiography. In C. Murchison, *History of psychology in autobiography*. Worcester, Mass.: Clark University Press, 1930, Vol. I, 31-62.

CANNON, W. B. 1929. *Bodily changes in pain, hunger, fear, and rage*. 2nd ed. New York: D. Appleton & Co.

CARMICHAEL, L., Editor. 1946. *Manual of child psychology*. New York: John Wiley & Sons.

CARPENTER, W. B. 1876. *Principles of mental physiology*. 4th ed. New York: D. Appleton & Co.

CARR, H. 1930. Functionalism. In C. Murchison, *Psychologies of 1930*. Worcester, Mass.: Clark University Press, 1930, 59-78.

CATTELL, J. McK. 1904. The conceptions and methods of psychology. *Pop. Sci. Mo.*, 1904, **46**, 176-186. Included in *1860-1944 James McKeen Cattell —man of science,* Lancaster, Pa.: The Science Press, 1948.

CHARCOT, J. M. 1877. *Lectures on the diseases of the nervous system*. London: New Sydenham Society.

CLAPARÈDE, E. 1930. Autobiography. In C. Murchison, *History of psychology in autobiography*. Worcester, Mass.: Clark University Press, 1930, Vol. I, 63-97.

1933. La genèse de l'hypothèse, étude expérimentale. *Arch. de Psychol.*, 1933, **24**, 1-154.

COGHILL, G. E. 1929. *Anatomy and the problem of behavior*. London: Cambridge University Press.

DASHIELL, J. F. 1939. Some rapprochements in contemporary psychology. *Psychol. Bull.*, 1939, **36**, 1-24.

DILTHEY, W. 1894. Ideen über eine beschreibende und zergliedernde Psychologie. In his *Gesammelte Schriften*. Leipzig: Teubner, 1924, Vol. V, 139-240.

1895-1896. Beiträge zum Studium der Individualität. In his *Gesammelte Schriften*. Leipzig: Teubner, 1924, Vol. V, 241-316.

DUNCKER, K. 1935. *Zur Psychologie des produktiven Denkens*. Berlin: Verlag Julius Springer.

1945. On problem-solving. Trans. by L. S. Lees. *Psychol. Monogr.*, 1945, **58**, No. 270.

DUNLAP, K. 1919. Are there any instincts? *J. abn. Psychol.*, 1919, **14**, 307-311.

EBBINGHAUS, H. 1885. *Über das Gedächtnis*. Leipzig: Duncker & Humblot.

1913. *Memory*. Trans. by H. A. Ruger and C. E. Bussenius. New York: Teachers College, Columbia University.

EDWARDS, J. 1754. *A careful and strict enquiry into the modern prevailing notions of that freedom of will which is supposed to be essential to moral agency, virtue and vice, reward and punishment, praise and blame.* Boston: Kneeland.

EHRENFELS, C. v. 1890. Über Gestaltqualitäten. *Vierteljahrschr. f. wiss. Philos.*, 1890, **14**. 249-292.

1937. On Gestalt-qualities. *Psychol. Rev.*, 1937, **44**, 521-524.

ELLIS, W. D. 1938. *A source book of Gestalt psychology*. New York: Harcourt, Brace & Co.

ELMGREN, J. 1938. Gestalt psychology, a survey and some contributions. *Göteborgs Högskolas Arsskrift*, 1938, **44**, No. 4.

ESTES, W. K., and SKINNER, B. F. 1941. Some quantitative properties of anxiety. *J. exp. Psychol.*, 1941, **29**, 390-400.

FENICHEL, O. 1945. *The psychoanalytic theory of neurosis*. New York: W. W. Norton & Co.

FORDHAM, M. 1945. Professor C. G. Jung. *Brit. J. med. Psychol.*, 1945, **20**, 221-235.

FRANZ, S. I. 1902. On the function of the cerebrum: the frontal lobes in relation to the production and retention of simple sensory motor habits. *Amer. J. Physiol.*, 1902, **8**, 1-22.

1907. On the functions of the cerebrum: the frontal lobes. *Arch. Psychol.*, 1907., No. 2.

FRANZ, S. I., and LASHLEY, K. S. 1917. The effects of cerebral destruction upon habit-formation and retention in the albino rat. *Psychobiol.*, 1917, **1**, 71-139.

FREUD, S. *Gesammelte Werke. Chronologisch geordnet*. Volumes I-XVII. London: Imago, 1940-1948. (*G*. with a number following on the Freud reference indicates *Gesammelte* and the volume.) NOTE: References in the text are to the original editions, but quotations are from the respective translations.

1900. *The interpretation of dreams*. New York: The Macmillan Co., 1913. 1st ed., German, 1900. (*G*. II-III.)

1901. *Psychopathology of everyday life*. New York: The Macmillan Co., 1915. 1st ed., German, 1901. (*G*., IV.)

1905. Three contributions to the theory of sex. Translated by A. A. Brill. *Nerv. and ment. Dis. Monogr. Ser.*, 1910, No. 7. 1st ed., German, 1905. (*G*., V.)

1914. *The history of the psychoanalytic movement.* New York: Nervous & Mental Disease Publishing Company, 1917. 1st ed., German, 1914. (*G., X.*)

1914a. On narcissism: an introduction. In *Collected papers.* Vol. 4. London: Hogarth Press, 1925. 1st ed., German, 1914. (*G., X*)

1916. *A general introduction to psychoanalysis.* Trans. by J. Riviere. New York: Boni & Liveright, 1920. 1st ed., German, 1916-1917. (*G., XI.*)

1920. *Beyond the pleasure principle.* New York: Albert & Charles Boni, 1922. 1st ed., German, 1920. (*G., XIII.*)

1921. *Group psychology and the analysis of the ego.* London: International Psycho-analytic Press, 1922. 1st ed., German, 1921. (*G., XIII.*)

1923. *The ego and the id.* London: Hogarth Press, 1927. 1st ed., German, 1923. (*G., XIII.*)

1926. *The problem of lay-analyses.* New York: Brentano's, 1927. 1st ed., German, 1926. (*G., XIV.*)

1927. *The future of an illusion.* London: Hogarth Press, 1928. 1st ed., German, 1927. (*G., XIV.*)

1930. *Civilization and its discontents.* London: Hogarth Press, 1930. (*G., XIV.*)

1932. *New introductory lectures on psychoanalysis.* New York: W. W. Norton & Co., 1933. 1st ed., German, 1932. (*G., XV.*)

1937. *Moses and monotheism.* New York: Alfred A. Knopf, Inc., 1938. Translated from articles in *Imago,* 1937.

1940. Abriss der Psychoanalyse. *Internatl. Z. Psychoanal.,* 1940, **25**: 9-67. (*G., XVII.*)

1946. *Selbstdarstellung.* London: Imago Publishing Co., 1946. 1st ed., German, 1925. (*G., XIV.*)

FROMM, E. 1941. *Escape from freedom.* New York: Farrar & Rinehart.

1947. *Man for himself, an inquiry into the psychology of ethics.* New York: Rinehart & Co.

GOLDSTEIN, K. 1939. *The organism, a holistic approach to biology derived from pathological data in man.* New York: American Book Co.

1940. *Human nature in the light of psychopathology.* Cambridge, Mass.: Harvard University Press.

1947. Organismic approach to the problem of motivation. *Transactions N.Y. Acad. Sciences,* 1947, **9**, 218-230.

GOLDSTEIN, K., and SCHEERER, M. 1941. Abstract and concrete behavior: an experimental study with special tests. *Psychol. Monogr.,* 1941, No. **239**, 151.

GUILFORD, J. O., and GUILFORD, R. S. 1936. Personality factors *S, E,* and *M,* and their measurement. *J. Psychol.,* 1936, **2**, 109-127.

HARRELL, W., and HARRISON, R. 1938. The rise and fall of behaviorism. *J. genl. Psychol.,* 1938, **18**, 367-421.

HARTLEY, D. 1749. *Observations on man, his frame, his duty, and his expectations.* London: W. Eyres.

HARTMANN, G. W. 1935. *Gestalt psychology, a survey of facts and principles.* New York: The Ronald Press Co.

HEIDBREDER, E. 1933. *Seven psychologies.* New York: Century Co.

HERBART, J. F. 1816. *Lehrbuch zur Psychologie.* Königsberg: Unzer.

1824. *Psychologie als Wissenschaft.* 2 vols. Königsberg: Unzer.

HILGARD, E. R. 1948. Theories of learning. New York and London, Appleton-Century-Crofts, Inc.

HILGARD, E. R. and MARQUIS, D. G. 1940. *Conditioning and learning.* New York: D. Appleton-Century Co.

HOBBES, T. 1651. *Leviathan.* London: Printed for Andrew Crooke.

HOBHOUSE, L. T. 1901. *Mind in evolution.* New York: The Macmillan Co.

HORNEY, K. 1939. *New ways in psychoanalysis.* New York: W. W. Norton & Co.

1942. *Self-analysis.* New York: W. W. Norton & Co.

1945. *Our inner conflicts, a constructive theory of neurosis.* New York: W. W. Norton & Co.

HULL, C. L. 1920. Quantitative aspects of the evolution of concepts. *Psychol. Monogr.,* 1920, **28,** No. 123.

1925. An automatic correlation calculating machine. *J. Amer. Statist. Ass.,* 1925, **20,** 522-531.

1928. *Aptitude testing.* Yonkers, N. Y.: World Book Co.

1930. Knowledge and purpose as habit mechanisms. *Psychol. Rev.,* 1930, **37,** 511-525.

1933. *Hypnosis and suggestibility.* New York: D. Appleton-Century Co.

1935. The conflicting psychologies of learning—a way out. *Psychol. Rev.,* 1935, **42,** 491-516.

1937. Mind, mechanism, and adaptive behavior. *Psychol. Rev.,* 1937, **44,** 1-32.

1943. *Principles of behavior, an introduction to behavior theory.* New York: D. Appleton-Century Co.

HULL, C. L., and others. 1940. *Mathematico-deductive theory of rote learning: a study in scientific methodology.* New Haven: Yale University Press.

HUME, D. 1739. *A treatise of human nature.* Vols. 1 and 2. London: Noon; Vol. 3. London: Thomas Longman.

1748. An enquiry concerning human understanding. In his *Essays and treatises on several subjects.* London: Pr. for A. Millar.

HUNTER, W. S. 1926. Psychology and anthroponomy. In C. Murchison, *Psychologies of 1925.* Worcester, Mass.: Clark University Press, 1926, 83-107.

1928. *Human behavior.* Chicago: University of Chicago Press.

1930. Anthroponomy and psychology. In C. Murchison, *Psychologies of 1930.* Worcester, Mass.: Clark University Press, 1930, 281-300.

1932. The psychological study of behavior. *Psychol. Rev.,* 1932, **39,** 1-24.

JACOBI, J. 1943. *The psychology of Jung.* Trans. by K. W. Bash. New Haven: Yale University Press.

1945. *Die Psychologie von C. G. Jung.* 2nd ed., Zurich: Rascher & Cie.

JACOBSON, E. 1932. Electrophysiology of mental activities. *Amer. J. Psychol.,* 1932, **44,** 677-694.

JAMES, W. 1890. *Principles of psychology.* 2 vols. New York: Henry Holt & Co.

1892. *Psychology, briefer course.* New York: Henry Holt & Co.

JANET, P. 1889. *L'automatisme psychologique.* Paris: Alcan.

1892. *L'état mental des hystériques.* Paris: Ruell.

1903. *Les obsessions et la psychasthénie.* Paris: Alcan.

1907. *The major symptoms of hysteria.* New York: The Macmillan Co.

JUNG, C. G. 1920. *Collected papers on analytical psychology.* Trans. by C. Long. London: Baillière, Tindall & Cox.

1928. *Contributions to analytical psychology.* Trans. by H. G. and C. F. Baynes. New York: Harcourt, Brace & Co.

KANTOR, J. R. 1924, 1926. *Principles of psychology.* 2 vols. New York: Alfred A. Knopf, Inc.

1929. *An outline of social psychology.* Chicago: Follett Publishing Co.

1933. *A survey of the science of psychology.* Bloomington, Ind.: Principia Press.

1947. *Problems of physiological psychology.* Bloomington, Ind.: Principia Press.

KARDINER, A. 1939. *The individual and his society: the psychodynamics of primitive organization.* New York: Columbia University Press.

KARDINER, A., LINTON, R., DuBois, C., and WEST, J. 1945. *The psychological frontiers of society.* New York: Columbia University Press.

KATONA, G. 1940. *Organizing and memorizing: studies in the psychology of learning and teaching.* New York: Columbia University Press.

KATZ, D. 1911. Die Erscheinungsweisen der Farben und ihre Beeinflussung durch die individuelle Erfahrung. *Z. Psychol.*, 1911, *Ergänzungsbd.*, 7.

1925. Der Aufbau der Tastwelt. *Z. Psychol.*, 1925, *Ergänzungsbd.*, 11.

1930. *Der Aufbau der Farbwelt,* Leipzig: S. A. Barth.

1935. *The world of colour.* Trans. by R. B. MacLeod and C. W. Fox. London: Stanley Paul & Co., Ltd.

KINSEY, A. C., POMEROY, W. B., and MARTIN, C. E. 1948. *Sexual behavior in the human male.* Philadelphia and London: W. B. Saunders Co.

KLUVER, H. 1929. Contemporary German psychology as a "cultural science." In G. Murphy, *An historical introduction to modern psychology.* New York: Harcourt, Brace & Co., 1929, 443-455.

KOFFKA, K. 1922. Perception: an introduction to the *Gestalttheorie. Psychol. Bull.*, 1922, **19**, 531-585.

1925. *The growth of the mind.* New York: Harcourt, Brace & Co.

1935. *Principles of Gestalt psychology.* New York: Harcourt, Brace & Co.

KÖHLER, W. 1925, 1927. *The mentality of apes.* New York: Harcourt, Brace & Co.

1929. *Gestalt psychology.* New York: Liveright Publishing Co.

1938. *The place of value in a world of facts.* New York: Liveright Publishing Co.

1940. *Dynamics in psychology.* New York: Liveright Publishing Co.

1944. Max Wertheimer, 1880-1943. *Psychol. Rev.*, 1944, **51**, 143-146.

1947. *Gestalt psychology: an introduction to new concepts in modern psychology.* New York: Liveright Publishing Co.

KÖHLER, W., and WALLACH, H. 1944. Figural after-effects: an investigation of visual processes. *Proc. Amer. Philos. Soc.*, 1944, **88**, 269-357.

KRUEGER, F. E. 1926. Über psychische Ganzheit. *Neue psychol. Stud.*, 1926, **1**, 1-123.

Kuo, Z. Y. 1928. The fundamental error of the concept of purpose and the trial and error fallacy. *Psychol. Rev.*, 1928, **35**, 414-433.

Landis, C. 1924. Studies of emotional reactions. *J. comp. Psychol.*, 1924, **4**, 447-509.

1940. Psychoanalytic phenomena. *J. abn. soc. Psychol.*, 1940, **35**, 17-28.

Laromiguière, P. 1815-1818. *Leçons de philosophie.* 2 vols. Paris: Brunot-Labbé.

Lashley, K. S. 1923. The behavioristic interpretation of consciousness. *Psychol. Rev.*, 1923, **30**, 237-272, 329-353.

1929. *Brain mechanisms and intelligence.* Chicago: University of Chiago Press.

1931. Cerebral control versus reflexology: a reply to Professor Hunter. *J. genl. Psychol.*, 1931, **5**, 3-20.

1934. Nervous mechanisms in learning. In C. Murchison, *A handbook of general experimental psychology.* Worcester, Mass.: Clark University Press, 1934, 456-496.

1935. Studies of cerebral function in learning. XI. The behavior of the rat in latch box situations. *Comp. Psychol. Monogr.*, 1935, **11**, No. 22, 1-42.

1938. Experimental analysis of instinctive behavior. *Psychol. Rev.*, 1938, **45**, 445-472.

1947. Structural variation in the nervous system in relation to behavior. *Psychol. Rev.*, 1947, **54**, 325-334.

Lashley, K. S., and Wade, M. 1946. The Pavlovian theory of generalization. *Psychol. Rev.*, 1946, **53**, 72-87.

Leeper, R. W. 1943. *Lewin's topological and vector psychology.* Eugene, Ore.: University of Oregon Press.

Lewin, K. 1917. Die psychische Tätigkeit bei der Hemmung von Willensvorgängen und das Grundgesetz der Assoziation. *Z. Psychol.*, 1917, **77**, 212-247.

1921-22. Das Problem der Willensmessung und das Grundgesetz der Association. *Psychol. Forsch.*, 1921-1922, **1**: 191-302, **2**: 65-140.

1935. *A dynamic theory of personality.* Trans. by D. K. Adams and K. E. Zener. New York: McGraw-Hill Book Co.

1936. *Principles of topological psychology.* Trans by F. Heider and G. M. Heider. New York: McGraw-Hill Book Co.

1938. The conceptual representation and the measurement of psychological forces. *Contrib. to psychol. Theory,* 1938, **1**, No. 4.

1940. Formalization and progress in psychology. *Univ. Iowa Stud. Child Welfare,* 1940, **16**, No. 3, 9-42.

1947. Frontiers in group dynamics. *Human relations,* 1947, **1**, 5-41, 143-153.

Liddell, H. S., James, W. T., and Anderson, O. D. 1934. The comparative physiology of the conditioned motor reflex. *Comp. Psychol. Monogr.*, 1934, **11**, No. 51.

Locke, J. 1690. *An essay concerning human understanding.* London: T. Basset.

MacLeod, R. B. 1947. The phenomenological approach to social psychology. *Psychol. Rev.*, 1947, **54**, 193-210.

Masserman, J. H. 1946. *Principles of dynamic psychiatry.* Philadelphia: W. B. Saunders Co.

Max, L. W. 1937. Action-current responses in the deaf during awakening, kinesthetic imagery and abstract thinking. *J. comp. Psychol.*, 1937, **24**, 301-344.

McDougall, W. 1905. *Physiological psychology.* London: J. M. Dent & Sons.

1908. *Introduction to social psychology.* 5th ed. (1912), London: Methuen & Co., Ltd.

1912. *Psychology, the study of behavior.* London: Williams & Norgate, Ltd.; New York: Henry Holt & Co.

1923. *Outline of psychology.* New York: Charles Scribner's Sons.

1924. Fundamentals of psychology. *Psyche*, 1924, **5**, 13-32.

1926. Men or robots? In C. Murchison, *Psychologies of 1925.* Worcester, Mass.: Clark University Press, 1926, 273-305.

1926a. *Outline of abnormal psychology.* New York: Charles Scribner's Sons.

1929. *Modern materialism and emergent evolution.* London: Methuen & Co., Ltd.

1930. The hormic psychology. In C. Murchison, *Psychologies of 1930.* Worcester, Mass.: Clark University Press, 3-36.

1930a. Autobiography. In C. Murchison, *History of psychology in autobiography.* Worcester, Mass.: Clark University Press, 1930, Vol. I, 191-223.

1932. *The energies of men, a study of the fundamentals of dynamic psychology.* London: Methuen & Co., Ltd.

1932-33. Experimental psychology and psychological experiment. *Character & Pers.*, 1932-1933, **1**, 195-213.

1936. *Psychoanalysis and social psychology.* London: Methuen & Co., Ltd.

1943. *William McDougall, a bibliography together with a brief outline of his life,* compiled by A. L. Robinson. Durham, N. C.: Duke University Press.

McGeoch, J. A. 1942. *The psychology of human learning.* New York: Longmans, Green & Co., Inc.

Menninger, K. A. 1938. *Man against himself.* New York: Harcourt, Brace & Co.

1942. *Love against hate.* New York: Harcourt, Brace & Co.

Meyer, A. 1897. A short sketch of the problems of psychiatry. *Amer. J. Insanity*, 1897, **53**, 538-549.

1908. The role of the mental factors in psychiatry. *Amer. J. Insanity*, 1908, **65**, 39-56.

Meyer, M. F. 1911. *The fundamental laws of human behavior.* Boston: Richard G. Badger (The Gorham Press).

1921. *The psychology of the other one.* Columbia, Mo.: Missouri Book Company.

Michotte, A. 1946. *La perception de la causalité.* Louvain: Institut Supérieur de Philosophie.

Mill, J. 1829. *Analysis of the phenomena of the human mind.* London: Baldwin.

Mill, J. S. 1869. Notes and annotations on J. Mill, *Analysis of the phenomena of the human mind.* 2 vols. London: Longmans, Green & Co., Ltd.

MORGAN, C. L. 1894. *An introduction to comparative psychology.* London: Walter Scott.

MÜLLER, G. E. 1911, 1913, 1917. Zur Analyse der Gedächtnistätigkeit und des Vorstellungsverlaufes. *Z. Psychol., Ergänzungsbd.,* **5, 8, 9.**

MÜLLER, G. E. and SCHUMANN, F. 1889. Über die psychologischen Grundlagen der Vergleichung gehobener Gewichte. *Arch. ges. Physiol.,* 1889, **45,** 37-112.

1894. Experimentelle Beiträge zur Untersuchung des Gedächtnisses. *Z. Psychol.,* 1894, **6,** 81-190, 257-339.

MURPHY, G. 1929. *An historical introduction to modern psychology.* New York: Harcourt, Brace & Co.

1947. *Personality, a biosocial approach to origins and structures.* New York: Harper & Brothers.

PARKER, C. 1920. *The casual laborer and other essays.* New York: Harcourt, Brace & Co.

PASCAL, G. R. 1947. The use of relaxation in short-term psychotherapy. *J. abn. soc. Psychol.,* 1947, **42,** 226-242.

PAVLOV, I. P. 1927. *Conditioned reflexes: an investigation of the physiological activity of the cerebral cortex.* Trans. by G. V. Anrep. New York: Oxford University Press.

1928. *Lectures on conditioned reflexes.* Vol. I. *25 years of objective study of the higher nervous activity (behavior) of animals.* Trans. by W. Horsley Gantt. New York: International Publishers.

1932. The reply of a physiologist to psychologists. *Psychol. Rev.,* 1932, **39,** 91-127.

1941. *Lectures on conditioned reflexes.* Vol. II. *Conditioned reflexes and psychiatry.* Trans. by W. Horsley Gantt. New York: International Publishers.

PETERMANN, B. 1932. *The Gestalt theory and the problem of configuration.* New York: Harcourt, Brace & Co.

PILLSBURY, W. B. 1911. *Essentials of psychology.* New York: The Macmillan Co.

PRINCE, M. 1913. *The dissociation of a personality.* 2nd ed. New York: Longmans, Green & Co., Inc.

REIK, T. 1940. *From thirty years with Freud.* New York: Farrar & Rinehart.

RENNIE, T. A. C. 1943. Adolf Meyer and psychobiology; the man, his methodology and its relation to therapy. *Pap. Amer. Congr. gen. Semant.,* 1943, **2,** 156-165.

RICHARDS, E. L. 1941. *Introduction to psychobiology and psychiatry: a textbook for nurses.* St. Louis: C. V. Mosby Co.

RITCHIE, B. F. 1944. Hull's treatment of learning. *Psychol. Bull.,* 1944, **41,** 640-642.

ROBINSON, E. S. 1932. *Association theory to-day, an essay in systematic psychology.* New York: Century Co.

ROGERS, C. R. 1942. *Counseling and psychotherapy.* Boston: Houghton Mifflin Co.

RUBIN, E. 1915. *Synsoplevede Figurer.* Kobenhavn: Gyldendalske Boghandel.

1921. *Visuell wahrgenommene Figuren: Studien in psychologischer Analyse.* Trans. from Danish. Kobenhavn: Gyldendalske Boghandel.

1930. Psychology regarded as a positive science. *Ninth International Congress of Psychology*, 370-371.

SACHS, H. 1944. *Freud, master and friend.* Cambridge, Mass.: Harvard University Press.

SEARS, R. R. 1943. *Survey of objective studies of psychoanalytic concepts.* New York: Social Science Research Council, Bulletin 51.

SHERRINGTON, (SIR) CHARLES S. 1906. *The integrative action of the nervous system.* New Haven: Yale University Press. New ed., 1947.

SKINNER, B. F. 1931. The concept of the reflex in the description of behavior. *J. genl. Psychol.*, 1931, **5**, 427-458.

1932. On the rate of formation of a conditioned reflex. *J. genl. Psychol.*, 1932, **7**, 274-285.

1938. *The behavior of organisms, an experimental analysis.* New York: D. Appleton-Century Co.

1940. A method of maintaining an arbitrary degree of hunger. *J. comp. Psychol.*, 1940, **30**, 139-145.

1944. Review of Hull's *Principles of behavior. Amer. J. Psychol.*, 1944, **57**, 276-281.

1945. The operational analysis of psychological terms. *Psychol. Rev.* 1945, **52**, 270-277, 291-294.

SMITH, S., and GUTHRIE, E. R. 1921. *General psychology in terms of behavior.* New York: D. Appleton Co.

SPEARMAN, C. E. 1923. *The nature of 'intelligence' and the principles of cognition.* London: Macmillan & Co., Ltd.

SPOONER, A., and KELLOGG, W. N. 1947. The backward conditioning curve. *Amer. J. Psychol.*, 1947, **60**, 321-334.

SPRANGER, E. 1928. *Types of men: the psychology and ethics of personality.* Trans. of 5th German ed., by P. J. Pigors. Halle: Neimeyer.

STERN, W. [sometimes L. W.] 1906, 1918, 1924. *Person und Sache: System der philosophischen Weltanschauung.* 3 vols. Leipzig: S. A. Barth.

1930. Autobiography. In C. Murchison, *History of psychology in autobiography.* Worcester, Mass.: Clark University Press. 1930, Vol I, 335-388.

1938. *General psychology from the personalistic standpoint.* Trans. by H. D. Spoerl from the German edition of 1935. New York: The Macmillan Co.

STEVENS, S. S. 1935. The operational definition of psychological concepts. *Psychol. Rev.*, 1935, **42**, 517-526.

1939. Psychology and the science of science. *Psychol. Bull.*, 1939, **36**, 221-263.

SULLY, J. 1884. *Outlines of psychology.* New York: D. Appleton Co.

TAPPAN, H. P. 1841. *The doctrine of the will.* New York: Dodd, Mead & Co., Inc.

TEAD, O. 1918. *Instincts in industry.* Boston: Houghton Mifflin Co.

THORNDIKE, E. L. 1898. Animal intelligence: an experimental study of the associative processes in animals. *Psychol. Rev. Mon. Suppl.*, 1898, No. 8. Reprinted with other animal studies in the same author's *Animal intelligence.* New York: The Macmillan Co., 1911.

1905. *The elements of psychology.* New York: A. G. Seiler.

1913. *The psychology of learning.* New York: Teachers College, Columbia University.

1931. *Human learning.* New York: Century Co.

1932. *The fundamentals of learning.* New York: Teachers College, Columbia University.

1933. *An experimental study of rewards.* New York: Teachers College, Columbia University.

1943. *Man and his works.* Cambridge, Mass.: Harvard University Press.

TILQUIN, A. 1935. Un "behaviorisme" téléologique, la psychologie de Tolman. *J. de psychol.,* 1935, **32**, 731-775.

TITCHENER, E. B. 1898. The postulates of a structural psychology. *Philos. Rev.,* 1898, **7**, 449-465.

1899. Structural and functional psychology. *Philos. Rev.,* 1899, **8**, 290-299.

1901, 1905. *Experimental psychology, a manual of laboratory practice.* Vol. I., *Qualitative experiments:* Part I. Student's manual; Part II. Instructor's manual. Vol. II. *Quantitative experiments:* Part I. Student's manual; Part II. Instructor's manual. New York: The Macmillan Co.

1909. *Lectures on the experimental psychology of the thought processes.* New York: The Macmillan Co.

1909-1910. *A textbook of psychology.* New York: The Macmillan Co.

1915. *A beginner's psychology.* New York: The Macmillan Co.

1929. *Systematic psychology: prolegomena.* New York: The Macmillan Co.

TOLMAN, E. C. 1920. Instinct and purpose. *Psychol. Rev.,* 1920, **27**, 217-233.

1922. A new formula for behaviorism. *Psychol. Rev.,* 1922, **29**, 44-53.

1923. A behavioristic account of the emotions. *Psychol. Rev.,* 1923, **30**, 217-227.

1932. *Purposive behavior in animals and men.* New York: Century Co.

1935. Psychology versus immediate experience. *Philos. of Science,* 1935, **2**, 356-380.

1938. The determiners of behavior at a choice point. *Psychol. Review,* 1938, **45**, 1-41.

1942. *Drives toward war.* New York: D. Appleton-Century Co.

1948. Kurt Lewin. *Psychol. Rev.,* 1948, **55**, 1-4.

VOLKMANN, W., VON VOLKMAR. 1875-1876. *Lehrbuch der Psychologie vom Standpunkte des Realismus und nach genetischer Methode.* Cöthen: Schulze.

WALLAS, G. 1908. *Human nature in politics.* London: Constable & Co. Ltd.

1914. *The great society.* New York: The Macmillan Co.

WARREN, H. C. 1921. *A history of the association psychology.* New York: Charles Scribner's Sons.

WASHBURN, M. F. 1908. *The animal mind.* New York: The Macmillan Co.

1915. *Movement and mental imagery.* Boston: Houghton Mifflin Co.

1922. Introspection as an objective method. *Psychol Rev.,* 1922, 29, 89-112.
1930. A system of motor psychology. In C. Murchison, *Psychologies of 1930.* Worcester, Mass.: Clark University Press, 1930, 81-94.
WATSON, J. B. 1913. Psychology as a behaviorist views it. *Psychol. Rev.,* 1913, 20, 158-177.
1914. *Behavior: an introduction to comparative psychology.* New York: Henry Holt & Co.
1916. The place of the conditioned reflex in psychology. *Psychol. Rev.,* 1916, 13, 89-117.
1919. *Psychology from the standpoint of a behaviorist.* Philadelphia: J. B. Lippincott & Co.
1924-1925. *Behaviorism.* New York: People's Institute Publishing Company. Rev. ed., New York: W. W. Norton & Co., 1930.
1936. Autobiography. In C. Murchison, *History of psychology in autobiography.* Worcester, Mass.: Clark University Press, 1936, Vol. III, 271-281.
WEISS, A. P. 1925. *A theoretical basis of human behavior.* 2nd ed., 1929, Columbus, Ohio: R. G. Adams & Co.
1928. Feeling and emotion as forms of behavior. In M. L. Reymert, *Feelings and emotions: the Wittenberg symposium.* Worcester, Mass.: Clark University Press, 1928, 170-190.
1930. The biosocial standpoint in psychology. In C. Murchison, *Psychologies of 1930.* Worcester, Mass.: Clark University Press, 1930, 301-306.
WERTHEIMER, M. 1912. Experimentelle Studien über das Sehen von Bewegung. *Z. Psychol.,* 1912, 61, 161-265.
1921, 1923. Untersuchungen zur Lehre von der Gestalt. *Psychol. Forsch.,* 1921, 1, 47-58; 1923, 4, 301-350.
1945. *Productive thinking.* New York: Harper & Brothers.
WEXBERG, E. 1929. *Individual psychology.* New York: Cosmopolitan Book Corporation.
WOODWORTH, R. S. 1938. *Experimental psychology.* New York: Henry Holt & Co.
WOODWORTH, R. S., and MARQUIS, D. G. 1947. *Psychology, fifth edition.* New York: Henry Holt & Co.
WUNDT, W. 1894. *Lectures on human and animal psychology.* Trans. from the 2nd German edition by J. E. Creighton and E. B. Titchener. London: Sonnenschein.
1896. *Grundriss der Psychologie.* Leipzig: Engelmann. Trans. by C. H. Judd entitled *Outlines of psychology.* Leipzig: Engelmann.
ZENER, K. 1937. The significance of behavior accompanying conditioned salivary secretion for theories of the conditioned response. *Amer. J. Psychol.,* 1937, 50, 384-403.

AUTHOR INDEX

Adler, A. 193-197, 257
 clinical methods of 196
 divergence of, from Freud 181,
  192, 193, 195, 197
 on dream interpretation 197
 on neuroses 196
 on social spirit 194
 on style of life 195, 207
 on superiority motive 193, 195
Alexander, F. 257
 clinical methods of 168
 on hostility motive 187
 on Oedipus complex 187
Allport, G. W. 257
 on personality 251-252
Anderson, O. D., on conditioned
  response 263
Angell, J. R. 257
 on animal psychology 31
 on functional psychology 30-32
Aristotle
 on faculties 12
 on laws of association 38

Bain, A., on association 45, 257
Bekhterev, V. M., on conditioned
  response 82, 257
Bentley, M., as pupil of Titchener
  30, 257
Berkeley, G., on association 41,
  257
Bernard, L. L. 257
 on environmentalism 225
 on instincts in society 224
 on sublimation 225
Binet, A. 257
 on introspective method 22
 on thinking 23
Bleuler, E., on schizophrenia 198
Bogen, H., on Stern's methods 248,
  257
Boring, E. G. 257-258
 history of psychology by 5, 38,
  126
 on operationism 119
 as pupil of Titchener 30
 on tonal senation 30

Breuer, J., talking-out method of
  160, 258
Bridgman, P. W., on operational
  definitions 116, 258
Brown, T. 43-44, 258
 on association 43
 on mental chemistry 43
 on relations perceived 44, 125

Calkins, M. W. 258
 on introspection 243
 self psychology of 120, 242-244
Cannon, W. B., on emotion 86, 258
Carmichael, L., on child development 234, 258
Carpenter, W. B., on unconscious
  cerebration 170, 258
Carr, H. 258
 on animal psychology 68
 on functional psychology 32
Cattell, J. McK. 258
 definition of psychology by 72
 pupils of 51, 99
Charcot, J. M. 258
 on hypnosis and hysteria 157
 pupils of 157, 159
Claparède, E. 258
 on functional psychology 33
 on the schools 33
Coghill, G. E. 258
 on development from whole to
  parts 233
 on organismic psychology 233-
  235

Darwin, C., influence of, on psychology 8, 48, 158
Dashiell, J. F., on *rapprochements*
  of the schools 254, 258
Descartes, R., reflex theory of behavior of 6
Dewey, J., on functional psychology
  30, 32
Dilthey, W., on "understanding"
  psychology 249, 258-259
DuBois, C., on psychoanalysis 262

269

SUBJECT INDEX